THE

THE SIXTEEN

THE SIXTEEN

The Covert Assassination Squad
that went Beyond the SAS

John Urwin

First published in Great Britain by Vision,
a division of Satin Publications Ltd.

Vision
101 Southwark Street
London SE1 0JF
UK
e-mail: info@visionpaperbacks.co.uk
website: www.visionpaperbacks.co.uk

Publisher: Sheena Dewan
Printed and bound in the UK by Mackays of Chatham Limited, Chatham, Kent

ISBN: 1-904132-14-6

This book is dedicated
to the memory of
the extraordinarily unique men
who were
THE SIXTEEN
especially
Dynamo, Chalky, Spot and Ken
whoever you were – wherever you are

CONTENTS

Contents

Preface

In the highly volatile and unsettled political situation throughout the Middle East during the 1950s, the threat of all out nuclear war was a very real possibility and the whole area was a seething hotbed of unrest. At that time no government could be seen to be responsible for certain tasks undertaken on their behalf; hence the need for a special unit such as The Sixteen. Seemingly accountable to no one, operating in such a unique and extremely covert way that there was never any real possibility of their discovery, their existence and operations were, and still remain, virtually untraceable.

Part of the group's cover, and one of the reasons that they were so successful, was that any information concerning the group or their operations was always on a strictly 'need to know' basis. When I joined them, in their opinion I needed to know very little, so I was never given any real detail as to how The Sixteen were originally formed. My thoughts on this remain purely speculative and are based mainly on the small amounts of information that were supplied indirectly by my colleagues in the group and from what I gleaned during various conversations that took place in my presence. Largely by piecing together these snippets of information, I concluded that they had existed or been in force for several years prior to my joining them and had been active in various countries throughout Africa and the Middle East, with their own well-established intelligence network.

I also gathered that this 'network' consisted of eight of The Sixteen who were dispersed throughout various parts of the Middle East gathering relevant information required for the operations that were to take place in those areas. How they achieved this and relayed this information back to the other eight of us was never explained to me but it ensured that right up to the moment we left to carry out an operation our information was extremely accurate. These 'intelligence gatherers' were also responsible for ensuring that hidden fuel dumps were in place en route and any other supplies required were available too. They also provided backup for all operations if needed, in order to help us achieve our goal and get back in one piece.

During all our operations we wore no means of identification, no badges, insignia, etc, but in order for anyone to identify themselves to us during an operation The Sixteen had devised a small, unique badge instantly recognisable as such only to another member of the group.

Why The Sixteen were formed in the first place is a matter of conjecture. At the time, I was young, excited at being specially chosen, and totally loyal to the group. I accepted what they told me without question, as they had instructed me that I must – which, in my opinion, is the way it should be. The curiosity came later. But at the time I was totally wrapped up in and fascinated by my training with them and the subsequent operations we carried out.

However, in the ensuing years, I spent hour upon hour trying to figure out the hows, the whys and the wherefores. I wondered if perhaps they had been formed as the result of some Thomas à Becket-style wishful thinking on the part of a high-ranking government official, maybe in the presence of some military top brass. But, again, this is purely speculation on my part.

I did not set out to write this book as any form of exposé. I came to the decision to tell my story for some very personal reasons and following world events over recent years culminating in the September 11 atrocities in New York and Washington. The subsequent statement by the British Defence Secretary, Geoff Hoon, that we in Britain needed a new type of special forces group proved to me that our so-called elite SAS were simply not up to the job. It also became obvious to me that after such a statement neither Hoon nor anyone in the government or MOD could be aware of the previous existence of such a specialised group as The Sixteen.

I deliberated long and hard before deciding to break my 40-year silence about their existence. I am still somewhat reluctant to make it common knowledge, but I wanted the British public, you the reader, to know that such a specialised group did indeed exist. I wanted to prove that despite dozens of books supposedly detailing elite special forces operations (but which in fact show these groups to be special only in the spectacular number of their failed operations), none of these has the correct training or expertise. In fact, it would appear that they do not even have the intelligence when writing a book or making a film to do so in a way that portrays them in a good light.

It is also of note that books based on supposedly factual events in the Gulf War are now the subject of in-depth investigations by the TV and press – those involved are being shown to have lied in their accounts. In the light of all this, I simply want to show how a special forces unit should be, could be and, in fact, was. Maybe this will prod the military hierarchy out of their inertia, and get them to start asking why it is that our special forces today do not have the unique training and weapons that this group had over 40 years ago.

So, why the need for The Sixteen all those years ago? Why no government or MOD acknowledgement of their existence? Why no records and no obvious chain of command?

My experience with The Sixteen tells me that at that time British Intelligence, the government and the MOD had been deeply infiltrated by Soviet controlled and operated moles. This was at a time when the Soviets were moving into several Middle Eastern countries following the Suez Crisis and providing nuclear know-how and financial support. The threat of war (possibly nuclear) was a very real one given the unstable political situation throughout the Middle East during the 1950s, and especially 1958. This also meant that no one nation wished to be seen as the instigator of a full-scale conflict.

However, certain key personnel were the targets of extreme covert operations due to their anti-Western policies and strong Soviet support, in particular President Nasser of Egypt, who was the key Middle Eastern figure at that time. A British government-backed plan to assassinate Nasser was mentioned during a television news item, following the revelation by David Shayler of a government plot to assassinate Colonel Gaddafi.

An attempt on Nasser's life was in fact due to be undertaken by myself and colleagues in The Sixteen. We planned it and were waiting to set off for Cairo when we were told to abort the operation. Other successful operations did, however, take place throughout the Middle East, the targets including Eastern bloc military and civilian advisers to various Arab nations.

Following the discovery in 1951 of Burgess's and Maclean's defections to the Soviet Union, it was felt that no employee of either British Intelligence or government departments could be fully trusted. A wise move given that even today there are still dimwits working for the government, MOD and Intelligence capable of leaving top secret documents, briefcases and laptop computers behind them in public places, taxis and the like. Besides, The Sixteen were there to carry out missions that no government could be seen to be endorsing.

This avoidance of government, MOD and British Intelligence sources would explain why these departments or offices either will not or cannot acknowledge that The Sixteen ever existed or undertook the operations outlined in my book. However, I think it is obvious that there had to be some high-ranking military personnel involved in the formation of the group. They must have ultimately instigated and controlled the various operations that we undertook and organised the complicated logistical arrangements involved in these operations. Although the others in The Sixteen never discussed these matters in detail (not in my presence, anyway) I got the feeling that a very few top brass alone knew the identities of each member of the group.

In answer to the obvious question as to whether they still exist and are operational, I can only say 'Who knows?' I certainly do not and, because of the way in which they were (and perhaps still are) organised, I think no one will ever know. That, of course, is exactly how it should be, the ultimate strength of The Sixteen and surely the true definition of the now overused and somewhat debased words 'elite' and 'covert'.

Everything about The Sixteen had to be different from anything known to the SAS or any other special forces units: the method of recruitment, the training, the exceptional skills and distinctive weapons, the ability to seemingly vanish into thin air, the absolute secrecy. No other operational unit had, or indeed has, these requirements or skills.

The Sixteen were unique in that their training gave them the ability to act in a universal role. They had to be able to operate anywhere and undertake operations that would be deemed impossible by conventionally trained and armed special forces. In order to achieve this they targeted their recruits and handpicked only those who possessed the necessary skills, both physical (gymnastic) and mental, and who could learn complex tasks very quickly. These abilities allowed them to successfully undertake a period of extremely intense training totally different to anything they had previously experienced. Only a very few possessed the necessary aptitude and attitude required to undergo this training.

By surviving the life-changing 'One Step Beyond' (a fear elimination process) they were also armed with the mental resources to absolutely control any given situation. This, together with their unique form of unarmed combat, weapons and techniques, turned them into a formidably awesome fighting unit.

To those who will undoubtedly question both the authenticity and plausibility of my story, I would say that while I fully understand such scepticism I can only point to myself as living proof that The Sixteen did infact exist.

Many ex-special forces personnel have been to my unarmed combat club and taken part in various events and initiative courses that I organise – without exception they have been unable to undertake even the most basic of these courses, which I base on the simplest of tasks set for me by The Sixteen. Over the last 40 years, I have also met many ex-special forces men from a variety of units and entered into extensive discussions with them regarding their training methods. Having watched their training exercises and programmes and been aware of how many men they injure or lose during their training, it has become even more obvious to me that the knowledge and skills I possess were, and still are, totally unique to The Sixteen and unknown to other special forces worldwide.

The US has proved, when saturating countries such as Iraq and Afghanistan with all their modern technology, that they still have learnt nothing from the Vietnam debacle, namely that these methods do not work against this type of foe. They have still not, at the time of writing, caught or disposed of Saddam Hussein, Osama Bin Laden or the Al Qaida forces. Now it looks like they are going back into Iraq to try to finish off the job that, despite all their high tech equipment and the SAS, they did not achieve in the first place. The US is trying to drum up support for this action from all their usual allies. It is also currently being reported that President Bush is considering using nuclear deterrents against several countries. Whether this is true or not is irrelevant – such reporting merely causes hostility and agitation, puts these countries on the alert and causes more individuals to want to undertake terrorist activities.

Because of our links with the US, all this puts Britain in serious danger. The risk posed by the fact that unauthorised and potentially hostile people seem to be able to get into our country easily by various means, including via the Channel Tunnel (our modern equivalent of the Trojan Horse), is another worrying factor. Recent world events lead me to believe that Britain will once again need the skills of a group like The Sixteen, and sooner than we think.

Acknowledgements

Writing this book has been a long, difficult task that could not have been achieved without a great deal of encouragement from a number of people. I am especially grateful to the following:

Robert Smith, my agent, for having the guts to go with it.

All at Vision for their help and hard work, and Martin and Helen Moss at Proof Positive.

All my family, who kept me going with their love and support.

Brian Stern, Kevin Fitzpatrick, Mark Jones, Chris Wood and David Bremner – the whole project would never have got off the ground had it not been for the vital part they played in initially encouraging me and giving me the confidence to do it. Many thanks, lads, for all your help and continued support – I couldn't have done it without you!

Last, but by no means least, my beloved wife, Helen, who brought me back to life again. Thank you, darling, for putting up with me; your endless patience, understanding and love got me through the difficult times.

1. The first death

Two jerks on the rope – my signal to go. Spot, who was also holding the rope, tapped my shoulder. 'OK, Geordie, off you go,' he hissed into my ear, then turning away whispered slightly louder: 'Chalky, Dynamo's on the ledge. You're OK to go.'

'OK,' came a faint reply from further along the cliff top where Chalky had set up another belay point.

Apprehensively, I readied myself on the edge of the cliff. No matter how many times I practised, it always gave me a weird feeling to launch myself over a precipice into a black void not knowing where the end of my rope was. As quickly and quietly as I could I abseiled down to where I knew Dynamo would be waiting below. The cliff face consisted of huge rocks and boulders interspersed with little shrubby bushes and smaller, looser rocks and stones, several of which I dislodged with my feet as I made my way down. They clattered ahead of me into the blackness below and, as I couldn't hear them hitting the ground, I realised just how high the cliff must be. But as it was pitch dark I had no idea just how far it was to the bottom.

As my feet made contact with solid ground, two strong hands suddenly grabbed my shoulder and pushed me hard against the face of the cliff. 'Take it easy, Geordie,' Dynamo's voice quietly urged. 'Be careful you don't move too far away; stay as close to the cliff face as possible. I think this track is only a few feet wide so try not to dislodge any boulders or anything like that. If we knock something over the edge and they hear us we could be in real trouble,' he whispered. 'We'll have to find out just how big this ledge is before the others get down. It could get a bit crowded.'

It was so dark that I could barely make out my own hands as I detached my nine inch dog-clip from the heavy rope and gave the signal for Spot to follow me. As he began his descent, Dynamo and I dropped to our hands and knees and inched away from the cliff face. For a few moments we fumbled around in the dark as we tried to find out just exactly how wide the track was. Moving only a fraction of an inch at a time and cautiously placing one hand in front of the other, I made my way forward for about three yards, then suddenly my outstretched hand felt only empty space beneath it and I realised that I was only a couple of feet from the edge. Picking up the smallest stone I could find, I dropped it over to see what would happen – but heard nothing. Carefully I shuffled backwards and whispered over my shoulder to Dynamo.

'I've found the edge, mate. You were right, it's only about nine feet away from the cliff face, so watch what you're doing,' I warned as Spot landed just behind us.

'We'll have to find a safe place to rest up until daylight,' Dynamo said quietly. 'Get your gear and try to find yourself a little hole somewhere, Geordie.'

I carefully crawled back to the cliff face to collect my bag and gear and then moved off to my left in order to investigate a little further in that direction. A slight scuffling noise stopped me in my tracks and then I heard Chalky urgently whispering:

'Hey, chaps, I'm over here. Are you all OK?' His voice sounded as if it was coming from a slightly higher position a bit further along the track.

'Yeah, we're all right. How about you? Where are you, Chalky? I can't make you out,' I replied as quietly as possible, turning my head towards his voice and peering into the blackness.

'Bloody well dangling in mid-air – I've come to the end of my rope,' he hissed. 'I can't see a bloody thing either, Geordie, but you sound a bit of a way off, over to my right.'

'Can't you try to swing across and drop off over this way or try to go back up and come down our rope?'

'No! There's too many loose rocks just here. If I dislodge any it'll make a hell of a racket. And I can't go back up; I haven't brought my rope keys.'

'Well, I'll try and work my way further along towards you then. Just hang on a minute.'

'Oh, very funny! Where the hell am I going to go?'

With my face pressed against the cliff, I slowly and cautiously began to feel my way along it with my hands outstretched fumbling along its uneven surface. Suddenly, without warning my left foot found nothing beneath it and I stumbled and almost fell – the track had completely disappeared. I desperately scrabbled for a handhold, digging my fingers into the cliff face to prevent falling any further, and quickly got my foot back onto the solid ground.

My voice came out in a hoarse whisper. 'Bloody hell, Chalky!' I exclaimed, 'I don't think there's anything under you, the flaming track peters out just here. Whatever you do, don't attempt to drop down. I'll go back for our rope and try to get it across to you.'

Warily I began to edge my way back towards Spot and Dynamo, whose quiet voices I could just make out as I fumbled towards them.

'We've come down in the right area, Geordie,' Dynamo said quietly. 'According to our map this used to be a very narrow road around the cliff past the front of the cave. There's not much of it still intact. It must've been washed away; in fact I think this bit of ledge is all that's left. But I've just been along it quite a way to our right and it gets a little wider further on, just where it leads around to the entrance of the cave where we saw those truck lights last night. The trouble is, it looks too open. If we go in that way we'll have no cover and we'll lose the element of surprise. If they spot us on the ledge we won't stand a chance: it's so narrow there'll be nowhere to go. We need to find a back way into this place. What's it like along that way?'

'Any sign of Chalky yet?' Spot asked before I had time to answer.

'Yeah, he's hanging over there to our left. He's come to the end of his rope with nothing beneath him, this track just disappears about 20 feet along that way,' I told them. 'I couldn't see him but he sounds OK. I think he'll need help to get down, though. I don't think he'll be able to manage it on his own.'

'Great, that's all we need! I always knew that silly sod would come to the end of his bloody rope one day!' Dynamo said evenly.

'But he shouldn't be. I reckon this cliff to be only about 110 feet and he's got a 120 foot rope.'

'I know what'll have happened: he's obviously come down from a higher point than us in the dark. But this track shouldn't run out just there,' Spot pointed out. 'According to our map it should go along that way for at least another 100 yards or so. There must have been some pretty heavy flash floods in the area, which would explain why so much of it's been washed away.'

Flash floods were a problem at this time of year especially in the mountains. Our journey up here in the dark had been fairly tricky for the same reason. We had encountered a similar hazard on the narrow track we were following where it had almost disappeared.

In order to avoid bumping into an army patrol or a group of terrorists, we'd been travelling without lights along a little-used and fairly steep track which eventually disappeared into nothing more than a goat track. As it had progressively narrowed to barely the width of the jeep, the vehicle's wheels had suddenly spun out over a sheer drop where the edge had been completely washed away. It had been obvious to us that the rest of our journey would have to be made on foot. So Dynamo had pulled the jeep off the track onto a small clearing beneath a cliff overhang and we'd concealed it as best we could behind some scrubby bushes and small trees.

We'd all closely studied a detailed map of the region before we set off, so we knew that we'd be able to follow this old track to where we believed the terrorists were holed up. It would be difficult in the dark due to the rough terrain but, by taking a circular route, we would eventually get to within 200 to 300 yards west of the area.

Earlier on our way up we'd caught sight of the tail lights of a truck across the gorge, which had been a stroke of luck for us, as we hadn't wanted to travel much further in the jeep and maybe alert the terrorists. By spotting it, we had saved having to search the entire vicinity for their exact location.

'They must be pretty confident that they won't be seen, to use their lights like that,' Chalky had commented dryly. 'Let's get to some higher ground and have a look around.'

We'd begun to climb, but had only gone a few hundred yards from the jeep when he'd suddenly stopped us and pointed ahead.

Following the direction of his outstretched arm, we'd been able to make out a small red glow and looking through our binoculars, we had clearly seen the dark outline of a man standing smoking a cigarette, lit from behind by a flickering light, possibly from a fire within a cave. Another stroke of luck: now we had their exact position.

We had grouped together, pulling our jackets over our heads, and checked our bearings on the map. It was obvious that by walking and climbing the rest of the way, we'd be able to manoeuvre into a position above and behind the terrorists where we could descend a cliff face with a drop of roughly 100 feet onto a narrow old track. Once on the track, we would be able to stay there until daylight, but failure to get it right would result in possibly having to abseil down more than 200 feet on ropes that were only 120 feet long. Although we had the ability to do this if necessary, it would have been a difficult descent.

Now it appeared that by abseiling down from a point further along the cliff top, Chalky had run into a bit of a problem, although neither Spot nor Dynamo seemed unduly concerned about the situation. 'We'll just have to leave him there until it's lighter,' Spot said casually. 'We might as well get this rope down now, Dynamo. We won't need it to climb back up if you think we can get around that way.'

'Here, I'll do it,' I told him and gave a yank on the light line, which Spot, as last man down, had brought with him. This light line was attached to a five inch metal wedge and tied onto the other end of our heavy rope, which was held in place by a highwayman's noose around a small tree about 10 feet from the edge of the cliff. The wedge was holding this noose in place and once it was removed, by sharply tugging on the light line the heavy rope was released and both it and the light line came crashing down at my feet.

Grabbing one end of the abseil rope, I quickly coiled it up, wrapped it around my shoulder and carefully felt my way back towards Chalky. I didn't like the idea of leaving him hanging in mid-air for over an hour; I knew just how painful the rope harnesses could be. Besides, it was freezing up here and it hadn't stopped raining for hours.

'Chalky,' I hissed. 'I'm going to try to throw a rope to you. Get ready!'

Although I could hear him and knew he couldn't be that far away, I only had a rough idea of where he actually was as I could see nothing at all; it was going to be difficult to get the rope to him. Feeling my way with my hands and feet, I got as close to the edge as I dared in the dark when my left hand brushed against a small bush at the base of the cliff. I tugged at it to see how good a hold it had, then swiftly tied one end of the rope around it, so that it would be easy to retrieve it if it fell when I threw it out to Chalky. I coiled the rest of the rope up and with difficulty threw it across to where I believed him to be. But it missed and I heard it fall past.

On my second attempt, I tried to throw it higher and further, hoping it would drop down on top of him, but again it was an awkward throw, right-handed between my body and the cliff face and once more the rope missed him. Gathering it up again, I decided to give it another go, but this time I would try it with my left hand.

'What's that racket? What are you doing, Geordie?' Dynamo's urgent whisper came out of the darkness to my right.

'I'm trying to get a rope over to Chalky.'

'Just leave it until it gets a bit lighter. You can't do anything in the dark.'

'OK. But I'll just give it one more go.'

Gathering the rope into extra loops in my left hand, I held onto a rock jutting from the cliff face with my right and leaned out as far as I dared, in order to swing it higher. This time it seemed to catch on something, so I gave it a yank.

'Have you got it, Chalky?'

'Have I hell!'

Just then, I felt the rope drop and as it fell past I made a grab for it. But, thrown off balance, I instantly lost my footing, fell over backwards into the dark and began to slide down an embankment on my back towards the edge. Desperately I twisted and struggled, trying to use my right leg to push my body over onto my front, all the while grabbing at anything I could to try to stop my fall. But still I slid downwards. Then suddenly, the back of my right knee hooked onto something and I came to an abrupt halt, upside down with my head and shoulders hanging into space. Immediately I froze solid, too terrified to move a muscle.

I was breathing heavily and could feel my heart pounding in my chest. I appeared to be caught up on a small bush or shrub, which was all that was preventing me from falling God knows how far. I gripped it as hard as I could with my leg. If I hadn't had my knee bent at that precise moment, or had been just a few inches further over, either way, I would have completely missed it and that would have been that.

Damn, I thought. My first job and already I'm messing it up. I was worried but tried to compose myself. Clearly, something was preventing me from falling further so I reasoned that if I could grab onto it I might be able to pull myself back up. I made a desperate attempt to get hold of the bush or shrub but the second I grabbed hold of it the whole thing bent towards me and my body began to slip. Instantly I froze again. It was obvious that if I tried to move I was going to fall; besides, I could not risk dislodging anything. There was nothing else for it: I was going to have to try to attract the attention of Spot and Dynamo and risk whispering as loudly as I dared.

'Dynamo! Spot!'

Immediately Dynamo's voice came back to me.

'Keep your voice down, Geordie! What's up?'

'Come this way, over to your left. I'm down here hanging over the edge. Hurry up: I don't think what I'm caught on will hold much longer!'

I heard them moving nearer to me.

'Where the hell are you?'

'Just a bit further along the ledge. You won't be able to grab me, I'm too far over. You'll have to throw a bloody rope, quick!' I whispered, trying not to sound too panicky.

My head was hanging into the blackness and although I couldn't see anything below, I knew it was a long way down and this little bush wasn't going to hold out forever.

'Where is it?' Spot asked.

'It's tied to a bush near the cliff face.'

I could hear Dynamo and Spot cautiously moving closer towards me, searching around for the rope I had been using. The next moment it was thrown in my general direction and fell heavily close by me and slightly to my left. Trying to grab it, I reached out as far as I dared but could feel nothing.

'Where are you? Say something so we can get a fix on you.'

'Down here. You need to be over a bit more to your left.'

Their next attempt fell right across my chest and immediately I grabbed it, pushed the noose over my shoulders and gave it a sharp tug.

'That's it, I've got it! Pull!'

Seconds later I was back on the ledge beside them. 'I thought I was a goner there,' I exclaimed in relief. 'Sorry about that, I was trying to get the rope across to Chalky and slipped.'

'Forget it, Geordie, forget it. Are you OK?' Dynamo asked.

'Yeah, I'm fine. But what about Chalky?'

'He'll be OK. He's been in worse spots than this; he's as hard as nails and besides if he gets cold he's got his gear in his bag with him!'

Spot put his hand on my shoulder. 'Come on, Chalky will have to stay there until we can see him; let's just hope no one else spots him before we do.'

'Get the CTCs out, Geordie, and come over here. I want to show you something,' Dynamo said and moved off. Deeply embarrassed, I followed them back along the ledge to where our bags lay and pulled out our camouflage topcoats (CTCs).

I always hated using these. They were cumbersome things made out of hessian and coated with a sticky glue-like substance on one side that had to be pulled apart before they could be put on. This sticky gel was used to pick up extra camouflage from the ground such as dust, dirt, small stones, leaves, pine needles, twigs or whatever happened to be in the near vicinity. The coat itself was very long and dragged along the ground behind for about two feet. Two straps, one just below each knee, fastened around your legs and a large hood covered your head. A cape-like flap was attached to the sleeves and the back of the hood. Once the hood was up, by lying in a small dip or hollow with your arms outstretched beyond your head, your body's outline would be completely covered and you would be flush with the ground. With all of the bits of twigs and gravel picked up by the sticky substance, it enabled us to blend into any surrounding area and become virtually impossible to see.

The three of us crouched closely together and pulled one of these coats over our heads. Dynamo turned on a small torch and shone it on the map he held.

'Judging by the shape of this cliff face, we've come down in the right place, which probably means that these guys can't be more than 80 yards or so away. There's nothing more we can do now, so we might as well find ourselves a cubby hole somewhere and rest up until daylight.'

'Don't forget to remove your sash,[1] Geordie, and try not to fall asleep. We don't want you "dropping off" in the night, now do we?' Spot teased. I crawled around for a few minutes until I found a small hollow in the ground, and using the flat of my hand tried to clear it of as many small stones as possible. I released the safety catch on my sash and laid it on the ground beside me before settling down flat out on my stomach. Then, pulling my CTC over my head and around me, I settled down to wait for daybreak.

I was desperate not to make another blunder and so kept as still as I possibly could despite the numerous small, sharp stones that were already beginning to dig into me. At least the discomfort prevented me from dozing off and accidentally knocking any loose stones over the edge. Some of these rocks and stones were the size of house bricks and would have made quite a racket tumbling down the cliff into the valley below, which would probably have alerted the nearby terrorists.

For over an hour we lay on the narrow mountain ledge, hidden under cover and waiting for first light. My limbs were beginning to go numb. Clenching my right fist, I tried to flex the aching muscles of my arm without moving around too much. I managed to wriggle about a little bit to change to a slightly more comfortable position but the straps holding my MK1 to my right thigh were digging into my flesh and starting to cut off the blood supply to my lower leg. God knows how Chalky must be feeling right now, I thought.

Hearing a slight noise nearby, I cautiously raised the edge of my cover an inch or so and peered out. A thin watery light filtered

1 A special belt-like weapon.

through the heavy night clouds and the air was damp with early morning mist. It was almost dawn. Peering through the gloom, I could just make out the dark bulk of Chalky's silhouette, hanging from his rope like a bauble on a Christmas tree. He was barely visible, as he had managed to get his CTC out of his holdall and pull it on. If I hadn't known where to look I simply would not have been aware that he was there at all.

He was suspended in mid-air about 15 feet to the left of me and roughly six feet or so higher up, just around a slight bend in the cliff face. A couple of small shrubs protruded from where the rock wall curved near to him and I realised just why I had been unable to get the rope to him in the dark: these bushes were in the way, no doubt what the rope had snagged on just before I had fallen. I realised that it was lucky Chalky had not attempted to drop down in the dark, as the ledge on which we had landed was totally missing directly below him and he was hanging over a sheer drop of at least 200 feet.

I could see why he'd had a problem coming down. Between our belay point and his, the cliff rose by approximately 10 to 15 feet, which accounted for his rope appearing to be too short to reach the ledge. Obviously, there was no way he could have seen that in the dark.

A movement to my right caught my eye and I saw that Dynamo and Spot were now on their feet and taking off their CTCs, so I quickly followed suit, relieved to be moving again and glad to be able to get rid of the damn thing.

We had no time to waste so we quickly set about getting Chalky down. Dynamo expertly threw a rope up to him, which Chalky pulled over his shoulders and fastened around his chest. Then the three of us began to slowly and carefully pull him towards us on the ledge, trying to prevent his rope from dislodging any of the rocks above, until we reached a point where we could not get him any closer. Chalky was still a few feet away and had no other option but to release his rope from the top by pulling on his light line. He immediately dropped when he did so and just managed to grab onto the ledge as his heavy rope, still attached to his waist, rushed noisily past him and disappeared into the blackness below. As he fell, we pulled on the rope around his shoulders and dragged him back onto the ledge, hoping and praying that nobody had heard us.

Chalky tried to stand but his legs instantly gave out. He sat down and began to rub them vigorously. 'Sorry, guys, but my pins aren't working properly yet. That bloody harness has cut off the circulation and I can't feel them. In fact, I can't feel much below the waist, I don't think anything's going to work for quite some time,' he whispered ruefully.

'You prat! You should have come down the same rope as us,' Spot told him. 'Well, I'd found a good, solid belay point up there,' Chalky explained.

He had been stuck in his harness for well over an hour gradually losing the feeling in his legs, which must have been agonising. Until now, I hadn't really appreciated just what he must have been going through. He tried to stand again, but couldn't straighten up. 'Listen, stay where you are for a while until we check things out,' Dynamo told him.

We could see an opening about 20 feet away and the three of us began to make our way cautiously along the ledge towards it, me in the lead with Dynamo and Spot following closely behind.

The cave 'mouth' was little more than a niche in the limestone but it appeared to go a lot deeper into the hill. From inside came the sound of dripping water but I was convinced I could also make out something else and decided to investigate. The opening was very narrow, but with some difficulty I eventually managed to squeeze my way in.

Although the cave interior was dark, by now it was gradually becoming lighter outside and through a series of holes in the roof several pale shafts of daylight filtered through and lit up the top of a huge pile of rubble that filled most of the cave. Over the years it must have been washed down from the roof to form the mound in front of me, which reached almost to the top of the cave, leaving a gap of no more than a few feet between it and the roof.

Sprays of water cascaded from the cave roof onto the top of the pile of rubble and ran in rivulets down its sides, as the beams of early morning light filtering through the holes in the roof produced a rainbow effect on the mist that the spray created.

Although I had a torch with me, I didn't want to use it in case it was spotted. So, peering through the gloom, I cautiously made my way further towards the back of the cave, but coming up against a solid wall and finding nothing further to explore I turned back.

As I edged along towards the entrance, a fine mist from the spray settled on my face and I paused briefly to wipe it away with my hands. A faint noise from above caught my attention and I looked upwards just as, over the top of the mound, appeared the largest and whitest dog I had ever seen. It paused for a moment, then suddenly came hurtling towards me down the slope, half running, half slipping, its huge feet slithering and scrabbling to obtain purchase on the wet scree. Its lips were drawn back in a ferocious snarl, its enormous jaws wide apart, teeth bared.

Instinctively I dropped onto my right knee and offered up my left forearm while simultaneously pulling out my boot knife with my right hand, which I then extended but kept concealed beneath my left arm.

The massive dog accelerated down the slope and leapt at me. As it did so, I pulled my left forearm back against my chest and pushed the knife in my right hand forward. It entered the animal's chest between its front legs, killing it instantly. The weight of the dog knocked me onto my back. Stunned for a moment by the sheer ferocity of the attack, I lay against the cave wall with the dog's warm, heavy body across my legs preventing me from getting up. I was sorry that I had had to kill the dog, but it had been either it or me at the time.

'Give me a hand then,' I whispered urgently to Spot, who by now had also squeezed through the opening into the cave.

'Jesus! This is some size, isn't it!' he exclaimed. 'Where the hell did this thing come from? I take it there's no way in through here?' He began dragging the dog off me, trying not to make too much noise. For all we knew it might be a guard dog belonging to the nearby terrorists.

'No, it's a good job I killed it; there's only that one entrance. You could say it's a "dead" end,' I whispered back, giggling. Spot grinned and turned to go but I grabbed his arm to stop him.

'Shh, listen, listen,' I said urgently. We stood very still, our ears straining to catch any sounds. A very slight, muffled noise, barely audible, was coming from over the mound. I carefully tried to get to the top of the rubble without dislodging too much of it, but it was wet and loose and I slipped back down.

'Watch it, Geordie, there could be another one up there.' We stood for a moment listening.

'Just leave it, Geordie. I can't hear anything, it's probably just the water coming through the roof,' Spot whispered and turned to leave.

But I could definitely hear something, and continued to scramble up the pile of rubble until I reached the top. Suddenly the reason for the dog's ferocity became clear. Hidden behind a smaller pile of rocks were two snow-white puppies curled together into a tiny mewling heap, their eyes only just open. It made me feel worse about the dog's death but I had no time to dwell on it; we had a job to do and I had to get on with it.

I took a quick look around but it was obvious that there was nothing else in the cave; we would have to look elsewhere. Joining the others, we continued our search. The next two openings were little more than clefts in the rock face and took no time to explore. A fourth initially appeared to be the same, but something caught my attention and made me squeeze just a little further into the gap than first appeared possible – it was the unmistakable smell of wood smoke. Swiftly I signalled to the others to hang back while I investigated further.

'OK,' Dynamo whispered. 'But don't take any unnecessary risks.'

Cautiously, I made my way into the crevice and after an initial tight squeeze I found that it opened out into quite a wide passage. The air was now filled with the strong smell of smoke and I quietly made my way towards its source.

The passage was damp and filled with the sound of dripping. Water poured down the walls from the roof to form large pools that spread across the uneven floor and I trod as carefully as I could to avoid splashing. Following the tunnel for a little way, I eventually emerged into a large cave where the way ahead was barred by a rock fall, similar to the one where I had killed the dog. Once again, the mound almost reached to the roof with only a narrow gap at the top, but this time I could clearly see the dull red glow of flickering firelight on the cave roof beyond and heard the sound of burning firewood spitting and cracking in the flames. This had to be them.

As I stealthily approached the rock fall, I began to hear the low murmur of voices coming from the other side, barely audible but unmistakable.

'I hope to God there isn't another flaming great dog at the top of this one,' I thought, as I cautiously began to climb up the incline of the mound towards a small gap between it and the cave roof.

The slope of the rock fall was not too steep but I had to move very carefully so as not to disturb any of the loose rocks and stones. The voices grew louder as I neared the narrow gap at the top and crept forward to look over the ridge into the cave beyond.

From what I could see, it appeared to be a moderately large cave but the majority of it was in darkness. Light rays penetrating through tiny gaps in the rocks to form a criss-cross pattern of thin beams did little to brighten the scene below. The main source of light came from the ruddy glow of a small fire around which were grouped four men who were partly dressed like soldiers, with Sten guns slung over their shoulders. I couldn't see if there were any others in the shadows but as there was a large entrance in the wall opposite to the mound, I knew that there could be more of them outside.

Quietly retracing my steps, I swiftly made my way back to the cave entrance and silently indicated to Dynamo and Spot that we should go back along the ledge to where we had left Chalky before I filled them in with what I had discovered.

Chalky was moving around now, slowly trying to bend and stretch his legs. He was hunched over and his legs still could not fully straighten.

'Do you realise you're two feet shorter than when we first left camp?' teased Dynamo.

'Oh ha, ha, very funny,' Chalky hissed, wincing and grimacing as the feeling began to return to his constricted blood vessels. The pain must have been unbearable.

'Well, that's it,' I told them quietly. 'I've found the back door. They're definitely there; I saw four but there are possibly more.'

'Can we get through from there into the cave where they are?' Spot asked.

14

'Yes, definitely. There's another big mound of loose earth and stones in there, just like the one in that other cave. It goes right up and almost touches the roof but there's a gap of about three feet at the top, enough to get through; that's how I could see their fire-light. I went as far as I could and only saw four of them but I think there might be more of them outside. There's a big opening in the wall directly opposite the mound, about 70 feet away, which is probably the main way in. There's water pouring in down the sides of the passage and the noise of that should cover any sound we might make, but it's pretty wet in there: we'll have to go through about three inches of water.'

'Good work, Geordie! OK then, if you're right there's only one main entrance into the cave,' Dynamo said quietly. 'Chalky, the blood should have reached your erogenous zones by now, do you think you can make your way around the cliff edge to the front of the cave?'

'Yeah, course I can! No problem!'

'OK, but don't make a move until you're sure we're in physical contact with these guys. Right then, check your weapons, and let's go and get the bastards before it gets too light,' Dynamo said removing his pistol from its straps.

'We'll have to try not to use these unless it's absolutely neces-sary,' Spot warned. 'The noise will carry for miles and we don't know how many more of them there may be about.'

I took out my MK1 to make sure there was a bullet up the spout, then replaced it in its straps before checking my boot knife and sash. Then, grabbing our holdalls, Dynamo, Spot and I made our way back to the narrow crevice and re-entered the cave.

I led them along the damp tunnel towards the rock fall, where we left our bags at the bottom of the mound. Then the three of us carefully made our way up the loose shale and peered through the gap at the top into the cave below.

Four men were grouped around the small fire, two squatting with their backs to us, one standing slightly to their right and the other kneeling opposite facing the mound. They appeared to be cooking something on the end of sticks, which they were poking into the fire. They kept their voices low, but every now and then would burst into laughter at the guy kneeling opposite. He seemed to be having a problem with a handgun in his belt, which he kept hitching up and adjusting. Suddenly he stood up and moved around the campfire so that now he too had his back to us.

Dynamo silently indicated that I should take out the guy nearest to me, on my left; he and Spot would take care of the others. Together we squeezed through the narrow gap between the embankment and roof but just as we prepared to roll sideways down the slope, we heard a slight scuffling noise from outside the cave and knew that Chalky must have had to act quickly. The terrorists instantly grabbed at their guns and began to move towards the cave entrance. It was our signal to act before they got too far away from us.

The three of us rolled down the steep slope in unison and I landed lightly on my feet about a yard behind my target. Immediately he spun around and paused for a brief second, a shocked expression on his face, before going for the handgun in his belt.

Instinctively I knew what to do: my training just took over, or I should say 'the machine'[2] took over. I blocked his weapon arm with my right hand and spun my body in behind him using the unorthodox and seemingly robotic movements of the machine. This ensured that his body was between his pals and me, allowing me to constantly check all around for where another attack might come from. Simultaneously my left and right hands cracked him hard on the side of the jaw and the left side of his head just behind the ear. Stunned, he staggered as I locked his head against my arm before I completed the special machine technique I had been taught and broke his neck.

I felt no resistance at all. There was simply a muted cracking sound, like dry wood on a fire, then his body went limp. I hung on to him for a brief moment while I checked the area for anyone in the shadows ready to take a shot at me, swiftly turning with my back to the cave wall. If there been anyone there, I would have used his body as a shield and his gun to take them out. Glancing quickly about me it appeared that the fight was over, as the cave was eerily quiet now. I let him go and his inert body fell onto its

2 A series of unique combat techniques known only to The Sixteen.

knees like a sack of potatoes before turning to land face down on the ground at my feet.

I looked at the lifeless shape for a brief moment, stunned by how easy it had been and how quickly it had happened – a matter of mere seconds. I knew exactly how the guy must have felt at that precise moment before he died, as I had experienced a similar movement during my training and had felt as though I were locked in a vice, totally unable to move.

I was still tense, ready for action and pumped up with adrenaline, when a nearby movement caught my attention. Immediately releasing the safety catch on my sash, I whirled around in case we had missed one of them in the shadows. In the same instant that I turned, I saw Dynamo in the flickering firelight as he dropped a body to the ground where it landed with a dull thud. He stood over it for a moment, his boot knife upside down in his right hand, then looked over towards me and seeing my hand hovering over the button in the centre of my buckle, he slowly smiled and winked.

'That's the way, Geordie,' he said quietly, then pointed towards the guy at my feet. 'But I don't think you're going to need it now. Check him, make sure he's dead.'

I replaced the catch on my sash. Once I hit that button, the spring was so powerful nothing could stop it. Dynamo had been well within its range and he knew it.

With my left foot, I flipped over the motionless body and as it turned the man's left arm fell into the nearby fire in a shower of sparks that shot into the air. The fire brightened and a bloody face was illuminated in the glow, its eyes blank and staring. A huge gaping wound at the throat and another deep slash to the wrist formed large pools of blood around the body. I knew exactly what the man had attempted to do and the moves Dynamo had made in order to have inflicted those particular wounds.

A strong smell of singeing hair and flesh brought me swiftly back to reality and, jumping over the body at my feet, I kicked its arm out of the fire before the flames could do much more than burn the skin. Looking up I saw Dynamo standing watching me, shaking his head. I realised that what I had done was rather pointless under the circumstances, since the man would not have been able to feel a thing. I had merely acted instinctively.

17

Beyond Dynamo two other bodies lay crumpled on the rocky ground. Spot was kneeling next to one checking it over. 'See if they're carrying any documents or papers on them, Geordie, then have a quick look around,' he told me.

The guy I had killed carried nothing on him other than a packet of cigarettes. I moved away from the fire towards the walls of the cave to see what, if anything, they had stashed about. There was a small army trailer filled with bits of weapons nearby but other than a few empty boxes there was nothing else. A slight noise at the entrance to the cave alerted the three of us and we turned in unison just as Chalky strolled in dragging a body behind him with one hand and carrying his sash in the other. The man's jaw was missing and his face was unrecognisable. The front of his white shirt was saturated with blood that glistened damply in the firelight. Several 'pineapple' grenades hung from fastenings on his belt. Chalky dumped the lifeless form against the cave wall.

'Well, he's going nowhere!'

'What the hell happened there, couldn't you have done a neater job than that?' Spot teased, nodding towards the dead man.

'Well, he shouldn't have jumped out of the bushes the way he did! I couldn't move quickly enough because of my legs, so I had to use my sash on him, didn't I?' Chalky indignantly replied. 'What else could I do? Anyway, look what he's carrying – he must've been planning to blow up half the bloody island!'

'What else is out there?' Dynamo asked.

'Well, there was only him but there's obviously been a lot of others, judging by the number of footprints. I've had a bit of a look around but there's nothing out there now. I think we're too late. It must be true about the Turks getting ready to invade because these guys were preparing for something big. They've been part of a full-size operation – there are empty ammo boxes and gun boxes lying all over and a stack of tyre tracks mainly from light trucks.'

'Well, I don't think they'll be so keen to use this place again. They won't feel safe hiding up here in future, not when they find this lot,' Dynamo pointed out. 'Come on, we're finished here. Grab those grenades and any weapons they've got and let's get back.'

Spot nodded towards the mound of rubble. 'Come on, Geordie, we'll go and get our ropes and bags from behind this lot.'

'Just a minute, Spot, I've got something to do.' And before he could reply, I dashed out of the main entrance to the cave leaving them to collect our stuff. The sky was lighter now and the still mountain air felt cool and fresh after the smoky atmosphere inside the cave. Thick radiation fog swirled heavily beneath me in the valleys below, screening them from sight as I made my way around the cliff face and returned to the first cave where I had killed the dog. Scrambling up the wet scree once again, I collected the two puppies and returned to the others.

When they saw me holding the puppies in my arms the three of them looked at me in astonishment and burst out laughing.

'Bloody hell!' Dynamo exclaimed. 'What a guy! He'd risk his neck just for a couple of puppies. Why didn't you just leave them?'

'What on earth are you going to do with them?' Spot asked, laughing and shaking his head.

'I'll take them back to the camp and try to find a home somewhere for them. I'll just say that I found them dumped by the roadside. I couldn't leave them there to starve to death, Dynamo, I mean it just wouldn't be British, would it?' I replied grinning.

The three of them burst out laughing again.

'You big softie,' Chalky teased.

'He'll learn,' Dynamo said. 'Come on, let's go.'

We left the cave by the main entrance and followed the narrow track for about 100 yards or so before leaving it. We had no way of knowing who was in the area and did not want to run the risk of coming across any terrorists who might still be in the vicinity, or possibly run into a British army patrol.

Although the early morning mist still covered the low-lying areas, it was growing warmer now and the air was heavy and still. The only sound was that of our feet on the gravel and loose rocks as we made our way back over the mountains to where we had hidden the jeep the night before.

We carefully approached the concealed vehicle checking the surrounding area in case it had been discovered, but it was well hidden and remained undetected. I climbed into the back with the two puppies; the seats were soaking wet where the heavy dew had dripped from the branches above and Dynamo was having trouble getting it started due to this and the dampness in the air. The battery was barely turning the engine over.

'That's all we bloody well need. Jump out, Geordie,' he told me. 'We'll have to bump-start it. It's just as well we're on top of a mountain.'

I did as he said and stood to one side holding the puppies as Spot and Chalky pushed the jeep out onto the steep track.

'Get in,' Dynamo yelled and we scrambled on board as the vehicle slowly began to freewheel then pick up some speed but, when he took his foot off the clutch, the wheels merely skidded as though the handbrake was still on. They just were not gripping on the loose stones and chippings of the track.

'Oh, bloody great!' he exclaimed. 'If this thing doesn't start soon we'll end up having to walk back. We'll just have to freewheel as far as we can and I'll keep trying the damn thing.'

The three of us began to bounce up and down to try to help the wheels to grip. Chalky and I were sitting in the back and I was being thrown about a bit and having difficulty holding on to both the jeep and the puppies. The two of us burst into an uncontrollable fit of laughter.

'You and your bloody puppies,' Chalky laughed and put out his hand. 'Here, give me one of them before you fall out of this damn thing. Lovely little chaps, aren't they?' he said, taking the fat little body I passed to him and stroking it.

I was grateful for the free hand; we were being jolted around a lot and I needed to hold on. The puppy snuggled into him and Chalky grinned broadly.

'Who's a big softie now?' I asked him.

Suddenly there was a huge bang and the jeep's engine burst into life. A cloud of belching black smoke shot out of the exhaust. Dynamo braked sharply and stopped the jeep then turned around in his seat.

'Hell, that's all we need. They'll have heard that in bloody Nicosia. I might as well have fired a 12-bore. And here's me thinking we were going to get back without a hitch as everything's gone smoothly so far.' The engine had stopped spluttering now and was running quietly.

'Well, at least you've got it started,' Spot pointed out as Dynamo crunched the vehicle into gear and we slowly began to make our way down the steep track. Chalky sat watching me, shaking his head, laughing and smiling as I clung on with one hand and cradled the puppy in the other.

'I might be soft but you're crazy, do you know that?' he said.

'Aye, but I took care of that Greek, didn't I?' I replied.

He looked at me steadily for a moment. 'Yes, you certainly did, Geordie. But you know, I think you need to be a bit crazy to belong to this outfit…so you're well and truly a part of the team now!'

'Those puppies could land you in a bit of bother when you get back, you know. People will ask questions about them,' Spot pointed out. 'You really should have just left them behind, Geordie.'

Dynamo shook his head. 'Just leave it, Spot, he'll learn.'

With the gradually lightening sky the visibility improved, and we began to catch brief glimpses of the trail ahead through the thinning mist as we descended slowly down the twisting track. Eventually we came across the bend where we'd had trouble on our way up the night before.

'Jesus! How the hell did we manage to get past here in the dark without ending up over the edge?' Spot exclaimed, speaking for all of us as we gazed in disbelief at the sheer drop where the washed-away track narrowed to the mere width of the jeep. It was no wonder our wheels had spun off in the dark – only Dynamo's fast reactions had saved us from going over. Obviously going down was going to prove to be much easier than going up!

We didn't talk much after that and I sat quietly stroking the warm little body on my lap. The gentle snuffling of the sleeping puppy reminded me of two rabbits I'd had as a kid. I had grown up in a rough, poor area of Newcastle where presents were rare in most houses and non-existent in mine. But on one particular occasion when I was about seven my father came home with two very small rabbits saying they were for me. I had hardly been able to believe it, as he'd never bought me anything before!

I had loved them and called them Floppy and Hick. In order to get money to buy bran and to make them a hutch, I had hunted around for old boxes and once the hutch was built, I had broken up what was left and sold it for firewood. I kept this up for several months and the rabbits grew sleek, plump and cuddly. They were Flemish Giants and as they grew began to live up to their name. I would rush home from school every night and dash straight into the back yard to see them.

Then one night my mother shouted down the stairs, frantically trying to stop me – but it was too late and as I had opened the back door, I'd seen their bodies hanging there, dripping with blood. My father had killed and gutted them to sell to one of his mates for his Sunday dinner! In that moment all my hatred of him had come to the surface. I had wanted to kill him and would never trust him again.

Suddenly my daydream was shattered, as a loud crack rang out and a stream of water cascaded onto us from the leaves above. Chalky pointed ahead. 'I think I spotted something that looks like a truck, over there.'

'Where?'

'Over there, about 800 yards in that direction.'

'How can you see 800 yards?' Dynamo queried, peering into the mist. 'I can't see a bloody thing.'

'Well, it was clear when I looked before. Over there, down on the other side of the river.'

Dynamo stopped the truck and we all peered in the direction Chalky pointed out, trying to see through the mist into the valley below. 'Ssshh! Be quiet: we might hear something,' Chalky said.

'Well, I'm not switching this bloody engine off for anyone. We might not get it started again,' Dynamo insisted.

'Look, we can't sit here all day,' Spot pointed out. 'There's only one way down here so let's get going. Chalky must have eyes like a bloody hawk. I can't see a thing either.'

Dynamo put his foot down and the jeep picked up speed. 'We need to get out of here quickly,' he said. 'That was definitely gunfire. It's a bloody good job whoever fired it is cock-eyed.'

I turned to Chalky. 'This is the only way down isn't it? So there's a good chance whoever fired at us will be waiting at the end of this track by the time we get to the bottom.'

Just then several more shots rang out and whistled overhead.

'I still can't see anything!' Dynamo exclaimed. 'Look, we might have to ditch this bloody thing and take care of the bastards. If there isn't a turn off soon, we're a sitting target in it!'

'Surely they can't be aiming at us, they're miles out. They mustn't be able to see us and are aiming at the sound.' As Chalky spoke, the mist swirled and cleared for a brief moment and through the break, we could just make out a British army truck and what looked like several soldiers on the other side of the river.

'Hey, it looks like our lot! Bloody typical, I might have known. Whatever happened to "Halt! Who goes there?"' he joked.

'It's a good job they can't see us properly, dressed like flaming terrorists in a bloody American army jeep,' Spot laughed back.

'We've got to get away from here. We can't take our own men out but we can't afford to let this lot catch us either,' Dynamo pointed out and abruptly veered off the track and headed the jeep straight up the side of the hill.

'Where the hell are you going?' asked Spot.

'Look, I know this area pretty well: there's a little dirt track on the other side of this, if we can make it. They won't be able to catch up with us, they can't cross that river here, they'll have to go a couple of miles further down and we'll be long gone by then.'

The hill was steep but relatively smooth and the jeep slid and skidded sideways across the rough surface as we sped towards the top. Once on the other side, we looked down the steep slope and beneath us could just make out the old dirt track in the distance that Dynamo had mentioned.

'There you are, I knew it.' Dynamo grinned. 'We're home and dry now, lads.'

2. A lesson learnt

Back at camp that night, I lay on my bunk unable to sleep, going over and over the vivid events of the previous night, barely able to believe what had happened up in the Troodos Mountains. It still seemed so unreal to me: my first operation as part of the The Sixteen. If it had not been for the puppies, I might have simply believed I had dreamt it all.

Unanswered questions whirled around and around in my head, and not for the first time I wondered just who these guys were that trained me. Where did they go after an operation once they had dropped me off, what happened to them, did they go back to a regular army camp like me? And what was it all about anyway, what was it in aid of and just who was behind it? Why were there only sixteen of them and what on earth had induced them to pick someone like me to be one of their group? But although I was desperate to hear the answers and learn more about them, I knew it was pointless to ask, as they had warned me from the start that I would only ever be told what I needed to know.

I had heard rumours that a special forces group called the SAS were operating on the island, and on one occasion while training with Dynamo I had asked him whether the The Sixteen were anything to do with them. But, as usual, I got little out of him; he'd merely laughed and shook his head.

'No, we're nothing to do with that lot!' he'd said emphatically. 'Don't ask questions, Geordie, you know the routine.'

Training with them had been an incredible experience. They told me that I needed to reach a stage of readiness in a very short period and, apparently, I had proved to be an extremely adept and quick pupil, surprising them with the speed at which I learned complex manoeuvres and techniques. I had loved every minute of my training and over the last few months I had quickly reached a stage where I feared nothing and felt almost invincible, so that by the time of my first operation I was raring to go.

But now that the adrenaline had faded, I began to feel a real sense of disappointment, almost of being cheated somehow. As I'd looked at those dead men lying in the cave, I had realised just how much I'd wanted to prove myself: I'd desperately wanted the opportunity to take on more of them. I had really wanted to use my sash and my boot knife, to be able to act like the machine they had trained me to be. It had been such an incredibly strong, powerful urge – unlike anything I had experienced before in my life.

Using my sash during training, I had seen the awesome, unstoppable power of the weapon and had been itching to use it ever since. With it I knew that I had the capability of ripping three or four men to pieces in seconds. But now I felt as though I had been given the best toy in the world and then told that I wasn't allowed to play with it.

For the life of me, I could not understand what had happened, just what it was exactly that they had done to me, and turned me into, in such a short period. I was not a vicious thug with something to prove and I certainly had not been out of control; in fact, it had been the complete opposite: I had been so totally, unbelievably in control. Yet, only three months before, I had been a shy, stammering, ill-educated lad.

Although I was good in the gym, being fit and agile, and had done a bit of boxing as a kid, I had always avoided any type of conflict or trouble because I felt that I couldn't fight my way out of a paper bag. Exactly what had happened to me in the cave I could not say, but afterwards everything was a total anti-climax. I experienced not only a deep sense of loss, but also an equally strong craving to feel so powerful again, and to be back in action as soon as possible.

Naturally, I had been dying to tell my mates what had happened when I got back to 524 Company but, for obvious security reasons, I couldn't. Besides, there was no way they would have believed me anyway. I might as well have told them that I had just seen a flying saucer as recount the incredible story of how I had been recruited and selected to serve with this ultra-covert outfit and trained as a professional assassin! Even I still found it difficult to believe. After all, who was I – a complete and utter nobody doing my national service in the Pioneer Corps; just how low can you get?

Eventually it had dawned on me just how good a cover it really was; in fact it was the best there could possibly be. Who on earth would ever believe such a fantastic story, for God's sake? I would never be able to prove a thing; I didn't even know where they trained me as they took me a different route each time! They certainly knew how to cover their tracks.

So I just kept my mouth shut and said nothing to my pals. It was difficult though, listening to all their boring tales about how much beer they had drunk and all the stupid antics they got up to when they had a few. Their other main topics of conversation were football, which they would go on and on about endlessly, and either women in general or their girlfriends in particular and how they just couldn't wait to get back home.

I could understand how they would think that I was a real bore, because most of the time I would refuse to go to the NAAFI (the army canteen) with them or join in their foul-mouthed discussions about women. It wasn't their fault: the poor buggers had nothing more interesting to talk about. But for once in my life, I had done something exciting and adventurous and I couldn't tell a soul. If only they'd known.

I would have loved to have been able to keep the puppies, but knew deep down that it was impossible. On my return to camp, I had managed to smuggle them back to my tent, but needed something to put them in as they were trying to crawl around all over the place. As it was Friday night there was no one about; all the lads were all down the NAAFI spending their pay. So I left the puppies hidden in the tent while I went to look for something suitable that would hold them.

Over at the NAAFI I managed to scrounge a cardboard box from one of the Indians who helped to run it and bought a couple of sausage sandwiches to feed the dogs with when I got back. Hopefully this would keep them quiet and help them go to sleep. It was quite a while since they had last been with their mother and they were obviously very hungry by now. I just hoped that they were old enough to eat solid food.

Of course, I should have realised that puppies are just like babies and cry a lot. Back at the tent they were trying to move around, squeaking and whimpering constantly. I had just taken them from their mother and they were obviously fretting for her. I was beginning to regret bringing them back to the camp, but what else could I have done? I could not have just left them there to die: after all, I was responsible for their mother's death. I suppose it is hard to believe that I felt so guilty about two puppies after I had just killed a man, but then again these dogs had not been going about murdering British soldiers and their families, as the local terrorists were doing all over Cyprus.

Taking the sausage meat out of the bread, I put some of it together with the puppies into the cardboard box, which I then pushed outside through the back tent flap. I had no idea what I was going to tell the lads I shared the tent with when they returned from the NAAFI: I just hoped that the puppies would go to sleep and not make any noise.

It was getting late now and I decided to write a letter home to my mother. I told her about my life at the camp but there was not very much to tell, so I jotted down a bit about the puppies, although not, of course, how I had actually come by them. Then suddenly it dawned on me just how daft I was being: I was on active service and censors vetted all letters home. If any army personnel read about the puppies, the poor things would be taken away and immediately destroyed. Wild dogs were a constant problem around the camp, roaming about looking for food, and orders were to shoot them on sight, so I really could not expect much sympathy for these two little scraps. I knew that I really had not given enough thought to how I was going to look after them. Spot had been right, they were going to cause problems and might get me into a lot of trouble; I could see that now.

Suddenly I felt very, very tired. It was about 48 hours since I'd had any proper sleep, having spent most of the previous night on a stony mountainside, and so, fully clothed, I lay down on my bunk and finally began to relax for the first time in the last couple of days. As the tension started to disappear at last, I realised just how relieved I was to be back safely, especially after almost being shot by our own troops. But weirdly, despite being glad to be back, I also realised just how much I was looking forward to the next operation. It was as if deep down inside I had a want, a driving force. I had never felt so alive as I had the previous night.

To play with danger the way I had done, to face death that way, to be so totally in control and have the ability to walk away without a scratch, had left me feeling almost invincible. I just wanted to be back with Dynamo, Spot and Chalky as soon as I possibly could.

They were all great guys who took their training very seriously but went about it in such a way that they made it seem like fun. They were always laughing, joking and poking fun at one another, yet I knew that I could trust them implicitly and rely on them totally. Bright, intelligent and well-educated, they knew exactly what they were about. With them, for once, I felt that I was among real men.

On our way back from the mountains, they had been full of praise for the way in which I had handled myself. Spot had leaned towards me in the jeep and said quietly: 'Believe me, Geordie, that's nothing, nothing! Not compared to what we have done and what you will be able to do.' I had been intrigued, wanting to know more, but he did not go into any further detail.

As I lay there thinking unable to sleep, someone began fumbling with the tent flap and eventually Bill Strickland stumbled noisily into the tent and immediately flopped onto his bunk. He had obviously been down to the NAAFI with the others for a skinful.

'Where've y'bin all week, Gsheordie?' he mumbled drunkenly into his pillow, his strong Lancashire accent even more pronounced than usual.

'Over at 518 Company, how about you?'

'Lucky bashtard, ah've bin diggin' bloody roadsh all week.' He was almost incoherent with sleep and booze. Just then, one of the puppies began to whimper and scratch at the box outside the tent.

'Wha..., wha's that noishh, Gsheordie?' Bill asked, trying to raise his head. 'Ee, ah thort ah heard myshe or shnakes or summat…' he slurred as his voice faded and he fell asleep. I crept to the back of the tent and slipping my hand through the flap dropped some more sausage into the box directly outside. I had just lain back down when Dave arrived back too. I closed my eyes pretending to be asleep: I didn't want conversation.

Unlike Bill, he was not the worse for alcohol and sat down to write a letter. Eventually I dozed off, but some time later, I woke to hear the two of them talking quietly. Opening my eyes I found them sitting on the opposite bunk each holding a puppy in front of him.

'Hey, Geordie, look wot we've found!' Dave said, holding the small white bundle out to me. Bill, obviously still drunk, swayed from side to side as he sat, staring hard and trying to focus on the puppy curled up in his hands.

'Look, lads,' I began to explain. 'I brought them in, I found them wandering about just outside the camp. I think their mother must be dead. You know what would happen to them if the sergeant found out: he'd have them shot straight away.'

'You darft bugger, this ain't a cat an' dog shelter. It woz probably our lot wot shot the muvver anyway. You'll be in real bovver if yor caught. You'll 'ave to get rid of 'em you know,' Dave grumbled in his strong Cockney accent.

'Shoft shod!' Bill mumbled.

'I know, I know. Look, Dave, help me keep them hidden over the weekend, mate, and I'll sort something out.'

Dave obviously wasn't keen. 'Yeah, well, OK. But only over the weekend, mind. You'll 'ave ter get sumfing sorted by Monday. I don't want ter gerrinter bovver over some darft bleedin' dogs,' he grumbled. ''Ere you, gimme that before you drops it.' He took the other puppy from Bill then returned them both to the box outside.

Dave was as good as his word and between the three of us we managed to take it in turns to look after the puppies over the weekend, each of us smuggling bits of food back after mealtimes. Late on Sunday night, when they returned from the NAAFI, Bill and Dave again tackled me about what I was planning to do with the puppies.

'Well, Geordie, this is it. What will you do tomorrer if we're all sent to work out of camp? D'you know where you'll be this week?' Bill asked, slightly drunk yet again.

'No, I haven't a clue. Look, we might not all get sent out and who-ever doesn't can take care of them, can't they?' I pleaded with them.

'That's easier said than done: don't forget that the sergeant 'as a good look around the tents when we go off every morning. You'll 'ave ter find somewhere else ter hide them,' Dave grumbled, obvi-ously keen to be rid of the problem.

'I know, I know! Just help me out for a little longer and I'll have a word with Lieutenant Stevens. He's sort of a pal of mine, but I'll not be able to see him until either Monday or Tuesday. I'm sure he'll be able to help us.'

They seemed reasonably happy with that, but I was beginning to wonder if I had done the right thing in rescuing the puppies. They were a real problem.

The following morning began like any other Monday, at 0600 hours, when the damn bugle blew. But on this particular Monday morning, my name wasn't called out for a working party out of the camp; instead I was told to report to the cookhouse, which was a relief. Once there I thought I might be able to sort something out for the puppies.

As soon as we were dismissed, I reported to the cookhouse to get my orders off the sergeant cook, then dashed back to my tent. The parade ground was deserted now so I grabbed the cardboard box with the puppies in it and dashed across to the cookhouse. There was a gap between the cook's sleeping quarters and the cookhouse wall that was only about a yard away from where I was working; I hid the box with the puppies in there before sneaking back into the cookhouse. I started to wash the stacks of breakfast pots and pans, knowing that after about two hours of this I would be finished until lunchtime and so free to go and look for Lieutenant Stevens.

For the next two hours I scrubbed and cleaned the dixies and pots and pans, sweat pouring from me. It was like an oven in the cookhouse! I couldn't understand how the cooks put up with the intense heat from about five in the morning until six at night, with only a short break in between. From my workstation, I could see across the parade ground as I scrubbed away and when I saw

Lieutenant Stevens striding across the other side of it, I immediately dropped the pan I was cleaning and ran after him. I knew that if anyone could help me with the puppies he could.

From the odd bits of conversation we'd had, I knew him to be a real dog lover and I hoped he would be able to help me find good homes for the puppies. I told him my slightly far-fetched story about finding them running around on their own outside the camp and although he seemed somewhat dubious about my explanation, he followed me over to where they were hidden. When he saw them, however, he gave me a long hard look. The puppies were so young they could barely walk.

He looked at me suspiciously. 'Urwin, I could get into serious trouble over this. Where did you say you found them?' he asked, picking one of them up and holding it in front of his face. 'They seem far too young to be taken away from their mother.'

'I found them over by the fence, sir, I think they may have been dumped there. I've fed them and they can drink and eat on their own.'

'Hmm. OK. Right, leave it with me, I'll see if I can get rid of them somehow,' he told me unenthusiastically, as he lifted the other puppy from the box. For one awful moment, I thought he might be going to have them put down.

'What are you going to do? You're not going to have them killed, are you, sir?' I asked anxiously. He looked at me steadily for a moment before replying evenly.

'What do you take me for, Urwin? I'll ask around a couple of other regiments on the island who use dogs as company mascots. They'll be perfectly all right, don't worry. Leave them here and I'll collect them later. Make sure you're not caught with them,' he warned as he handed the puppies back and marched off.

At every opportunity, I slipped out from the cookhouse with scraps of food and even a little milk for them. Then at about two in the afternoon another sergeant, a huge fat bloke from 518 Company officers' mess, strode into the cookhouse.

'Well, well. Look what I've got here! Who's responsible for this? You know there's not supposed to be dogs anywhere on the camp and especially not near the food,' he bawled.

As I looked up, my heart sank. He was standing holding one of the puppies by the scruff of the neck. I had worked under him briefly in the officers' mess and for some reason he did not like me one bit.

'They're going to other regiments to be trained as mascots,' I told him.

'Is that a fact? Who says so?'

'Lieutenant Stevens,' I blurted out, quickly taking the puppy from him. 'They belong to Lieutenant Stevens; he asked me to look after them for him.'

He looked at me for a moment with his narrow, piggy eyes, then appeared to accept my explanation.

'Well, get them away from here,' he ordered, nastily. 'You always seem to be at the bottom of something or other, don't you Urwin?'

'I don't know what you mean, sarge,' I said, trying to sound truthful. Just then the sergeant cook strode over to us and spoke abruptly to the fat sergeant.

'What's going on here? Leave that lad alone; he's working for me not you. Anyway, what the hell are you doing over here, you fat slob?'

'OK. OK. Keep your hair on! I only came to borrow a couple of tins of corned beef,' the fat sergeant said defensively. 'There's no need to be like that.'

'Here, then,' the sergeant cook said, throwing a couple of tins towards him. 'Now push off.'

The fat sergeant gave a belligerent look in my direction then waddled off.

'You want to keep well away from that one, Urwin,' the sergeant cook warned me with a nod at the other's departing back. 'He's a nasty piece of work, so don't you go making an enemy of him.'

Lieutenant Stevens was as good as his word and came back for the puppies early in the afternoon; I was so relieved that they were going to be looked after.

'Don't do this again, Urwin!' he warned, and then in a friendlier tone asked, 'By the way, whatever happened to that stammer of yours?'

'Sold it, sir,' I replied, cheekily.

He just smiled and shook his head as he walked away with the puppies. I never saw them again. Once I had explained to Dave and Bill what had happened when they returned to camp that night, I never mentioned the puppies again.

I realised that I should have listened to Dynamo and the others and trusted their judgement when they had warned me. I simply could not afford to draw any undue attention to myself at all. I had learnt an invaluable lesson: I had to keep a low profile at all times.

That night as I lay dozing on my bunk, I thought back over the events of the last few days and months. Just how had it all come about? How had I, an ordinary 18-year-old Geordie lad, become part of such an elite and highly covert assassination squad?

3. In the army now

It seemed like only yesterday that I had said goodbye to my mother and sisters at Newcastle central station to head off to Wrexham, North Wales, in order to undergo six weeks of basic training before starting my two years of national service.

I had always been very close to my mother and had not wanted to leave home when I received my call-up papers. But the only choice I had been given was that I did not have to go into the forces if I was serving my time as an apprentice, learning a trade. I wanted to be a mechanic and had a job at a local garage, but right from the start I had known there was no future in it for me there. I was not being properly trained – just used as a dogsbody, a grease monkey, the butt of constant taunts and jokes about my terrible stammer.

Mam and I discussed my going into the army. Naturally she was very upset about it: she didn't like the idea of my being away from home with the real possibility of being killed as, at that time, there was still so much trouble and unrest throughout the world after the War. However, a couple of days after receiving the papers, I was outside messing about with my motorbike when Mam called me into the house. Putting her hand on my shoulder she stared at me for a few moments and then said quietly: 'Do it, son. Join the army and get away from that miserable, moaning father of yours. It's probably the only chance you'll get to see a bit of the world and maybe better yourself.'

'But what about you, Mam?' I asked, concerned at how she would cope with him if I were not there.

'Never mind me,' she replied. 'Just you do it!'

I told her that I would think about it, but I really had not wanted to leave her alone with my father. Although small and slightly built, he was an ex-boxer and a vicious bully who over the years had taken his drunken temper out on both her and me. As a direct result of his treatment, I had developed a dreadful stammer, and by the time I was 12, my mother had already made two desperate attempts to take her own life (both of which I had discovered). Who would look after her if I were not there?

However, the following day matters were taken out of my hands when the foreman at work announced they were paying off two of the other lads and me. Obviously, that changed everything and I felt as though I really had no choice in the matter: good jobs were not that easy to come by. It seemed as though I was destined to go into the army.

Two days later, another letter arrived from the army giving the date and time for my medical at Chester-le-Street, which I passed with flying colours the week before my 18th birthday on 28 November 1957. When they asked me which regiment I wished to join, I must have looked a bit blank. I knew little about the army at that time, so I told them that I would like to do anything that involved mechanical work. One of the recruitment staff made a note of this and told me I would hear from them in a few weeks' time.

In the meantime, however, I knew I had to find work quickly as my mother relied on my extra money to make ends meet. After spending a couple of days looking around, I eventually managed to get a job at Tizer, the soft drinks manufacturer, where I worked for about two months. I had almost forgotten about the army when the letter arrived giving me the date to report for training at Wrexham.

So, that had been that. I was given only a week to sort everything out and I went through all manner of emotions. I was both excited and terrified. I had never been away from home (or even out of Newcastle) before, and thought that crossing the Tyne Bridge was going abroad!

Well, this is it, I thought, now I'm bound to meet some sensible and intelligent people. This shows just how naïve I was and how little I knew about the army then.

My mother and sisters came to the station to wave me off, but my father had refused when Mam asked him to come with us. Deep down I was glad of that: he was one person I definitely would not miss.

'Don't worry son, you'll be all right. Write when you can!' Mam shouted from the platform, suddenly looking so small and helpless that I wanted to jump straight back off the train. I waved and waved until they were out of sight and the train slowly made its way across the High Level Bridge over the River Tyne. My home town gradually disappeared as I watched with a sinking feeling in the pit of my stomach, feeling nervous, scared and lonely, not knowing what to expect.

I tried to imprint the scene in my mind, fearful that I might forget it while I was away. Down on the river below, small motor-boats were moving around on the water, reminding me of the many times I had spent on one just like them with my Uncle George; I wished with all my heart that I was down there in one of them, anywhere in fact other than where I was and where I was going. In the distance, through the archway of the Tyne Bridge, I saw the old horse trough where I used to stop when I'd taken my Dad's horse, Jackie, for a ride when we lived there. My eyes had filled with tears and I felt choked to be leaving it all behind.

Feeling very nervous and a bit lost, I sat back in the dingy compartment as the train sped south and wondered just what the next two years would bring.

RPC (Royal Pioneer Corps) 524 Company was based about three miles outside Wrexham and consisted of little more than a large number of wooden billets around a parade square, together with a gym, a NAAFI and a guardhouse near the main gate. I hated it on sight!

Most of my basic training was done in the middle of winter in the bitter cold. After a week of marching for miles and miles around the parade square in the snow and being shouted at every inch of the way, I began to find both it (marching) and the rifle drill very easy. Unfortunately, some of my mates found it more much more difficult to learn and because of this they were constantly shouted at and humiliated, which really angered me. Then, to my great embarrassment, the drill sergeant made me number one marker, as I'd been one of the best turned out on parade and the best at marching. I had been singled out just for walking and swinging my arms and keeping my back straight!

I don't know what I had expected, but I became disillusioned with the army very quickly. I suppose I had hoped that I would meet real men, people with common sense, and that with everyone coming from a variety of backgrounds and all walks of life, things would be different here. But all the lads could talk about was the same old stuff – football, women and drinking, just like back home. Once again, I just did not fit in at all.

When the lads went off to the NAAFI drinking, I would go down to the gym and work out on the parallel bars and rings. Usually there would be no one else around and I had the place to myself, which was great. I loved anything to do with gymnastics; it was something I excelled in at school. The other lads in my billet thought I was crazy and tried to persuade me to go to the NAAFI with them, but I was just not interested.

One night in the gym, the drill sergeant, another Geordie, joined me.

'How's it going, lad?' he enquired in a friendly way.

'OK, Sarge, b-but the army's s-so d-different to wh-what I thought it would b-be. I w-want to b-be a mechanic b-but I don't think I've g-got much chance of th-that here,' I told him. I had quickly realised that I was never going to learn anything with this outfit.

'Let me give you a word of advice, lad,' he said. 'You're not like these other morons. If you want to have an easy life in the army, you either box for the company or become a PTI. Your basic training will be over in four weeks and I suggest you put your name down now.'

I was grateful for his interest and decided to do as he suggested: make life as easy as possible by putting my name forward for something I enjoyed, and ask to be considered as a PTI (physical training instructor). However, when I made enquiries I was told that I was probably wasting my time, as they would only train me if I became a regular. This meant signing on for a minimum of three years that would follow on immediately from my two years' national service, which I had absolutely no intention of doing. Despite this set-back, I still spent all my free time in the gym working out and practising. I loved being active and the feeling of being strong and fit.

Shortly after our basic training was over, we had our passing out parade. A lot of the lads' families turned up but Mam just couldn't afford it. I was disappointed; she would have loved it and would have been very proud of me.

Rumours began to spread around the camp that we were being transferred, to another camp at Stratford-on-Avon in two days' time. I decided to spend what little time I had left at the camp in the gym, as I might not get the chance to work out for a while. I had been trying to train myself on the pommel horse, as I had seen the PTIs working on it and thought I would like to give it a go. But I was making a right mess of it, banging my knees until they were sore. As I practised, I gradually become aware of someone watching me and stopped what I was doing. Looking around, I was surprised to see a guy standing in the corner of the gym, arms folded, dressed in a black and red PT instructor's T-shirt and black trousers. I hadn't heard him come in.

'You're doing it all wrong, Geordie,' he called out to me. 'Here, I'll show you.'

I couldn't remember ever having seen him around the camp and had been surprised that he knew my nickname. I watched in utter fascination as he began to effortlessly swing his body around, as though it weighed absolutely nothing. He made it look so easy and as he worked, he kept on talking to me.

'You're a good gymnast, Geordie. I've been watching you for a while. I understand you like boxing.'

'H-how d-do you know that?' I asked him. 'It was wh-when I was a k-kid; anyway I w-wasn't that k-keen.'

'Never mind how I know, I might be able to help you. I understand you now want to be a PTI. Why?'

'Well, it d-d-doesn't look as though I'm going to g-g-get anywhere e-else in the army, they t-t-tell me th-that being a PTI is one w-way of making life more c-comfortable. I've j-j-just f-found out wh-what kind of outfit this is. I'd b-be b-b-better off w-working f-for McAlpine's!'

'Just what were you expecting?' he asked.

'I w-wanted to g-get s-some kind of t-trade, b-be a mechanic or s-s-something, b-but I've been t-told that if I want to g-get any-where I n-need to s-s-sign on f-for at least th-three years f-full t-time after doing my n-national s-service, so I've g-gone off the idea. I f-feel as though I've b-been d-duped in s-some way.'

'What else did you have in mind, if you had a choice?'

'If I can't b-be a PTI I w-want to b-be transferred t-to an active r-regiment, d-doing s-s-something a b-bit more exciting. I thought that w-was wh-what the army w-was all about. If only I could be t-transferred into s-some k-kind of a fighting unit; anything w-would be b-better than this f-flaming mob.'

'Is that what you really want, Geordie?' he said quietly, stopping what he was doing.

'Y-yes, I'm n-not in the habit of w-wasting time b-by s-saying things I d-don't mean. It t-takes me t-too long.'

He laughed at that and then continued on the pommel horse.

'Well, you've certainly got the determination. I've been watching you trying to do things in here and I can see that once you get into something you like to finish it. You're a quick learner too; you remember physical movements very quickly, don't you?'

'I-I s-s-suppose s-so. H-how is that g-going to h-help me?'

'It will, believe me! Don't do anything now, don't put in for a transfer or anything like that. We need you where you are right now.'

I opened my mouth to ask him more, but just then the Geordie sergeant came in and, to my surprise, the PTI immediately stopped what he was doing and came right up to me.

'One of us will contact you at Stratford,' he whispered then quickly left.

'E-excuse me?' I shouted after him but he just opened the door and walked out as if he hadn't heard. I thought that it had to be some kind of wind-up or practical joke.

'Who was that?' the sergeant asked.

'I h-haven't the f-foggiest idea.' I replied truthfully. 'H-he was sh-showing me how to w-work on the p-pommel horse. He w-was pretty good w-wasn't he? I th-thought you w-would know him.'

'Well, I've been here for over two years and I've never seen him before!'

'Are w-we g-going to S-stratford?' I asked, changing the subject.

'Now how do you know about that? Never mind, it'll be

common knowledge soon enough. Yes, you're leaving soon, but I don't know where you're going,' he told me.

I just shrugged and carried on training. Wherever the army decided to send me, I had little say in the matter. But I was unable to stop thinking about the stranger. All his talk of 'we' and 'one of us' had totally baffled me. Who the hell were 'we'? In fact who the hell was he? I hadn't a clue what he was talking about or why anyone would be remotely interested in someone like me, from a regiment like this.

The following Saturday morning our platoon had left Wrexham for Stratford-on-Avon and more rumours started, this time about us going abroad, in fact the other lads had talked of nothing else. But all I was able to think of was my 48-hour pass to go home. I was longing to see my family.

I was at the Stratford camp for about a week before I gave any more thought to the stranger in the gym. So far, no one had bothered with me at all. So much for his talk about someone contacting me, I thought. I knew it had been a wind-up!

More rumours began to spread about being posted abroad. The newspapers were full of reports about the escalating trouble out in the Middle East, and the lads talked about it constantly. But I didn't care: I had finally been given my 48-hour pass and I could hardly believe it. I would be going home and that was all I was able to think about. I was so excited, even though I knew I would spend most of those 48 hours on a train. But at least I would get to see my Mam and my sisters again, for the first time in three months; it had seemed more like three years and had been really awful.

But it was not to be. Despite our passes, we had all been stopped at the camp gate and told that they had been rescinded. Instead of heading off for home, we were taken to one shed for a load of jabs, which left our arms stiff and sore, and then to another where we received an issue of tropical kit. In what must have been hours but felt like mere minutes, we were herded aboard trucks bound for Southend airport and informed that we were on our way to Aden.

The army convoy drove straight onto the airport runway and we jumped out to an utterly amazing scene: thousands of troops stretched in every direction as far as the eye could see. The place was full of hustle and bustle, the air filled with noise: the roar of planes taking off and trucks racing around. Thousands of marching feet and hobnailed boots crunched on the runways, as sergeants screamed out orders. My unit formed part of an airlift in which we were told some 18,000 troops were flying out to the Middle East.

'Christ, the Third World War must have started!' someone commented, as we lined up to board our plane, a twin-engine Dakota. And for all we knew at that time, he could well have been stating the truth.

Inside, the plane was noisy, cramped and uncomfortable. We sat in long rows down either side making little or no conversation, each man lost in his own thoughts. This was partly due to the noise of the plane, which made it difficult to talk without shouting, partly because we were beginning to feel the effects of all of the jabs, but mainly because we were all stunned by the speed of it all. One moment, we were about to go home and the next we were on a plane with dozens of other soldiers most of whom we had never seen before, heading towards God knows what in the Middle East. We had heard all kinds of rumours about what was going on out there and knew that a lot of our lads were being killed, but we did not really know what to expect.

Whether it was always the intention for us to land in Malta I am not sure, but our plane diverted there when it developed engine trouble. Looking out of the window, I saw thick black smoke coming from the port engine.

'Hey, look at this,' I said, nudging the lad next to me.

'Eh! What?'

'Look, the flamin' engine's on fire! I don't think we're going to make it!'

'F... off, Geordie, try it on someone else!' he said, thinking I was winding him up.

'No, honest, look,' I insisted as the intercom suddenly crackled into life: 'Sorry about this, gentlemen. Apparently we have trouble with our port engine, but don't worry, chaps, we have two. We'll just have to make a little unscheduled stop at Malta,' the pilot had cheerfully informed us in a poncy, upper class accent that was pure 'Battle of Britain'.

His announcement was met with a variety of moans, groans and comments:

'Oh, bloody great, we're going to snuff it before we even get there. Just my flaming luck!'

'Don't worry, old boy, we've got another engine, don't you know, eh, what!'

'That's right, old bean. Toodle pip, chocks away!'

'Shut the f… up, this is serious.'

'Oh Jeez, I think I'm going to be sick.'

The incident had certainly woken us all up from our previous stupor! Now we were quiet for a different reason – we were all bloody terrified!

Our landing at Malta was very hairy and I for one thought we were not going to make it. The pilot seemed to be coming in at an alarmingly steep angle and I remember the immense, almost tangible, feeling of relief when we heard the tyres screech as the plane bumped along the runway and finally stopped. We all just sat there a bit numb, grinning stupidly at one another, as we realised we had landed safely in one piece.

'Thank God for that!' the lad sitting next to me had muttered. 'Mind you, it'll just be my luck to get shot at the other end the minute I get off the bloody plane!'

I don't remember a great deal about Malta, as all we really saw of it was the airport where we were given orders to change to other planes, which split most of us up. I was told that I would now be going to Cyprus together with several other men who trained with me at Wrexham, three of whom stand out for no reason other than their oddly similar names: Dave Hatfield, Dave Bradfield and Dave Buckfield.

The airport had been busy, noisy with numerous planes coming in to refuel and hundreds of troops en-planing and de-planing with all of the usual army paraphernalia. I had time to buy a postcard to send off to my mother. It had a picture of the local hospital – an old fort – on it and I merely had time to write: 'Mother – Cyprus – didn't get weekend pass – will write and explain when we get there', before we were on the move again. It would be almost two years before we were back in England and I saw her again.

For a young Geordie lad like me, arriving in Cyprus was like being in a dream. The airport was ablaze with lights and noise, and as the plane doors opened we were bombarded with a variety of strange, alien smells mingled with petrol and diesel fumes. The night air that hit us was warm and humid.

We were given no time to look around. As soon as we de-planed we were quickly shepherded onto waiting trucks, issued with empty rifles and dispatched to our final destination. Only the officers' revolvers and a handful of the escort troops' guns were loaded.

Our vehicle formed part of a large convoy of canvas-covered Bedford trucks, which eventually set off into the pitch-black night. None of us knew where we were going or what to expect when we got there. Just outside the airport gates we caught a glimpse of several market stalls covered in fruit, and I recall seeing oranges and watermelons, their vivid colours brighter than anything I could ever have imagined. I was briefly aware of tiny white painted houses and narrow cluttered streets, but once we left the built-up area around the airport, we saw nothing apart from a brief glimpse of one another when the lights of the following vehicle lit up the back of the truck or when a cigarette would light up someone's face briefly.

The canvas sheet at the back of the truck had been pulled to one side with the tailboard up and every so often, out of the opening, we saw the lights of a small town or village in the distance. The roads were quite smooth for short distances but then we would hit rough patches and be tossed all over the back of the truck. Constantly being thrown around like that after the long, uncomfortable flight together, with the warm night air and petrol fumes, had begun to make some of the lads feel queasy. By this time we were all very tired and groggy from the long journey and the effects of our shots.

'I'm bloody beat! I wish we were there!' the lad opposite me had grumbled as, almost stabbing me with his cigarette end, he was thrown against me yet again, practically landing on my knee.

Then just as we hit another large bump in the road, we heard a loud crack like a truck backfiring and the guy sitting next to me suddenly keeled over and lay still, face down in the bottom of the truck. The convoy had come to an abrupt halt and I went to help him up, thinking he had simply been jolted out of his seat, when we heard several more loud cracks and the truck engines and lights were switched off! As I tried to lift him, my hand made contact with his back. To my surprise it was warm and damp. The realisation of what had actually happened instantly hit me: he had been shot! In that moment, all hell broke loose.

'Snipers!' a voice nearby bawled.

'Get out of the trucks! Take cover!'

Everyone seemed to be yelling, shouting and screaming at once as, frightened and confused, we dived out of the back of the truck, bashing into one another in our haste and falling over our rifles. We landed painfully on top of each other, unable to see in the pitch black. Having received no training for this kind of situation, we desperately scrambled about in the dark trying to find whatever cover we could and, once found, kept our heads well down. It was a terrifying experience, lying there in the dark, clinging to the steep hillside with no idea what was below us, bullets thudding into the trucks in front of us and burying into the ground only feet from where we lay.

We were all carrying rifles but had been issued with no ammo. Even if we had had bullets, I doubt whether most of us would have been able to use them: we would have been too scared of hitting one of our own guys in the dark. We knew there had to be hundreds of us scattered all around but couldn't see a thing. Above the noise of the intermittent gunfire, officers and sergeants could be heard shouting:

'Stay where you are, lads, and keep your heads down!'

'Keep under cover and don't move.'

'What's he on about, "don't move", I couldn't bloody move if I wanted too, I'm so scared,' one of the lads crouched next to me grumbled. 'And even if I could, where the bleedin' hell would I move to, for chrissake?'

'Watch where you put your hands, there's bloody snakes and things around here,' another nearby voice mumbled.

'Oh Gawd! Bullets and snakes,' the first lad moaned. 'That's all I bloody need.'

'Sarge! Sarge!' I shouted. 'There's someone in the back of our truck, I think he's been hit and he's in a bad way. He needs help.'

I knew the sergeant had heard my shout for help as he instantly began to call out for a medic. I wondered how the lad in the truck was doing; with all that blood around, I thought he might be dead.

The sky ahead and above us flashed with gunfire and I guessed that the snipers must be somewhere on the hilltop in front of us. Some of our guys were firing back, as there had been occasional flashes, followed by the loud crack of gunfire, further along the hillside.

It seemed as though we lay there for hours. As dawn broke, we began to see our surroundings more clearly. Like much of the island, the area was mainly barren and rocky with some scrub and a few thorny bushes. As the light increased, the alien landscape became more visible.

On a hilltop in front of us, silhouetted against the gradually lightening sky, we saw four or five terrorists, now captured, being marched down the hillside towards us, their hands above their heads. They had managed to keep several hundred British troops pinned down for hours in the darkness. What became even more apparent as it grew lighter was the fact that British soldiers had been surrounding their position the whole time.

We were given orders to get back into the trucks as quickly as possible and clambering back into ours I saw the large pool of blood on the floor, where the lad who had been shot had fallen. Obviously, during the night, the medics had somehow been able to get to him and move him to a safer place.

'Let that be a lesson to you all,' the sergeant warned us. 'Don't underestimate these bastards. They're well armed, well trained and bloody determined. Soldiers, women, kids – they don't give a shit. So keep well away from them and watch your backs at all times. This isn't a bleedin' holiday camp.'

As the trucks moved off we all sat quietly, trying not to look at one another or at the pool of blood that now stained the truck floor. No one spoke or asked where he was. Any thoughts we may have had of being on a 'paradise island' had been quickly dispelled on that very first night, as the full reality of the situation hit us all. This was to be no holiday in the sun!

I later discovered that the young lad who was shot was eventually shipped back to England. Apparently, the bullet had entered his left shoulder, travelled along and through his body to exit from his chest on the right-hand side, causing considerable internal damage. The rumour around the camp was that he lost the use of his right arm due to his injuries.

We were stunned when we arrived at our 'camp' – it was virtually non-existent. We had to make it ourselves over the next couple of weeks from the surrounding, mainly barren, area, and were kept busy putting up tents, organising cooking facilities, digging latrines and eventually erecting a perimeter fence.

The camp, in the middle of nowhere and surrounded by barbed wire, looked more like a prison. There were no towns in the near vicinity and, to begin with, none of us had the remotest idea of where we were in relation to where we landed at Nicosia. There was no wildlife as such either, with the exception of lizards, which could be seen scuttling about or basking on rocks. Days and nights were filled with the incessant chirping of crickets and buzzing of insects. The days were baking hot, the nights warm and oppressively humid. There was nothing to see and nowhere to go other than the camp NAAFI or the long walk down to the beach at Episkopi.

There were about 300 of us stationed at 524 Company, D Platoon, four to every tiny tent, dust and ants in everything we touched. Each tent was equipped with two bunks down either side, about six inches off the ground, with a couple of planks of wood running down the middle. This meant that at least there was something to stand on other than the ground. But when we did stand up our heads touched the top of the tent and we kept knocking each other over, as we all tried to get dressed at the same time in the tiny space between the bunks, still half asleep.

To top it off, a little wimp of a sergeant would come along every morning, screaming his bloody head off and bashing the sides of the tents with a stick. This just caused even more confusion and made matters worse, although he probably thought it would make us get dressed quicker! We really needed no encouragement to escape from the cramped confines of the tiny tents and get to the mess tent as soon as possible, as we always seemed to be hungry.

Once the battle between the four of us trying to get our clothes on was over, there would be a mad dash to get washed and shaved.

We only had half an hour to do this before breakfast. Half an hour might seem quite a while, but when there are hundreds of men all trying to get washed at the same time, it really isn't very long at all. To perform our ablutions, we used what looked like a couple of wooden troughs, roughly 30 feet in length. About every yard or so a pipe stood up with a tap stuck on the top of that.

Of course, the next dash was to the toilets (or latrines as the army calls them). These consisted of lines of steel buckets with wooden seats on the top, surrounded by a four-foot wall of hessian sacking. We would all sit there trying not to look at one another, discussing how hot the weather was yet again in order to cover our embarrassment, while at the same time trying to prevent ants from climbing up our legs. We also had to dodge some huge buzzing things, which looked like bees but were called horseflies. Following this came breakfast and we just couldn't wait.

In a large, sideless marquee, where wind and dust passed straight through, we were doled out pitiful portions of greasy eggs, stringy bacon and dried-up porridge mixed with dust and grit. Even before we had time to finish, we were rousted out for works parade, with barely enough time to say 'hello' to one another. Before leaving the tent, we had to wash our mess tins and plates in two small tin baths set up on a trestle table. Hundreds of us had to use the same water and it was always thick with grease, even though the kitchen staff kept changing it. If you were one of the lucky ones who managed to get to the water first, you might just end up with clean kit.

After breakfast we would line up on the parade ground, a level area surrounded by tents with a flagpole stuck in the middle. And, as we stood to attention, small whirlwinds called dust devils would whip past us, making us grab onto our hats and each other. Through the swirling dust, we would see that stupid little sergeant coming towards us trying to hold onto his orders and shouting at the same time.

4. On the beach

I had never heard of Cyprus until we landed there. But one important thing we all learnt from the moment we arrived was just how much the Cypriots hated us.

The Greek Cypriots, under General Grivas, wanted self-government and what they called 'Enosis', union with Greece, despite almost a third of its citizens, who were of Turkish descent, being bitterly opposed to this. In 1923, Turkey signed an agreement that gave up all claims to Cyprus, which then became a British colony in 1925. However, after the War, Britain refused to give Cyprus the right to self-government and by 1955, the Greek Cypriot freedom-fighters (EOKA) began an armed struggle for liberation. This came to a head during 1957-58 with the outbreak of serious riots and fighting between Greek and Turkish factions. Due to the strategic importance of the island's proximity to the Middle East, Britain was forced to pass a special emergency powers act and increase its presence on the island, in order to protect its military installations there and to control the increase in hostilities.

The British troops taken to Cyprus were told that they were there to keep the peace between the Greeks and the Turks and to protect government property. However, the Greeks mainly regarded us as the enemy and did their utmost to get rid of us, and did not seem to care how they went about it! They were not satisfied with just killing British troops: there had also been incidents involving the deaths of British servicemen's families too. The situation there at that time was similar to the one that would eventually erupt in Northern Ireland years later.

It certainly made no difference to the terrorists that my unit was in Cyprus mainly to repair roads and supply the fighting troops, not to take part in any peacekeeping exercise: they still would have liked to get rid of us all. This frustrated me as, from what I could see, we had been given little or no training to deal with a dangerous situation like this. In fact, we were treated little better than POWs and had to set up camp virtually from scratch.

The living conditions at our campsite were very basic and had hardly improved since we moved in. The planners in their wisdom must have chosen the most barren piece of rocky wasteland they could find in the area to build this particular camp. I hated it the moment I saw it and I continued to hate every minute of it.

Our washing facilities were as basic as the toilets and, although drinking water was regularly brought to the camp in two-wheeled mobile tanks, these stood on the main compound in full sunshine for most of the day, so the water was always warm. Digging latrines was especially difficult due to the hard, sun-baked, rocky landscape. I was not impressed. This was not what I had expected of army life: I could have stayed at home to dig roads like a navvy and probably earned a darn sight more than army pay.

Having experienced at first hand the terrorist activities on our first night, I was understandably nervous sitting on a tin bucket (our toilet facilities) surrounded by a four-foot wall of hessian. I fully expected to have my butt shot off at any moment. It certainly did not give me peace of mind or help my stuttering! Even in my crowded home in Byker, I had had a lot more privacy than here. I found having someone else coming in when you were on the toilet then sitting down right next to you very difficult to get used to.

My mate Dave Buckfield burst into the latrines on this particular occasion. He had a painful expression on his face as, like most of us in the camp, he was suffering from dysentery. He sat down next to me.

'Ere, 'eard the good news, Geordie?' he said in his strong Cockney accent.

'Wh-what's that?' The only good news I could be given was that they were shipping me back home!

'They're only settin' us bloomin' free this weekend. We can go down to the bloody beach on our own! Well, that's not strictly true, there 'as to be at least three of us, an' one of us will 'ave to carry a rifle. You coming, mate?' I shook my head. 'You'll 'ave to come otherwise we won't be able to go, there 'as to be three of us! C'mon, it'll be a larf!'

Some great news! It certainly did not cheer me up; all I wanted was to get back home, away from the heat, the flies, the smells and the deadly dull routine which had set in during our first couple of weeks at the camp. So far, we hadn't been given any proper recreational time since we arrived and so this first 'weekend off' was an eagerly anticipated event, and most of the guys wanted to go to the local beach about a couple of miles from the camp.

Although in general I got on well with people, I wasn't really 'one of the lads'; I didn't fit in. I didn't drink at all, had never tasted the stuff, whereas they all drank a lot. I was very self-conscious about my stammer and tended to keep to myself. I was also very disillusioned with army life, which to me appeared to consist of endless navvy work, then going out to get blind drunk afterwards. Luckily, the two lads I shared a tent with, Bill and Dave, were good fun. The three of us got on very well and shared a lot of laughs. The two of them kept on at me, pestering me to go with them.

'Come on, Geordie, it'll be a laugh.'

'C'mon, mate, 'ave some fun!'

In the end they convinced me to go with them and so, when Saturday morning came, we grabbed a couple of blankets to take with us as we had been warned that the sand got so hot you couldn't lie on it. Before we were allowed to leave the camp, we had to report to the 'stupid little sergeant' who woke us every morning. He gave us a lecture on what to expect when we got to the beach and what time we had to be back. Then he went on about making sure that we kept covered up and did not get badly sunburned, or fire the rifle by mistake. Though what the hell they thought we would be able to do with the three rounds we were given was beyond me!

After this lengthy talk, he eventually let us go and as we left the camp we felt as though we had just been let out of prison and rejoined 'normal' life once more. If it hadn't been for the fact that we were carrying a rifle, we could easily have forgotten that we were soldiers. We were just a group of young lads laughing and joking together as we walked along, cheered by the prospect of having some ordinary fun.

We were all wearing standard army-issue shorts, short-sleeved army shirts, white socks and black sand shoes. The shorts were horrendous: huge, baggy things that flapped around our knees like something a music hall comedian would wear. In an attempt to get these terrible things to look half-decent, most of the lads paid a local Greek bloke to take them in. This reduced the flapping effect and made them look much smarter.Unfortunately, as new arrivals we had not been given the opportunity to either buy any suitable clothes or have these alterations done yet, so we flapped our way along the hot dusty road.

It took about 20 minutes to get down to the beach, which was a couple of miles away at Episkopi. There were troops everywhere, all heading in the same general direction. Those of us who had only recently left Britain in the middle of winter were still becoming acclimatised to the weather and to us it was baking hot; yet the summer hadn't even started in earnest yet. We couldn't get to the beach quickly enough. All we wanted to do was get into the water to cool ourselves down.

Eventually, we came to a fairly long tunnel that had been blasted through the huge rock cliffs. On the top of these cliffs were several houses, which were used as married quarters. The tunnel was dark and dank, but once we got through to the other side a beautiful, golden sandy beach appeared in front of us. The sea was an incredibly bright blue colour that I had never seen before, its surface sparkling and glinting in the fierce sunlight. It was like a scene from a Hollywood movie.

The long, wide golden bay stretched off into the distance to the left of the tunnel and formed a crescent-shaped bowl that was surrounded on three sides by steep, craggy cliffs. Also to the left of the tunnel, and some way from its entrance, was a golf course for officers' use only. The track from the tunnel continued, across a wide area lightly covered with scrub, towards a cluster of huts standing on the beach itself. These huts sold refreshments, cold drinks and hot dogs, although God knows it was hot enough without hot food too. You had to run like hell over the beach to the water, as the sand was so hot it actually burnt the soles of your feet.

The layout of the beach was just as the sergeant had described it, divided into sections: one for officers and their families near to the tunnel, one for other ranks, and a further section for families and children out of sight of the surrounding hills and possible snipers. Apparently, there had been a number of occasions where shots had been fired at servicemen on the beach and we were told to keep the rifle with us at all times. This meant one of us carrying the rifle just in case we had to defend ourselves and taking it in turns to keep watch while the others swam, and was the reason we had been warned to always go swimming in groups of at least three.

We made our way along the crowded beach, away from the officers' area, and found a spot about 100 yards from one of the refreshment huts, which was covered with Coca-Cola signs. By the time I had laid the blankets out on the sand, Bill had already stripped down to his trunks and run off towards the sea.

'Stay 'ere, Geordie, with the rifle an' our gear,' Dave said. 'I'll go an' get some cold drinks an' sandwiches. We can go an' join 'im later.'

I lay on the blanket using Bill's clothes as a pillow, and idly watched a nearby group of blokes who were playing a noisy game of volleyball. Dave was only away a few minutes, but when he got back sweat was pouring from him. He plonked himself down on the blanket beside me.

'Gordon Bennett,' he panted. 'It's hot enough to fry a bleedin' egg.'

'Well, wh-why don't you go and join B-bill for a s-s-swim, the w-water looks g-great?' I told him. 'I'll w-watch our g-gear and go when you g-get back b-but don't b-be all day, I don't w-want to b-be roasted alive!'

'OK, Geordie. Cheers, mate.' He winked and ran off.

I sipped the ice-cold drink and rubbed the bottle across my forehead and chest to help cool me down. For the first time since I had arrived on the island, things were starting to look up a bit and I thought that if this was the way most weekends were going to be spent, then my time in the army might not be too bad after all. Although I felt a little more relaxed, I was still very homesick and missed my mother and sisters a great deal. Knowing that it would be at least 18 months before I saw them again just made it worse; a year and a half on this god-forsaken island!

I finished my drink and lay back. It was growing even hotter now and the beach was packed with groups of off-duty servicemen lounging about while others played football or volleyball, and in the cordoned-off family area, the married men sunbathed and picnicked with their families. It was very easy to spot any new arrivals from England; they were generally lily-white and looked like ghosts. Until the three of us had arrived on the beach we had imagined that our newly acquired suntans made us look like bronzed Hollywood film stars. But now looking around at the host of well-tanned bodies, I could see that Dave, Bill and I still easily fell into the 'ghost' category.

Getting sunburnt was considered a serious offence. NCOs constantly warned us about the dangers of getting burnt, and how much damage the strong sun, and its reflection off the sand and sea, could do to our eyes. To help prevent this, we had each obtained what passed in those days for army-issue sunglasses. These consisted of a long piece of celluloid with a V shape cut out and a small hole at each end through which a rubber band was tied. When you put the band over your head, with the V inverted over the bridge of your nose, the plastic wrapped around your cheeks and shielded your eyes very effectively. Generally, drivers of motorcycles and open vehicles used these as protection against dust and insects, but the plastic in theirs was clear, unlike that in the pair that I now put on. These had been modified and the clear strip replaced by an almost opaque layer of dark, bottle green plastic. In fact, they were so dark that I could barely make out the nearby game of volleyball, and the guys playing it now only appeared as shadows, while the rest of the beach disappeared into a green haze.

A figure emerged from the direction of the volleyball game and came into my line of vision gradually growing larger and larger as it neared me. I watched him lazily until, eventually, he blocked out the sunlight, casting a shadow over me. I removed the sunglasses in order to see him better but at first could not make out his features, as the sun was behind him.

'Hiya, John, or should I say Geordie,' he said as he flopped down beside me on the edge of the blanket.

Before I could speak, he raised his hand and said, ' Don't say anything. Just listen for a moment. Do you remember a chap talking to you in the gym back in Blighty during your basic training? He told you that you would be contacted in Stratford, but something happened back then and we couldn't make contact with you at that time, then your lot were shipped over here. Well, Geordie, I am that contact.'

I had never seen him before and the fact that he knew my name took me by surprise. I was not sure what he was talking about at first, then suddenly it came back to me and I remembered.

'Oh, th-that's r-right. Y-y-y-es, I r-remember the g-guy,' I stammered.

My eyes had acclimatised to the bright sunlight by now and I saw him clearly for the first time. He was an extremely fit, good-looking bloke, deeply sun-tanned and dressed like the rest of us in army-issue shorts, although his had been tailored to fit him very well.

'How would you like to have a change, a chance to do something more exciting?' He paused before carrying on. 'Think about it for a moment. Would you like a drink?'

'W-well, y-yes, OK,' I replied as he stood up and dashed off.

I didn't know what to think! I was not quite sure just what he meant by 'excitement'. But I was so fed up with the way things were going anyway, I would have done anything to get out of the boring routine back at camp and the nightmare prospect of another 18 months of the same stretching ahead of me. From what he said, I had visions of maybe being transferred to an active unit where, perhaps, I might be patrolling the streets. I felt that anything would be better than what I was currently doing but I did not understand why he would need to meet me so secretly for that.

I looked over to where he stood at the Coke stand and my Mam's words came to me: 'Shy bairns get nowt, John. If you don't push yourself you won't get anywhere.'

I watched the guy now running back towards me, a Coke bottle in each hand, and in that brief moment decided to take a chance and go along with whatever he said when he returned. What had I to lose?

'Y-yeah, OK, I'll g-give it a g-go,' I told him before he had time to sit down or speak. He smiled slowly and handed me one of the cold bottles.

'Great stuff! Right, we'll be in touch soon. Catch you later.' And with that he ran off in the same direction he had come from.

I was surprised at him leaving so quickly: I had expected him to tell me more and maybe arrange the date and time for another meeting. I stood up and looked around to see if I could see him anywhere but he had completely disappeared. Replacing my sunglasses, I lay back on the blanket and thought about our odd conversation. I got the impression that he could have been an officer as he was very well spoken and sounded well educated and confident. But I knew absolutely nothing about him and really he had told me little more than the guy in the gym back at Wrexham.

For security reasons, we had been warned to be extremely cautious in our dealings with strangers and what we discussed with them. There was a lot of terrorist activity on the island and spies and infiltrators were all around, looking for information which could be useful to them. But, for some strange reason that I could not explain, I instinctively felt that I could trust this guy. Besides, I thought, he must have something to do with the army, otherwise how was he going to be able to change things for me? It was weird though, the way he knew all about the guy who had spoken to me back at Wrexham and the intended contact at Stratford-on-Avon.

Just then, Bill and Dave ran up the beach and flopped down beside me on the blanket, breaking my chain of thought.

'Eeh, t'water's great, Geordie, you want t'get in there,' Bill said.

'Who was that geezer you were talking to?' Dave asked casually as he dried himself down.

'Oh, him? He's j-just one of the lads from the c-c-camp, Dave,' I replied, which apparently satisfied their curiosity, as they didn't pursue the matter further and the whole thing was so strange that I pushed it to the back of my mind.

It was very hot now and my turn to go for a swim. The shimmering sea looked so cool and inviting, so, leaving them in charge of the rifle, I headed over the scorching sand down to the water. Everyone was having a good time, noisily playing games, splashing one another and generally larking about in the warm water – so different from the North Sea, which was freezing even at the height of summer. I had borrowed a pair of flippers and, putting them on, swam out to a wooden pontoon anchored a little way off the beach from where people were diving into the crystal-clear water.

There were several porpoises (or dolphins – I never could tell the difference) swimming around the pontoon. They really seemed to enjoy being near to the people swimming, and bumped into us with their noses. Now and then, someone would shout 'Shark!' for a joke and everyone in the water would panic and frantically look around for the tell-tale dorsal fins. For all I knew, the porpoises could well have been sharks and, at first, they scared the life out of me.

The three of us stayed on the beach until the end of the day when everyone gradually began to pack up their belongings and head back to the camp. As the light quickly began to fade, we reluctantly prepared to leave too. Our day of freedom seemed to have been so short. Still stripped to the waist, we headed back towards the camp through the cool, dark tunnel, our voices echoing as we laughed and joked. It was still very warm and we walked along to the sound of crickets chirping in the velvety night air. In the distance, the lights at the camp gates shone brightly while the rest of the camp remained in virtual darkness, lit only by a few scattered light bulbs.

As we walked back up the dusty track, Dave and Bill chatted to one another, discussing whether to go to the NAAFI when they got back and I began to think again of my conversation with the man on the beach. The total strangeness of it all really hit me. It was weird to think that someone could be 'watching me' all of the time, as the guy had implied. I went over and over in my mind what he had said, as Bill and Dave chatted on by my side. By the time we reached our tent, I realised just how chuffed I was to have been singled out this way; to be considered a bit special by someone. Although unsure of what it was all about, I was also quite excited at the thought of having the opportunity to do something 'different'.

It was a warm sticky night and I tossed and turned, unable to sleep. The conversation on the beach kept on going through my mind. Suddenly, a thought occurred to me: the plane I had travelled in from England had been forced to make an emergency landing in Malta and as a result our original destination of Aden had been changed, which was how we ended up in Cyprus. Or so we believed, you could never tell with the army.

Bloody hell, I thought, how did he know that I would be here? Would he have made contact with me in Aden if I'd ended up there? Had that been the original plan? Who the hell are these people and how did they get all this information? And just why have they chosen me?

I spent a restless night worrying about just whom I might be dealing with and what I was possibly getting myself into. My brain buzzed with a hundred and one questions and I couldn't sleep.

During the early hours there was a loud commotion from a nearby tent, a lot of screaming and yelling. The racket jolted me out of a fitful doze and I rolled out of bed to see what was going on. But, in my haste, I had completely forgotten about the mosquito net over my bunk and immediately became entangled in it as I stood up. Struggling to break free of the damn thing, I tripped over the duckboards on the ground, overbalanced and landed heavily in a heap on top of Bill, who was sound asleep in one of the other bunks. He instantly woke up in a major panic.

'Wh-what is it? What's going on, Geordie, what's happening? What's that noise outside, are we being attacked or what?'

'G-give us time, Bill, m-man, I'm t-trying to g-get out of this flaming n-net.'

Eventually I managed to rip a hole in the material, and peered out through the tent flaps. Two guards were dragging a guy from a nearby tent and judging by the racket he was making, he was in agony. As they passed beneath the light in the middle of the parade square I saw what looked like a huge balloon on his back. In fact, the majority of his back was covered in one enormous blister, which made him look like the hunchback, Quasimodo.

'What the hell's going on, Geordie?' Bill asked again.

'Christ, Bill, you w-wanna s-see the size of the b-blister on this g-guy's b-back,' I replied.

'Serve t'noisy bugger right', Bill grumbled, 'We were warned about getting burnt. He's in trouble now; he'll be in for a court-martial. At least we might be able to get some bloody kip.' And, satisfied that we were not about to be attacked by terrorists, he lay down and went back to sleep.

I climbed into my bunk and eventually dozed off, but it felt as though I had only been sleeping for about five minutes before that 'stupid little sergeant' was bashing the side of the tent and scream-ing his bloody head off at us to get up.

On parade that Monday morning, the officer on parade told me to report to Lieutenant Stevens. As soon as we were dismissed, I went over to his tent, knocked on the pole and waited.

'Who is it?'

'Urwin, s-sir.'

'Ah, yes. Come in.'

I pushed through the tent flaps and went inside. Lieutenant Stevens was sitting at his desk looking at some papers. He was a young, boyish-looking bloke of about 27 or so, slightly built and just under six feet tall. I usually got on well with him but he seemed to be annoyed with me for some reason that I couldn't think of. His manner was curt and he eyed me suspiciously.

'What have you been up to, Urwin? How did you manage to get yourself detailed over to 518 officers' mess?' he demanded. I was as surprised as he was.

'The officers' m-mess, s-sir? I h-haven't a clue, s-sir.'

'Well, that's where you're going so you'd better report to 518 Company straight away. You'll get further instructions over there,' he said, dismissing me abruptly.

I had no experience of an officers' mess at all. Besides, it was generally considered to be a bit of a 'cushy number', kept for those who deserved some type of merit, which certainly explained Lieutenant Stevens's raised eyebrows at my selection. But I wasn't complaining; I would get better rations and would not have to parade or do any guard duties. My first thought on being told to report to Lieutenant Stevens was that it might be something to do with the guy on the beach. But now I was just confused and didn't know what the hell was going on!

At 518 Company officers' mess, I was greeted with a mixture of deep suspicion, disbelief and a great deal of resentment by the kitchen staff and mess orderlies. They simply could not understand how a stuttering Geordie could possibly have been given the position of head waiter. However, they had their orders and went through the motions, showing me how to lay tables and serve food. I was just as baffled as they were and, although it was certainly an improvement on digging latrines, I didn't know why I had been sent there any more than they did.

I wanted to be a 'real soldier' and thought that if this had anything to do with the guy on the beach then I had been well and truly conned. This was neither funny nor exciting. I just couldn't believe that this could be what he had meant. Besides, why would 'they' (whoever they were) go to all that bother, all of that secrecy, merely to stick me in the officers' mess? It just didn't make any sense.

I wondered if perhaps it was because one of these officers was to be my next contact, but how would I know and why had the guy on the beach not simply explained more to me? I just wished that he had given me more information. But, for now, I would simply have to wait and see, and hope that it would not be too long before everything became clear.

The officers' mess was a large wooden construction, consisting of four pre-fabricated units, which together formed a square. One large rectangle formed the dining hall, with windows on two adjacent sides and doorways on the other two. A long, highly polished table stood in the centre surrounded by chairs; along the longer, windowless wall were draped flags and regimental regalia. On this same wall was a doorway into a smaller, squarer room that was fitted out with a bar, although for some reason there was no actual door attached to this opening. The bar led through to another room, which held a full-size snooker table.

The second doorway, on the shorter windowless wall, led directly into the kitchen area via a set of swing doors. The kitchen formed one short wall of the dining hall and was the length of the bar area beyond.

I was kitted out in the regulation white jacket, red waistcoat, white shirt and black tie, and black trousers with a red stripe down the outside of each leg. To my utter horror, I was told that I had been given the task of reading the menu out to the officers, and then to wait in order to take their individual orders.

The menu consisted of soup and a main course followed by a pudding. As I looked at it the nightmare grew, partly because of my stammer and self-consciousness, but also because I didn't even know what half the stuff on the menu was, or how the words should be pronounced!

The officers came through from the bar area in dribs and drabs, then sat around the table chatting to one another. Suddenly, one old boy with an enormous moustache pushed the papers he had been reading into his breast pocket, looked up at me and then glanced around the table.

'Well?' he bellowed. 'Are you going to get on with it?'

'Y-yes, s-sir. R-right a-away, s-sir,' I stammered.

'What! What's this?' he roared in his loud, plummy voice. He glanced around at the others, then stood up and turned his chair to fully face where I was standing at the head of the table before sitting down again. Then he glared at me and leaned forwards with his knees wide apart and one hand resting on each knee.

It was totally intimidating. My first attempt to read out the menu was a complete disaster. I simply could not get past the word 'soup'! I was supposed to be saying, 'For soup there is a choice of …' but all I managed was 'F-f-f-for s-s-s-s-s-s-s…' before I stopped dead, flushed and very embarrassed.

I tried again, but with no more success than my first attempt, which several of the officers found very amusing. However, the old boy was very definitely not amused at all.

'What the hell is going on here?' he loudly demanded to know, his face turning slightly red. To my surprise, another officer leaned over the table and beckoned to him. The old guy bent forward and listened intently as the younger officer whispered something to him.

'What? What's that you say? Well, why wasn't I told this before?' he said as he listened. Then he turned back in his seat to face me, leaned back in his chair, crossed his legs and tweaked the end of his large bushy moustache. He continued to look at me very, very hard for a few long moments, weighing me up.

'Look, if you can't say it, why don't you try to sing the bloody thing!' he said loudly.

I thought it had to be the stupidest thing I had ever heard. But he was deadly serious, so with a little hesitation and feeling a complete idiot, I did it – I sort of read the menu in a singsong way, which to my amazement worked with almost everything but 'asparagus'. I don't know why, but for some reason I just could not get my tongue around that one flaming word.

From then on, I gradually lost my stammer day by day.

Most of the officers were pleasant and reasonably friendly towards me, especially the old guy. He seemed very pleased to see that his remedy for stuttering was working and he always made a point of speaking to me. Unfortunately, my popularity with the officers did little to improve my relationship with the other orderlies. If anything it seemed to make them even more resentful.

They were suspicious of me from the start, mainly because I was an unknown who had landed a plum job and they were not exactly sure why I had been given it but, generally, they left me alone. The main exception to this was the sergeant cook, a big, fat, ugly bloke, who was constantly having a go at me, demanding to know how I had got to be so pally with the old boy. He didn't believe me when I told him that I hadn't a clue why the old guy seemed to like me and was more pleasant to me than the other orderlies, or why I had been given this job in the first place. He went on and on at me, constantly bringing the subject up whenever he saw me.

He had been having a go at me one afternoon and after he'd gone one of the other orderlies, who had seen him talking to me, came over.

'Here, a word of warning, pal. You don't want to be getting too matey with that one,' he warned quietly. 'Watch your back at all times, and if he drops a spoon, don't you bleedin' bend over to pick it up.'

'Why? What d-do you mean?' I asked.

'Why? 'Cos he's a bloody big pouf, mate, bent as they come and nasty with it, that's why, so watch out! He's only in here 'cos he's a good cook and he'd be given a right hard time of it in the normal camp. Serve the bugger right an' all it would!' he explained. 'Bloody soddin' queers, I hate them!' he said vehemently, almost spitting the words out. 'If I had my way the whole f...in' lot of them would be stuck up against a wall and bleedin' shot!'

I hadn't a clue what he was talking about, but realised it was obviously something he felt very strongly about and really felt I needed to know. I was simply that innocent, that naïve.

'Thanks for the warning. I'll certainly k-keep an eye on him,' I told him anyway, wondering what on earth I had to watch out for and just what exactly was a 'pouf'. I suspected that it was something that I should be aware of. But I didn't really want to ask any of my mates for details as they liked nothing better than to take the mickey. They were already giving me a rough time about losing my stammer and 'getting all posh' and 'full of myself' from being around the officers so much.

In all, I spent about two weeks working in the officers' mess during which time my stammer improved noticeably every day. It seemed little short of a miracle to me that such a terrible affliction, which had been with me most of my life, was all but cured in so relatively short a period and in such a simple way.

5. Initiation

I picked up most of the basics of working in the officers' mess relatively quickly. While I did not exactly enjoy it, it was better than what I had been doing so far and had obvious advantages to it. But, as I was preparing the table for Sunday lunch, the fat sergeant cook called out to me.

'Forget about that, Geordie, you're leaving right now. Report on parade tomorrow morning,' he ordered.

'On parade? Eh, why?' I asked warily, still cautious about him after the warning I had been given.

'How the hell do I know? Probably for your next cushy job,' he sneered. 'I've just received orders, so forget about that and beat it.'

Typical, I thought, just when I'm beginning to get the hang of things and getting to lose that awful bloody stammer. I was a bit miffed at losing the perks and the decent food I had been getting, too.

'But, sarge, what about my dinner?' I asked, as I hadn't eaten yet.

'Tough! Just beat it, will you, Geordie,' he growled nastily.

'That's great, isn't it,' I mumbled under my breath as I turned to leave.

'What was that?' he demanded, giving me a look that made me move pretty quickly.

'Nowt! I'll never understand this army,' I muttered over my shoulder.

I couldn't understand why I was suddenly no longer needed in the mess, but then I hadn't understood why I'd been sent there in the first place. Although I hadn't been there long I had learned the job quickly: the fat sergeant cook had even admitted that much. So, I didn't think it could be because I wasn't very good at the job and, besides, they had known I had no experience when they gave it to me.

Typical army logic, I thought as I made my way back to the tent. But at least it has helped me to get rid of that damn stammer.

It was very hot and I spent the rest of the day lounging around with Bill and Dave, just messing about taking daft photos to send back home. But that night when we turned in I wondered what was going to happen the following morning and what crummy job I would be given next.

'Back t'digging 'oles tomorrow, eh, Geordie?' Bill teased.

'Looks like it, mate,' I groaned. 'Nothing lasts forever, especially if it's good.'

On Monday morning I lined up on parade waiting for orders. 'Urwin!' shouted the officer on parade. 'You're on detachment'.

'Sarge, surely there's been a mistake made here?' I said looking at the papers he handed me.

'Yes, too bloody right, Urwin. I had a nice little job lined up for you here on latrine duty. You've had it too cushy in the officers' mess, lad. I'd like to know who's responsible for these bloody orders,' he barked.

'But they're sending me out with a truck.' I was surprised to say the least. I had hardly been out of the camp since we arrived and hadn't a clue about getting around the island, so how was I supposed to know where to go?

'Just do as you're bloody told, Urwin, and report next door,' the sergeant snapped and marched off. I did as he said and went to the nearby 518 Company depot and handed over the papers to the officer in charge, a sergeant, who allocated me a truck.

'Right, lad. Report to the ordnance depot at Dhekélia,' he ordered, giving me the papers I would need to hand in at the gate when I got there. I jumped into the passenger side of the assigned truck and sat there for a few minutes waiting for a co-driver. Suddenly someone banged loudly on the side of the truck.

'You still here? What the hell are you waiting for?' the sergeant bellowed.

'Eh! But where's the other bloke, sarge?'

'What other bloke? What are you talking about?'

'Well, the driver,' I explained.

He looked at me blankly. 'What driver? You're the driver, you pillock!'

'Me? You're kidding, though, sarge. The furthest I've been out of camp is to the beach and back.'

'Tough!' he snapped. 'There's a map in there above your head: use it. You can't go wrong; there's only one bleedin' road straight to the place, it'll take you five minutes. You're the driver, NOW GET MOVIN'.'

I did as he ordered and set off unable to believe that they were actually letting me take a truck out on my own. After driving along for about 10 minutes in the direction of Limassol, I noticed this guy standing at the side of the road near to a parked jeep. As far as I could see, he appeared to be alone.

As I drove closer, he stepped further into the road, put his hand up and waved at me to stop. I looked around but could still see no one else, just this guy on his own. I wondered if he might have broken down, but we had been warned about the dangers of terrorist traps, so I put my foot down and sped towards him. There was no way I was going to get caught out on my first trip.

He was wearing a short-sleeved army shirt and shorts and looked like an ordinary soldier except that there was something vaguely familiar about him. He obviously expected me to stop, as he stood right in the middle of the road until I was almost on top of him and had to jump to one side to avoid being hit. As I shot past him, I got a good look at his face and recognised him instantly – it was the guy from the beach.

Immediately I slammed on the brakes and screeched to a halt in a cloud of dust. I looked in the wing mirror but for several seconds he was obscured from my view by the choking dirt and sand. When it eventually settled I saw him beckoning to me and reversed to where he was waiting at the side of the road, dusting himself down with a hanky.

'Hello there, Geordie, it's me,' he said calmly with no reference to the fact that I had almost run him over and covered him with a fine film of brown dust. 'Remember?' he went on. 'We met on the beach a little while ago.'

'Yes, of course I do. Sorry about that,' I apologised, indicating the dust that covered his clothes. 'I thought you might be a flaming terrorist or something, I only realised who you were as I passed you,' I explained. 'Besides, when nothing happened the other week I thought you must have forgotten about me.'

He grinned broadly and shook his head. 'Come on, get out of the truck, Geordie. Just leave it,' he said calmly.

'What! Leave it?' I was concerned: the truck was my responsibility and there would be hell to pay if anything happened to it. 'I can't just leave it. I'm supposed to take it to Dhekélia.'

'No, you're not.'

'But I've got written orders.'

'Well of course you have,' he agreed, smiling. 'Don't worry, it's all been taken care of. It'll be here when you get back.'

'What do you mean "when I get back"? From where?'

'You said you wanted a change, some excitement. Well, believe me you're going to get it. This is it, Geordie, lad!' he told me with a grin, his manner so casual and friendly yet at the same time so positive. He jumped into the jeep and slapped his hand on the passenger seat.

'Come on, Geordie, get in. Stop worrying, I've told you your truck will definitely be there when you get back. I promise you.'

I couldn't explain it, but there was a real honesty about him, just something so compelling about the guy that made me believe what he said; the truck would be taken care of. For all he sounded like an officer he certainly did not act like any other officer I'd come across in the armed forces. He made me feel great and totally at ease. I jumped into the jeep and left the truck at the side of the road. As we drove off, I looked back at it, unable to believe what I'd just done.

We sped through the rocky hills and barren landscape into the middle of nowhere, or so it seemed to me, and travelled for roughly 20 minutes along a dusty, narrow road. As we rounded the base of a steep, rock-strewn hill, suddenly, to my surprise, we came in sight of what appeared to be a rusting old aircraft hangar standing well back from the track.

There was a fairly large flat area in front of it and I supposed it might have once been an airfield. But it seemed an odd place to have one, out here in the middle of all these hills. I wondered if it might have been used for helicopters or something like that. There were a few outhouses and sheds close by, all pretty dilapidated and run down; nothing appeared to have been used for a long time. The badly neglected concrete areas of ground were cracked and broken, with parched brown tufts of grass pushing their way through. Nearby a couple of large lizards basked lazily in the sunshine while others scuttled around in the dry grass before apparently disappearing into thin air.

The guy parked the jeep, jumped out and began to walk towards a small door in the side of the ramshackle old building.

'Follow me, Geordie,' he said and we went inside. It was just as decrepit inside as it was on the outside: dirty, rusting and falling to bits. Although I hadn't known what to expect, I was surprised to see that the building was not empty.

Three men were training together using some form of unarmed combat. They were young and extremely fit-looking, with lean, muscular bodies and faces. By the look of them, I guessed that they were all older than me by five or possibly six years. They all wore long trousers and plimsolls and were incredibly agile, moving around making very little noise, not shouting or screaming at one another. I had never seen anything like it before in my life. They were using real knives and what looked like a bayonet, and seemed to be going through some well-rehearsed routine. (I later discovered this was not the case: they were genuinely trying to catch one another out.)

With their dark hair and deeply tanned bodies, two of them looked like locals, although the other one was quite pasty-looking. Suddenly a terrible thought occurred to me: what if they were terrorists? I was frightened and nervous, and very concerned about what was going to happen to me. I realised that I had stupidly dropped myself in it. I had allowed myself to be put in this position despite all the warnings. I hadn't a clue where I was and as they suddenly stopped what they were doing and began to walk towards me, I panicked and turned around to get back out of the door. But the guy from the beach was already putting the bolt in it. I was trapped.

He placed his hand lightly on my shoulder and said in his quiet confident way: 'Let me introduce you to your future team-mates, Geordie.'

Still feeling very apprehensive, I turned back to the three men who were now standing directly behind me. Seeing them more closely grouped together, I became even more aware of just how powerfully built they were. They gave the impression that nothing could stop them, that they could simply walk through a brick wall if they wanted to. And there was something else too, something very odd about these men: they didn't appear to blink very often. They kept looking straight at me in a penetrating and direct way, almost as if their gaze was going right through me.

I expected my hand to be crushed by theirs when they shook it, but instead it was the complete opposite: their handshakes were firm but very gentle. Their general air of absolute confidence was overwhelming and I felt totally out of place standing next to them, like a cabbage in the middle of a strawberry field.

'Hi, Geordie, we know all about you,' the slightly shorter one in the middle said.

Well, I thought, if that's the case what the hell am I doing here?

'Just call me Dynamo,' he went on, then smiling he stepped forward and shook my hand. 'This is Spot and that's Chalky.' They both looked at me intently as they also shook my hand.

'Nice to have you with us, Geordie,' Chalky said and grinned.

The one called Spot merely took my hand and winked. They spoke quietly and confidently. To my surprise, their accents were pure English public school, very calm and very precise.

'Spot, bring Geordie a cup of tea up,' the guy from the beach said, indicating for me to follow him as he led the way up a short flight of wooden steps and into a room at the top. As I followed him, I glanced around at the area in which they had been training and saw what looked like several tailor's dummies, the heads of which appeared to be held on by small springs attached to the necks. I had no idea what they would be used for, nor the several old wooden doors standing against one wall with knives stuck into them.

Dynamo and Chalky had now quietly returned to the middle of the floor where they stood surrounded by several turnips suspended by strings at shoulder level from the beams above. It was all very strange; I was fascinated and very curious to find out more.

At the top of the stairs, I entered a very small, dingy room with a table and two high-backed wooden chairs stuck in the middle of it. An empty window frame, with only a few broken fragments of glass remaining, formed part of the wall between this room and their training area beyond. Through this opening, I saw that they had now resumed their training (although why anyone would choose this dump to train in was completely beyond me). What seemed even stranger was that the British army would be using such an out of the way, run-down and decrepit place as this for a training area.

It was fascinating to watch them. I couldn't tear my eyes away and itched to be able to join in and learn what they were doing. I was so engrossed that at first I didn't realise I had been spoken to until I felt a light tap on my shoulder.

'Do you want this tea, Geordie?' the guy from the beach said, smiling. 'Why don't you sit down here?'

I had been so absorbed in watching Dynamo and Chalky I hadn't even noticed that Spot had been in the room. I sat in the chair the guy indicated, but immediately jumped to my feet again as I heard several loud slapping noises coming from the training area. Looking through the window frame, I saw that the turnips were now swinging about wildly on their strings. Some of them were split in half, while others had huge chunks missing out of them. They had apparently been used as targets yet I could see no obvious weapons that could have caused such damage to them. Spot had now re-joined Dynamo and Chalky, but the two of them did not appear to have moved from where I had last seen them standing. For the life of me, I could not think what could have inflicted such an amount of destruction in the split second it had taken to demolish all those turnips. I sat down again and looked at the guy opposite me in utter amazement.

'Impressed?' he asked calmly.

'Yeah. But how did they do it? What on earth destroyed those turnips?' I asked him.

'Never mind that now, you'll find out later. By the way, call me Ken.'

The table we sat at was bare except for my cup of tea. It appeared to be very old with some of the knots pushed out of the wood, and there were marks on it where knives had scratched the surface, and several names had been carved into it.

'You obviously realise that things like this don't just happen overnight. This hasn't just been a random decision. We've gone to a lot of trouble to get you here,' Ken said, 'and a considerable amount of time has been spent observing you before selection. I don't want to have to go into an explanation as to how or why we arrived at that decision, but be aware that we don't do anything without a very good reason,' he said slowly, emphasising his words, then paused briefly before continuing. 'So, just accept it, Geordie. There is one very important thing that you must understand: nothing of what you see or hear can ever be repeated. Officially, this place does not exist.'

Somehow, I didn't think so. I thought. This has got to be a dream or maybe a nightmare.

'But why am I here?' I asked him, still confused.

'Well, as Dynamo rightly said, we know all about you, Geordie. We've been watching you for a long time now and have brought you here because we think you have the necessary ability and skills to join us. With the right training, we know you will become just what we are looking for.'

Now I knew I was dreaming. Me have the same skills as these guys? He had to be joking.

'I need to explain some things to you and as I have a lot to say we are going to be here for quite a while,' Ken went on. I noticed that it was very quiet now. There was no noise coming from any activity in the training area outside the room, which had apparently ceased and the men had gone, although I had not heard them leave. Now Ken and I appeared to be completely alone. I presumed Spot had brought in the large tea urn that stood in the corner of the room; as he had said, it looked as though we were going to be here for some time.

Ken was speaking to me again. 'Now concentrate on what I'm saying.'

'Look, Ken, what about my truck?'

'Forget about it, Geordie, it will be exactly where you left it when you return,' he reassured me. 'We'll make sure you're back in plenty of time; your truck will be waiting, your papers will all be in order and no one will suspect that you have been anywhere other than where you should have been. Trust me.'

I silently prayed that he was telling the truth. I would be in a lot of trouble otherwise.

'I see the stammer has gone. We knew our little plan would work!' he added with a wry smile.

'Eh! So, it was you lot! How on earth did you manage that?' I had been right to think there was something strange going on. It was no wonder Lieutenant Stevens had not been able to understand the orders. But Christ, just who were these people and how were they able to arrange stuff like that?

'Forget about it, it's just not important,' Ken said.

He sat chatting to me in a calm, friendly way for a while, asking all sorts of questions about me and then about my sense of duty and loyalty to my country. I answered him as best as I could but mainly just sat at the table feeling very uncomfortable, not really knowing what to expect next.

He rested his arms in front of him on the table and sat quietly watching me for a few moments, then he leaned towards me and stared straight into my eyes. It was unnerving; I couldn't meet his gaze and kept looking away from him in embarrassment. Without taking his eyes off mine, he took a coin out of his pocket and started spinning it on the tabletop, and just kept on staring at me the whole time.

'Just look at me, Geordie,' he said quietly. 'I need your attention. Concentrate. You must understand what you are about to embark on. We have all experienced fear at some time in our lives. It can be a real problem and will get you killed. When you are confronted by someone who wants to kill you, you have to be in complete control at all times. If fear gets in the way you will surely die. So, Geordie, if you listen to me carefully and concentrate on what I am saying, then I am sure we can do something about it.

71

Don't ask how, just concentrate. Are you afraid of dying?' he asked, still playing with the coin, his manner totally relaxed and casual.

I couldn't understand where all this was leading to. 'I've not really thought about it; I suppose so.'

'Well, I'm sure you won't have heard of the "One Step Beyond", Geordie, but this is a process by which we make you look at life in a totally different way. We hope this will give you the ability to cope with anything and to make you unafraid and ensure that you never suffer from fear again.'

'I don't really understand,' I said. It was true: I honestly had no idea what he was talking about.

'Neither did I, Geordie, neither did I,' he said, his gaze on me even more intense and direct. 'I can see that you're a little shocked by all of this, aren't you?'

'You can say that again!' I replied emphatically.

'Do you want to go ahead and continue?'

'Well, I don't quite know what I've let myself in for but I'm intrigued by what little I've seen so far and I'm not backing out now. So, yes, I do.'

'That's the way, lad. I thought that's what you would say. Right, let's get on with it then.'

In a flat voice, devoid of all emotion, he began to talk about life. For hours, he spoke about the effects of getting old, and how quickly time would pass and how soon I could die. On and on throughout the rest of the day he kept repeating similar things over and over again, emphasising the need to have a definite purpose for doing anything, even for simply living. He spent hour after hour convincing me that life just wasn't worth living. I didn't understand what he was doing or why, or what was happening; he was driving me crazy.

'What's the point of going on, for what purpose?' he kept asking. 'At the end of the day, you are going to die, no matter what. Life is pointless, futile. In the end you will grow old, and you can't stop it.'

After several hours, he produced a folder and showed me pictures from it to add emphasis to his words. There were pictures of old people, sick people, people with grotesque deformities, hideous illnesses, wasting diseases. He pointed out the inevitability of it all.

On into the night he talked. His voice never wavered, never altered its speed or inflection. I was becoming totally confused and disorientated, my head hurt and my body felt numb. I just wanted things to end there and then, but he kept on and on spinning that damn coin and eyeballing me constantly.

Repeatedly, hour after hour, his voiced droned on telling me how life simply was not worth living. And all the time he watched me with that unnerving, steady gaze. Eventually, his words began to run into one another and his voice became one long repetitive sound coming from far off in the distance. I was so tired and my eyelids weighed so heavily that I could barely keep them open. I wanted him to stop but he just kept on and on, monotonously. I was unable to focus properly any longer and his face was now just a blur on the other side of the table: his features appeared to have all melted together into a pink blob that made a constant droning noise.

Abruptly he stopped spinning the coin and, putting his hand beneath the table, he drew out a service revolver, which he then placed directly in front of me with the handle pointing my way.

'This will solve your problems,' he said very quietly and pushed it towards me. Everything he said suddenly made sense and I could see that he was right. I was only 18 but I didn't want to live a useless existence for years and years just to grow old and sick. To die for what, nothing! Life was pointless, so why bother to prolong it if death was inevitable anyway.

Tears poured down my face, blurring my vision even more and I could barely make out the gun in front of me. I reached out fumbling for it and then picked it up. I was shaking badly; the gun felt so heavy, it seemed to weigh a ton.

Ken was now sitting very still, staring directly at me and I couldn't look away from him. I placed the gun at the side of my face and he smiled slowly as I tried to squeeze the trigger. But nothing happened: my finger just didn't seem to be able to exert enough pressure to pull it. Slowly he reached out, grasped my wrist and gently took the gun out of my hand.

'Don't be stupid, Geordie,' he said, softly. 'There's another way.'

Completely exhausted and totally confused, I put my head onto my arms on the table top, too numb to speak, and closed my eyes.

Ken picked up both the gun and our cups, then pushed back his chair with a loud scraping noise, stood up and softly walked towards the tea urn. He filled my cup with tea, poured one for himself and brought them both back to the table. Then he replaced the gun underneath it.

Even though I hadn't been physically knocked about, I felt as if I had. I was utterly exhausted and my eyes were still unable to focus properly. Nothing felt real, my body and mind were numb and I simply could not believe or understand what was happening to me.

Although I could see his lips moving, the words seemed to be delayed, reaching my ears seconds later. All I wanted was to rest my head on the table and go to sleep forever, but he told me to drink my tea. He was completely relaxed, sitting back in his chair drinking, and now he no longer stared at me.

Gradually my head began to clear again and I relaxed slightly. Then, when I least expected it, his whole tack changed. He leaned forward again, placed his elbows on the table and looked directly at me once more.

'You just can't give up, Geordie. Yes, of course you're going to die, we all are, it's inevitable, but your mother didn't go through the pain of childbirth to bring you into this world for nothing,' he went on quietly. 'You don't want to disappoint her, do you?'

Now I was really confused. 'But you just said that living was a waste of time,' I moaned pathetically.

'Yes, I did. But it doesn't have to be that way. Look at it this way: none of us knows just how long we've got, so what the hell is there to lose? You were brought here for a purpose, Geordie, you are very important to us. The things that you are about to embark on would be a nightmare to any ordinary soldier. You can leave now if you want, but if you stay, by tomorrow I can guarantee you will fear nothing! We understand that you will want to tell people what has happened here, but no one will ever believe you and besides you won't even be able to remember most of what you have just gone through.'

Ken talked on throughout the remainder of the night and into the morning. He now told me just how important life was: which was the complete opposite to what he had been telling me before. I was so confused and desperately tired; I just could not understand how any of this was going to get rid of my fear.

'Well, Geordie, you will find this very hard to believe, but I don't think you will be frightened to take risks or fear death any longer because of what you have just been through,' Ken told me. 'You will know without a doubt that death is inevitable. But, because you will no longer be frightened of death, you will have no fear of that inevitability; it will be just a game to you and the game is to stay alive.

'You don't know what, if anything, is beyond death. Heaven and hell is here on earth and life is what you make it,' he continued. 'So you might as well enjoy life to the full. You will grow older, but you can control your ageing by keeping fit and active, by staying young in mind and body, by not smoking or drinking and by keeping an open mind. You see, if you rid yourself of the fear of death itself, and prevent things happening to you, by having the ability to totally control and handle any situation, then you won't be afraid to do things, to take risks. It is simply the fear of death that holds us back. Death is still inevitable but how you die can be controlled.'

Although I still didn't fully understand everything that he had told me, I began to see the truth in what he was saying. Awareness helped you to achieve control. He had spent hours breaking me down and then building me back up again, and while he had done it, something very strange had happened to me. It was as though overnight I had suddenly grown up, gone through a rite of passage or passed some form of test. Without him saying so, instinctively I knew that I had come through it in the way that he had hoped, or known, I would.

I felt an incredible sense of lightness, of release, as though a huge weight had been lifted from me. The next thing I knew was the loud clattering of pots, which woke me with a start. Groggily lifting my head from the table, I realised that I must have fallen asleep at some point. Spot, Chalky and Dynamo were noisily carrying food containers into the room, which they dumped onto the table in front of me.

'Come on, Geordie, old boy, we've got lots of work to do!'
Dynamo said cheerfully.

'Aw, can't I just go back to sleep?' I mumbled, as, still dazed and
unsure of my surroundings, I tried to rub the sleep from my eyes.

'No, no time for that. Life's too short,' he said, nudging me bois-
terously.

'I see you've made it then? Do you feel OK?' Spot asked.

'Made what?'

'Never mind, we'll tell you later. Come on, have something to
eat,' Chalky said, pushing a plate towards me.

Oh, the delicious smell of that food! For a few moments, I
looked down at it unable to remember the last time I had eaten
and then realised that it had to be well over 24 hours ago: no
wonder I felt so hungry. They had prepared porridge, a huge mug
of steaming hot tea, sausages, eggs, bacon and fried bread. I ate the
lot.

Dynamo slapped me on the back. 'Have we got a surprise for
you, when you're finished!' he said, grinning.

I glanced at my watch. It was just after 9 am. I had been in that
room since 9 am the previous day. I was utterly exhausted, my
head hurt and my bladder was bursting. But despite this, for some
inexplicable reason, I felt light-headed and strangely elated. As we
sat talking and eating, they made me feel as though I was already
one of the team. I felt completely relaxed in their company. It was
as if I was among old friends and it was a great feeling.

'When you've done, go downstairs with the lads and we'll get
you kitted out, Geordie,' Ken said. I was surprised that he seemed
to show no adverse effects from the last 24 hours and, apart from
the dark shadow of stubble around his chin, he looked and
sounded no different than he had this time the day before. Spot
looked over at me and smiled. 'Well, Geordie, you're one of us
now. You just don't know it yet.'

I was still uncertain about what had taken place and unsure of
exactly what he meant by 'us' but I felt that somehow he had
managed to put my feelings into words almost as if he had read my
thoughts. Talk about the 'change of life'! From the very first
moment I met my 'team-mates' and went through the 'One Step
Beyond', it was as if I had just woken from a long sleep. The 'One

Step Beyond' seemed to have brought me to life properly for the first time; almost like a rebirth. The person who had entered this little room yesterday certainly was not the same guy sitting in it today. And although a lot of things were still unclear to me, one thing I knew for certain: I did not have that cabbage feeling any more.

Dynamo seemed to be constantly on the move, pacing up and down the room. He gave the impression that he was full to bursting with energy and needed to burn some of it off quickly. Yet when he spoke he sounded neither agitated nor impatient; his voice was as calm and controlled as the others.

'Come on then, Geordie, let's be having you, laddie,' he said, in a strong Scottish accent, much to my surprise.

Even given the short time I'd been in their company I had already grown to like them all. I enjoyed their easy banter and the way they joked and laughed at one another. I could see that I was going to have some real fun with these guys.

I quickly finished what I was eating and, taking my mug of tea with me, I followed the three of them down the short flight of wooden stairs into the training area. Ken did not join us.

I looked at these three young guys: they were complete strangers, yet for some reason I knew instinctively that they were the kind of people I had wanted to be around all of my life: real men. That they wanted me to be a part of their team was hard for me to believe, but I had been in that room with Ken for 24 hours and we hadn't been in there all that time because he liked the sound of my voice. Naïve I might have been but stupid I was not, despite what my father told me.

'Well, how do you feel now, Geordie?' Dynamo asked.

'It's strange: I should feel exhausted but I don't. In fact I feel bloody marvellous.'

'Good! OK, come over here.'

Dynamo made his way towards a nearby bench and picked up a canvas holdall, which he then opened up and laid out flat like a sheet in front of me. Fastened inside it was a strange-looking belt, three boot knives and a 9mm Browning MK1 semi-automatic pistol. There was also a steel bow in two halves and a metal crossbow, together with some of the strangest looking arrows I had ever seen. They were headless and fitted with two small black rubbery flights and one large flight, like a plane's rudder, with a swivel attached at the tail end. There was also a large selection of peculiar shaped arrowheads that could be pushed onto the arrows.

Spot and Chalky had followed us and, as the three of them talked to me about the equipment in the bag, they kept referring to something called 'the machine'. My curiosity got the better of me. 'What's this machine you keep talking about?'

'It's very difficult to explain but you'll find out,' Chalky replied. 'You have to learn the moves of what we call "the machine" because its techniques will then give you the ability to use the sash and the rest of your equipment to great effect and with deadly accuracy.'

Again, I had no real idea what he was talking about and although desperately keen to learn, I had already begun to realise that the way in which they operated was very precise and specific. I would get to know what I needed to know as and when they felt I needed to know it.

'Is that what you were doing when I arrived yesterday, training together?'

'That's right.' Dynamo nodded.

'So what happened to those turnips, how did they get cut to pieces like that? And what exactly do you mean by "the sash"?' I asked, eager to know more.

Dynamo smiled and moved a couple of yards away. Then he winked at me and appeared to slap at his belt buckle. Instantly, there was a rushing, whistling, whip-like sound and the upper half of his body pivoted with amazing speed. All of a sudden, the remaining bits of turnip hanging nearby disintegrated. He turned and took one step towards me. Once again, I heard the whistling sound yet saw nothing. Frozen to the spot, I watched in stunned amazement as Dynamo's torso moved with incredible speed and a tin mug and bottle, which were standing on a nearby table only inches from my hand, appeared to vanish into thin air.

'That's what you call the sash, Geordie,' he said, grinning broadly, as a blurred shape sprang back around him. He slapped at his waist again and his belt, if in fact that was what he had used, was fastened back in place.

It was astonishing. I simply could not believe what I had just seen: it had happened so quickly. I had never seen anyone move at such amazing speed and to such effect. His movements had been so powerful, so exact, almost mechanical in their precision, yet at the same time fluid and smooth. I had worked on a farm for two years after leaving school and knew just how difficult it was to cut a turnip, even with a sharp knife. The weapon he had just used appeared to be nothing more than an ordinary belt, yet it had sliced through them like a hot knife through butter.

I marvelled at the confidence being able to use a devastating weapon like that would give you. The sheer element of surprise and the effect on your enemy when confronted with it would be overwhelming, especially as they were bound to assume they were dealing with an unarmed, defenceless person. Even if armed themselves, they simply would not have time to use their weapons and would be torn to shreds before they had time to realise what was happening.

For some time, they chatted to me about the various weapons they used, which all seemed to be for close-combat use. Not for the first time I wondered just who the hell they were and what exactly they wanted with me.

My initial nervousness and fears on meeting these people had now completely gone. They made me feel different, more relaxed and comfortable than I had ever been before in my life. It was intoxicating and I was eager to discover and learn more, to find out why I felt this way. Chalky nudged me.

'OK, Geordie?' he asked with a smile.

'Yeah, sure, what other surprises have you got for me?' I replied.

'Well, you must understand that what you are about to learn will change your whole way of life and thinking,' he said. 'The good news is that I don't think you will ever feel scared of anything again. But the bad news is that before you can begin to think of using any of this equipment, you must learn the moves of what we call "the machine" and as there's no time like the present we'll start right now with the basics.'

He moved away from the bench into the centre of the floor and indicated for me to follow him. 'Now, concentrate,' he said quietly.

'There are 150 basic moves, which will eventually lead to around 7,000 combinations. These moves cover the use of all the weapons you see in front of you. Just follow me and copy what I do.'

Seven thousand combinations of movement! That will take the rest of my life, I thought. But, I did as he said and exactly followed every movement he made as he began a series of smoothly fluid, sequentially numbered moves. To my surprise, I picked it up very quickly and even found it easy to copy each of his actions. Chalky was obviously very surprised too, but also pleased at the speed with which I learned.

For the remainder of that day and the best part of the evening, they all showed me just what they meant by 'the machine'. It involved using a defined sequence of unusual hand and body movements, whilst keeping the head and neck rigid so that they moved as one with the shoulders and upper body. For some reason these movements appeared to come naturally to me and I found them very easy to do. The others watched me closely and seemed to be impressed and excited by my ability to learn very quickly.

'Eyup, Geordie, we knew thaa'ud get to grips wi' it reet quick, lad,' Chalky said with a straight face, in an excellent example of a broad Yorkshire accent.

'Aye we've picked us t'right man for't'job arlreet.' Spot nodded in agreement, equally seriously.

They had me in stitches all day with their antics and by constantly changing their accents (which they were all very good at). I hadn't a clue where any of them actually came from. Ken had already warned me that it was pointless to ask questions of that nature because, for security reasons, I would never be told anything other than their nicknames and they would know nothing other than mine.

Later that night they gave me a further demonstration of what could be done using 'the machine' moves in conjunction with 'the sash' and the 9mm MK1 pistol, which explained the presence and relevance of the dummies and the moving targets.

Ken took off in the jeep around 9 pm and they gave me a small tent to sleep in, which I pitched near to theirs just a few yards outside the building, or hangar as I thought of it. The four of us sat talking for a while, enjoying the cool evening air after the stifling heat of the day. My mind was buzzing with questions and I was eager for more information.

They gave me a lot of information about the equipment but told me not to worry about anything else: I would find out soon enough. They told me nothing about themselves but I had had a chance to observe them more closely during the day.

Dynamo was a real 'live wire'; he quite literally hummed with energy. He was slightly shorter than me, about five feet nine, with dark hair and a well-developed muscular physique. From his antics during the day, I could tell that he was an extremely fit and agile gymnast.

Spot-On, or just plain Spot, was very strong-looking with dark brown hair. He was the tallest of the three, possibly around five eleven, and I suspected that he must be around the same age as Dynamo, about 24. Apparently, he was an uncanny marksman and his shooting, whether with crossbows, pistols or rifles, was always 'spot-on', hence his nickname.

It appeared that Chalky, who I had thought was probably called White, was actually given his name because no matter what he did or how often he was in the sun his skin remained very pale. I could understand that, he was a bit pasty-looking, but, like the others, he was dark-haired, muscular and very fit. He appeared to be slightly older than the other two, somewhere around 28, and was roughly my height.

Ken was a lean, fit, six-footer, and well spoken. I guessed he was about 30.

As I lay down that night, I felt both exhausted and exhilarated. For the first time ever I was in really good company, my kind of people if you like, who shared a common bond and had the ability to laugh and joke with one another without resorting to smutty remarks or bad language. For once, to be 'part of the gang' or 'one of the lads' did not involve filthy references to women, or sex, or alcohol: and I had loved every minute of it.

Ken arrived early the next morning with our breakfast and for the rest of the day I trained with Dynamo, Spot and Chalky, going over what I'd learned the day before. At about 1500 hours Ken drove me back to the spot where he'd stopped me just over 48 hours before, but which now felt like weeks ago. The truck was there as promised, and inside on the driver's seat was a sheaf of paperwork, all in order! Whatever it was that I was supposed to have being doing, someone else had either done on my behalf or they had fixed it to ensure there would be no awkward questions when I got back to camp.

'When will I be coming back?' I asked him, eager to continue with my training.

'You've got to go back now because you'll be expected,' he replied. 'And we don't want to draw too much attention to you or have anyone becoming suspicious. But we need to have you up to scratch quickly, so we'll probably pick you up again sometime next week: it'll take us that long to fix it. It won't be a problem getting you out of camp. Your lot are always working outside on detachment anyway, which is very considerate of them and very convenient for us,' he added, laughing. 'Don't worry,' he assured me. 'We'll arrange it soon. I've heard a lot of good news about you from Chalky; he reckons you've learned a lot faster than we'd anticipated.' He paused and smiled. 'But then, we always knew you had the qualities we were looking for. Catch you later!'

And with that, he spun the jeep around and drove off. I stood watching for a while as he disappeared up the dusty track, then climbed into the truck. I felt great and was eager to get back to camp to tell someone about what had happened. But as I started the engine I remembered that I couldn't tell anyone where I had been or what I was doing. Besides, who the hell would believe me? I scarcely believed it myself.

Although Ken had assured me that everything would be OK and no one would suspect a thing, I was unsure of the reception I would receive on my return. And so, a little apprehensively, I drove off in the direction of the camp, which after driving for roughly 10 minutes, I saw in the distance.

There was a small queue of vehicles waiting at the gates. The guards were stopping everyone and examining their paperwork before checking around for explosives, as they always did. Although I knew that things had taken place in the last couple of days that had drastically changed my outlook, up until this point I hadn't really been aware of any outward effects. But now, as I pulled up behind a staff car in the queue of vehicles and one of the guards looked up from the papers he was examining to stare at me, I stuck my head out of the window and shouted at him.

'Hoi, get a move on!'

I would never have dared to say something like that before and could hardly believe I had just said it now. The two officers in the staff car turned around and glared at me. But for some reason I simply didn't give a toss and just stared back at them. I could not have cared less, even when a belligerent-looking guard came over.

'Now then, what's all this bleedin' racket? What the hell are you shouting about, mate?' he angrily demanded. I handed him my papers and he gave the truck a quick look over before glancing at them. 'You're back early!' he said accusingly but passed them back without further comment and waved me through.

I drove straight to 518 depot to drop off the truck, then handed in my papers and dashed back to 524 Company to get washed up for tea. As I crossed the parade ground, I came face to face with that 'stupid little sergeant'. His eyes narrowed suspiciously as he recognised me.

'Well, well, back already, Urwin? I'm gonna have you on latrine duty tomorrow, lad,' he bellowed as he marched purposefully towards me.

'That's what you think. Get stuffed!' To my utter amazement, I had muttered my thoughts quietly but audibly as we passed. He instantly stopped and stared hard at me but either he hadn't heard me properly or simply preferred to pretend that he had not. After a couple of seconds he merely spun on his heel and stomped off. But for the rest of that week he was as good as his word, and had me digging latrines in the baking heat: pure backbreaking hard labour.

I thought about Dynamo, Chalky and Spot constantly, going through in my mind the moves I had learned with them as I dug in the blistering heat. I had no idea when they would contact me again, which was very frustrating, but all I could do was wait.

I felt as if they had crammed a whole lifetime into those 48 hours and had let me see what life could be. Like a prisoner serving a life sentence on death row, prison or punishment no longer holds fear for you, when you have nothing left to lose because you cannot be punished any more. So, if you are going to be in jail for the rest of your life what the hell have you got to lose?

My fear of dying was removed. Any risks I now took would be lessened because of the very fact that I no longer feared death. If I was going to die anyway then I might as well die taking a risk, doing something exciting, living life to the full rather than just hanging around for illness or old age to carry me off.

In just 48 hours they had changed my life forever.

6. The machine

My mind was in turmoil for the first few days following my initiation process, as I tried to understand and come to terms with just what exactly had taken place. I felt so different, as if a huge barrier had been removed and I was ready to face anything. But I didn't know why or how someone just talking to me could have changed me so radically. Surely Ken hadn't slipped something into my tea, had he, I wondered for the umpteenth time? I did not think that I would ever fully comprehend just what had happened to me and perhaps that was just as well.

But one thing I did know for sure: the few moves I learned from Dynamo, Chalky and Spot in the short space of time I was with them were now indelibly engraved on my mind. When Ken had first approached me on the beach, he had asked if I wanted to do something more exciting, but in my wildest dreams, I would never have thought that he meant anything like this. I was itching to get back and learn more.

Nothing felt real to me any more. It was as if I was detached from everything; I wandered around in a bit of a daze. Unfortunately, this did not go unnoticed.

'What's the matter, Urwin, dreaming about home again? WAKE UP, LAD!' the sergeant bawled at me as he passed by.

He could not have been more wrong. Home was the last thing on my mind right now. For the first time since we landed, I wasn't thinking about home or my family, which just goes to show the effect of Ken's 'talk'. Previously, just like for most of the lads, thoughts of home were always on my mind.

But now I just could not stop thinking of those moves and that sash. Jesus, I thought, what a weapon! And then there were those strange-looking arrowheads. What on earth could they be used for? I felt like a kid on Christmas Eve, barely able to wait until the following day.

The sergeant was nothing if not determined and if there was a hole to be dug, he had me digging it. He always seemed to be on our backs for one thing or other, and each time he passed us, he made some kind of crack. I was not a religious person but by Friday afternoon, I was almost praying that Ken would pick me up again and soon.

'Well, enjoyed your week, Geordie?' the sergeant said, as we finished our work. 'See you bright and early Monday morning, I've got another "cushy little number" lined up especially for you,' he smirked and strode off.

Bill, who was in the working party with me, overheard him. 'By 'eck, Geordie, you're popular. 'Ee must really like you, 'e dun't do that for everyone,' he joked.

'That's right, you can see I'm one of his favourites from all the "special" treatment he's giving me,' I laughed back.

'Miserable sod!' grumbled another lad. 'He's probably just got a "Dear John" letter from home.'

'Nah, it's 'is piles playing 'im up,' Bill sniggered.

'Yeah and he's taking out on me. Still, I can't do anything about it. I'll just have to put up with it.'

'It keeps him happy, Geordie,' Bill said.

'Aye, well, if he's not careful this hole'll be six feet deep, specially dug just for him.'

It was easy to think that the sergeant had it in for me, but he didn't really: he was just a typical sergeant. They all seemed to get some kind of kick from shouting and screaming at us all the time.

During the week and over the weekend whenever the lads went off to the NAAFI and I was left on my own, I secretly practised the moves Chalky and the others had shown me. From what they said, I knew that one day my life was going to depend on my ability to perform these movements. I was incredibly proud that these guys had chosen me and I was determined not to let them down. I wanted to be really good at the moves before they picked me up for training again, whenever that might be.

On Monday morning I stood on parade with my fingers crossed, hoping to be sent out of the camp again and, if I were, that they would be waiting to pick me up once more. I thought that if I had to spend another week with that sergeant screaming at me I would end up practising the moves on him. The officer on parade shouted out various names and assigned duties, until eventually there were just four of us left. But, as everyone else so far had been assigned to working parties outside, my heart sank and I gave up any hope of being sent out too. The sergeant called us over and looked down at his sheet.

'This can't be right,' he muttered, checking down the list of names. 'Everybody can't be working out of camp. Wait here you lot,' he ordered and marched over the parade ground to Captain Myers. He began pointing at the sheet then over at us and from where we stood it looked as though they were having a pretty heated discussion. Suddenly the officer shouted at the sergeant who immediately came to attention, saluted, spun around and came tearing back towards us, his face all red and puffed up. He looked as though he was about to burst into flames.

'Right,' he screamed. 'You three are going to Famagusta and you, Urwin, you're assigned to a camp just outside Limassol. Now move yourselves! Get on that truck, Urwin!'

He seemed furious to have to send me out on a working party but I couldn't get into the back of the truck quickly enough. I grinned and waved at him as we drove off. Brilliant, I thought, I'm going to be on my own; this could be it.

'Sorry about that surprise you had lined up for me, sarge,' I shouted cheekily. 'Maybe next time, eh?'

He glared at me. 'Don't forget, Urwin, you're here for a long time. You can't avoid me for ever,' he bawled, and then strode off shouting and screaming at everyone he met. Captain Myers was still standing on the parade ground and as our truck drove off towards the gate, he turned and stood looking at me. Then, to my surprise, he slowly smiled and nodded. What's all that about, I wondered; surely he can't have anything to do with The Sixteen, can he?

As we drove along, I thought about the possibility of it. Perhaps someone at my camp would have to know, otherwise how else could it be arranged for me to get outside assignments when it suited Ken and the others? But who could it be, Captain Myers or maybe Lieutenant Stevens? I thought of the many possibilities among the various officers and NCOs, but none of them immediately sprang to mind as a likely candidate.

We had only driven for a short way towards Limassol when my thoughts were interrupted as the truck stopped abruptly at a cross-roads just outside the town and the corporal shouted my name. I jumped out of the back and went to where he was leaning through the cab window.

'OK, Geordie, the camp's just down that road a bit, you can't miss it,' he told me.

I looked along the deserted track where he pointed. 'What am I supposed to be doing there?' I asked.

'How the hell do I know? Just report to the gatehouse, it's orders. Here,' he said, shoving some papers into my hand. 'We'll pick you up here again 1600 hours on Friday. Have fun.' He banged his hand on the outside of the door and the truck immediately drove off.

I stood watching for a moment as it speedily disappeared then turned to walk in the direction he pointed and there, to my surprise, was a jeep and in it sat Chalky, grinning from ear to ear. I had neither seen nor heard him arrive.

'Hi, Geordie, hop in,' he said cheerfully.

'Bloody hell! Where did you spring from?' I asked as he spun the jeep around and we shot along the track.

'Remember Ken's little poem, Geordie, "I saw a man who wasn't there"? Only believe half of what you see!' he said, enigmatically referring to the slightly amended version of a well-known poem Ken had told me when summing up how The Sixteen operated.

As I hadn't been out of the camp very much since arriving in Cyprus, the route Chalky took as we left the main road and headed towards the hills was totally unfamiliar to me. It was mainly unpopulated, the dry and barren scrubby hills having only an odd tree dotted about here and there, but that was all it had in common with the route Ken had taken.

Like Ken, Chalky drove at breakneck speed for about half an

hour as I clung on, desperately trying to avoid being flung out of the jeep. Gradually I thought that some bits of scenery were beginning to look vaguely familiar and then as, we rounded the base of one of the hills I realised where we were. Once again, we were at the dilapidated old hut they used for their training purposes, but we had arrived by a totally different route.

Chalky didn't check his speed but drove straight up to the building, braking at the very last moment. We skidded to an abrupt halt in a cloud of dust and dirt, mere inches from the rusting old door and scattering several lizards, some of them about a foot long, which had been basking in the sun nearby. As before, the place appeared to be deserted.

Chalky immediately grabbed what was left of the windscreen and to my surprise, vaulted straight over it onto the jeep's much-dented bonnet.

'Come on, Geordie, don't just sit there getting a tan. There's work to be done,' he laughed over his shoulder then disappeared inside the building. I quickly followed him in, my eyes taking a couple of seconds to adjust from the glare outside.

Dynamo and Spot were already training and I stood watching them for a few minutes, totally fascinated, taking in every move they made. It was amazing, and I didn't want to miss a thing. Their actions were so smooth, so accurate, now I could see why they called it 'the machine'. It was incredible to watch. I wanted to be just like them and was determined that nothing was going to stop me.

From the way they were together, I realised that they knew each other fairly well and I suspected that they had worked together for some time but I still knew nothing at all about them, only their nicknames. I didn't know where they normally served or who with (if in fact they did), what their full names were, whether they were married or even what part of Britain they came from because they constantly changed their accents. All I knew was that I, for some reason, had been specially chosen to become the fourth part of this particular team, which in itself was part of The Sixteen.

I stood there watching them, looking around taking everything in. Then Dynamo stopped what he was doing and came over to me.

'Right, Geordie, come and have a seat and a cup of tea and I'll put you in the picture on how we do things around here.' I followed him over to a small, old table and did as he suggested.

'As you've probably been told,' he said, smiling, 'we're a covert unit, and I mean just that. We've been very successful so far and what makes this possible is that only a handful of select people know of our existence. It is these people who make it possible for us to operate. Do you understand?'

I nodded. 'Yes, of course.'

'Good! Ken told you that as soon as you started your training we would begin to explain what we do and why. Well, as you can see we're obviously not a dancing club!' he smiled. 'We're a group of sixteen men trained in a specific, unique way who currently operate throughout the Middle East; you could say that this is a training ground for us, but I'll tell you more about that later. We mostly operate in fours and we were three until now: you are the fourth. Don't ask how we became three!' He grinned, stopping me as the words formed on my lips. He paused and drank some more of his tea, then stared at me briefly for a moment before continuing quietly.

'You could say that we are assassins, for want of a better word. We carry out the operations that armies and governments can't be seen to do. We belong to no country, or rather no country will acknowledge our existence, if you know what I mean.'

Again, I nodded. Although it was what I had suspected, it still came as a bit of a shock to hear him say it out loud. My mother had told me to join the army to see the world and better myself, but I don't think she had quite meant in this way!

'So, Geordie,' he continued, 'to all intents and purposes, you're still just a private in the Pioneer Corps. Nobody is ever going to believe otherwise and that's exactly how we want it. No matter what you do with us, or how successful we are, there will be no recognition of it. If anything should happen to go badly wrong on any of our operations...' He paused briefly and looked at me very directly, 'And I think you know what I mean by that, old boy?'

'Yes, I think so. No one would acknowledge me, I'd be classed as a deserter or something, is that it?'

'Yes, something like that. Remember, because this is important, this unit does not exist, we do not exist, and you do not exist.' He paused briefly then continued. 'You can still back out; it's not too late,' he warned, leaning forward and resting his arms on the table. 'But once we've trained you, I'm afraid that's it, so this is the point of no return. What's it going to be?'

'Back out, not on your life! I wouldn't miss this for the world!' I said emphatically. 'I'm certainly going nowhere with the outfit I'm in, just digging flaming holes, pitching tents and being screamed at for the rest of my time here.'

'OK, then, but there is something else you need to consider. We're not going to put you through all of this training for nothing. We'll need you to become a regular so you'll have to think about signing on for at least another three years. Don't worry too much about it at the moment; we'll tell you when.'

I hadn't expected that. 'If I do, would I be able to get some leave to go home and see my family?' I asked.

'Yes, of course you would. Don't worry about that now, though; we'd arrange that later on.'

'Dynamo?' I interrupted him. 'Before I start on this training, can I ask you something?'

'Yeah, sure, what do you want to know?'

'You all knew what I would say before I said it, didn't you? You knew I wouldn't say no after what I saw that day?'

'Yes, of course. It's like I said, we know you, Geordie, we know all about you, even more than you know about yourself. We wouldn't have gone even this far if we thought there was the slightest chance that you would back out. I know it must seem confusing to you right now, but it will all become clear to you through time. Just wait and see.'

As we talked, Spot and Chalky were now training nearby and it struck me just how indistinguishable from one another they were. It was impossible to differentiate the actions of the two men now training from those of Spot and Dynamo when I arrived. They all seemed to thrive on what they did and appeared to have limitless amounts of energy.

Dynamo was talking again. 'This is what it is all about. We take the seemingly impossible and make it possible, and we do most of it by using the equipment you have already seen. We've been doing this type of operation for a long time now and as I said no one has any idea that we exist and that's how we intend it to stay, and that's how it's going to be. Anything else before we get on?'

'Well, yes, just one more thing. I've never once heard any of you guys raise your voices, yell or swear at one another like they do all the time back at camp. Why's that?'

'It's simple: we don't need to be bullied into what we do, we do it willingly and with pride. Besides, we have nothing to fear, that's why.'

'What's that got to do with shouting?'

'Well,' he said, leaning back in his chair and crossing one leg over the other, 'let's put it this way, Geordie. Not having the ability to cope with a situation results in a lack of confidence and this in turn leads to fear and then panic. Shouting and swearing acts as a substitute for courage; it gives false courage. People who are trained under those conditions don't know any better and resort to shouting and swearing themselves because that is all they know. It generally means that they have something to cover up, and that something is usually fear. They use it in the hope that because it scares them they believe it will scare others or the enemy. If you have the confidence, but mostly the ability and skills, to deal with any situation, then you control that situation. And because you are in command of that situation, then you have no fear and you need nothing to back you up. For most of them out there, without gunfire they have nothing to back them up. So I think that speaks for itself doesn't it, Geordie? Besides, old boy, swearing is best kept for when you bash your thumb with a hammer, don't you think?'

He paused, smiling, then drained his cup. 'One other thing, we don't need either gung-ho brawn or educated idiots in our unit. The sort of people we have here are like-minded and quick thinking, athletic and persistent. They have the ability to learn quickly and act as an integral part of a team and, most importantly, have common sense. We don't drink, have never drunk, we don't need it because we don't have a problem, so we can do without the Dutch courage. We always need to be in control. We have no room here for armchair commandos,' he said, then laughed and winked before continuing.

'Yeah, of course, we knew you'd say yes. We've already got a damn good idea of how you're going to turn out! Remember that with us, Geordie, you're part of a team of highly skilled men not just a number. You might not feel that yet but, judging by what we've seen so far, you soon will once you've completed your training. Nowhere in the world are soldiers trained like this, you can be. sure of that. This is what gives us the edge and as long as our skills are unknown to others, we will always have that edge. We have to be trained in these particular skills because we're on our own. I'm afraid no one will ever come to our rescue. You see, because our operations are covert and most take us right into the heart of enemy territory, we can have no backup from other forces. No one will come to our aid if we were to get into difficulties; how could they? Remember, we do not exist.

'No matter what country we may have to go into we try to dress, and look, as much like the locals as we possibly can. We don't go in uniform, armed to the teeth with huge packs on our backs. For a start, I rather think that might defeat the object of the exercise and give us away, don't you?' he laughed, shaking his head.

'And, if you're carrying a rifle or a backpack, not only do you stand out like a sore thumb but you lose the ability to move quickly; they make you clumsy. Besides, there is just no way you can carry enough ammo with you for a rifle so, once you've used up what you can carry, it's totally useless to you. No, that kind of stuff is best left with an army on the battlefield, not for the kind of jobs we do. Whatever we want we locate in the region we're in, so we either buy it, or find it and "borrow" it! That is why it is vital that we have only the kind of people who can quickly and clearly assess a situation, weigh up the various options and adapt easily to a totally different set of circumstances.'

He got up from the table and helped himself to more tea, 'Want another?' But before I could answer, he filled my cup too and sat down again.

'Right, where were we? Oh yes! There is nothing new in the idea of operating in disguise: the main problem is getting caught under those circumstances. Obviously we would be classed as spies and shot. More than likely, after being tortured to find out why we were there. These are the facts, Geordie. If for some reason we were to find ourselves in the position of possibly being discovered, if it looked as though that were inevitable, we would simply take control of the situation and allow it to happen. By not being dressed as soldiers or carrying any visible weapons, we lessen the possibility of being fired on immediately. They are more likely to approach you, warily of course, if you look like them. They will probably want to know what you are up to first and it is then, when they get close enough to realise that you are not what you first appeared to be, that your life is at its greatest risk. Being dressed like the enemy enables us to get very close to them, to move among them even, but the problem with this is that on close inspection, especially in an Arab country, it becomes obvious very quickly that we are not who we seem to be. It is at this point that we must immediately decide what action to take. The people in this area in particular are extremely excitable: they panic easily and are very trigger-happy. We cannot afford to take any chances. They could shoot us straight away and as we have no way of knowing this, we must take them out. Are you with me so far?'

'Yes, I understand.' It was all becoming clearer to me now; Dynamo was answering a lot of the questions I had been dying to ask.

He pushed back his chair and lightly sprang to his feet. 'You still have a lot to learn, Geordie, and there's no time like the present, so let's get started. Follow me.'

I did as he asked and we went over to where Spot and Chalky had continued to practise while we talked. Dynamo pointed towards them.

'This is not basic unarmed combat, Geordie, it is a science! Let me explain. You, or rather we, have to have the ability to get out of any scenario in which we might find ourselves; this type of combat in conjunction with our weapons is what makes that possible. The four of us have to work together in such a way that if we are confronted with one, two, or even ten, armed men we know we have the ability to take them out. But to do that we have to draw them in, we need for them to be only inches away to execute what we need to do. What makes this possible is that we have the element of surprise: we will not be dressed like soldiers, we will not appear to be armed. Ten heavily armed men surrounding four unarmed men would feel under no threat and totally in control of the situation. They would relax and have no idea that the four men they think are their prisoners actually have the ability to dispose of them all. Still with me?' he asked, but raised his hand to silence me before I could interrupt by asking questions. I nodded and he went on.

'Although we might allow ourselves to appear to be captured, and let our "captors" believe they have the upper hand, we can't afford, under any circumstances, to allow ourselves to be tied up. Once that happens they might start beating you or just blow your bloody brains out and we can't take the risk of that happening. If it appears that this is what is about to take place, then that is the point when we take them out. There is no other option: we cannot allow them to get rough or physically damage us in any way because once hit you become weakened and can lose the ability to fight back. So, any indication that one of them might be going to get violent, or make a move to use a rifle butt, punch, hit or kick us, then that is the time we take them out. And what makes this possible is "the machine". It's all about controlling a situation that appears to be controlled by someone else. Remember it's one thing to be surrounded by just a few men but that situation can only get worse and the next thing you know you're in prison or surrounded by an army.

'The full range of moves that we are going to teach you covers every form of attack, whether this is by knives, batons, rifles, pistols, revolvers, whatever. I know this will seem totally impossible to you right now. But for example, take someone coming at you with a knife,' he said, picking up a nearby bayonet. 'If the guy tries to slash your face then suddenly changes direction and aims for your stomach instead, you have no way of knowing that is what he intends to do until he actually moves. His whole action takes merely a fraction of a second, but your recognition of what he is about to do takes a fraction of a second longer, by which time your guts will be hanging out.'

To demonstrate what he was saying, Dynamo swiftly brought the bayonet in his right hand up towards the left side of my face. Instinctively, I raised my hands to prevent him and leaned backwards away from the blade. But I was too late; the bayonet was already touching my cheek.

'What will give you the edge and make it possible for you to counter his attack is knowing what he is going to do before he actually does it. This you will learn in time. But by anticipating every move it is possible for him to make with a knife, you then have the knowledge to stop him. You must begin to learn to know your enemy, how he operates, what he is likely to do in a given situation. You will learn how to recognise from the moves he makes whether he is carrying a knife or a gun, and act accordingly.'

Dynamo smiled. 'The moves you are about to learn will give you the ability to cover the whole area of your body that is vulnerable to his attack, at one and the same time. It will also give you the ability to turn his attack to your advantage, disarming and disabling him and then using his weapon against him. Judging by what we have seen so far you have the ability to learn the moves so quickly that it's only going to take a matter of weeks for you to get to grips with this. Which is just as well, as we need you to be up to scratch as soon as possible.'

'Chalky!' he called out. 'Take that bayonet and attack me with it in a slashing movement to the left-hand side of my body, either to my face or wherever you want, so that I can demonstrate to Geordie the exact move that stops it.'

Chalky picked up the bayonet and swiftly did just as Dynamo asked. Dynamo's reactions were unbelievable. He appeared to anticipate Chalky's move before it was made. His movements seemed almost robotic, yet were carried out with the most incredible speed and precision. He stopped the attack Chalky had aimed at his stomach not his face, with a move that enabled him to block the knife blow from Chalky's right hand in such an unusual way that he ended up standing behind Chalky, who by now he had disarmed.

'That is how it is done,' he said. 'The reason I did it in this way was to show you how it then becomes possible to use the disarmed person as a shield if there is more than one attacker. In time, we will show you how it is possible to use "the machine" to take out other attackers at the same time before they have realised exactly what has happened. Of course, I knew what Chalky was going to do, because I asked him to do it, but I didn't know where he was going to attack me, or exactly when. But even if he had changed his mind and attacked in a totally different manner, I, or rather "the machine", would have stopped it.'

'There are 10 to 15 different ways to stop that particular move,' Chalky said, 'which would enable Dynamo to be in the position he would want to be in if for some reason he was surrounded. It would make no difference whether the attacker was using a gun or a knife. But the really clever stuff is in knowing how to keep your enemy from shooting you straight away, getting him to come close enough to you without alarming him, which then enables you to take him and any others out.'

Dynamo's actions had really impressed me. What he had done was brilliant and I was itching to get started.

'One final thing to remember, Geordie,' he said. 'We go in and do the jobs that others cannot be seen to be doing. We succeed where the regular army have failed, or we help them to achieve their objectives without them actually being aware of it, but we do it in such a way that no one country is seen to be responsible for any outcome. When we eliminate someone we have to be able to get back out so rather than drawing attention to ourselves and having the whole country chasing after us we try, wherever possible, to make our jobs look like accidents or suicides. We work in total and utter secrecy. Think about it: that is the whole definition of the word "covert".

'Right, I can see by your face that you understand what I've been talking about and I know that you want to get on with it, so let's get cracking.'

Chalky took me over to a nearby table on which stood one of the canvas bags. He took out two boot knives, a sash and an MK1.

'This is it, Geordie. You're going to have to get used to wearing these so you must train with them on all the time. You'll find that all of these weapons coincide with the movements of "the machine". Now you're dressed to kill, let's teach you to kill.'

The training was incredibly intense: from first thing in the morning to last thing at night we would spend about four to five hours solidly going over something then have a short break, followed by another four to five hours. Although it was stiflingly hot and uncomfortable in the old hut, I just did not want to stop. That was the strange thing about it: the more I learned the more I wanted to know; it was addictive. At last, I was really beginning to understand what they meant by 'the machine'.

No matter which of them I was actively training with at any one time, their moves were always precisely the same, completely identical. It was uncanny. Although by this time I had only learnt about 70 moves, I could feel something happening to me as we repeated things over and over, not only to get them right but also to ensure that they became like second nature. Following one particularly long session with Spot, I stopped for a moment to wipe the sweat pouring from my brow.

'Had enough?' he asked. 'Do you want a break?'

'No way,' I replied.

Spot grinned. 'You've got the bug. I remember when it first hit me I didn't want to stop either. It's a strange feeling isn't it, powerful, as though you could walk over anyone? Yeah, I remember it well, Geordie. You feel good now, but wait until you know all of the moves, you'll feel incredible. You'll probably end up like Dynamo and we'll have to tie you down for a few days,' he laughed.

'It gets as bad as that, does it?' I said, laughing back at him.

'You'd better believe it! You don't know what you've let yourself in for.'

'What exactly do you mean?'

'Well, I don't want to put you off…'

'I don't think you'll be able to do that,' I interrupted him.

'OK, then. I remember the first job I did,' he went on. 'Afterwards, when we got back, I felt really strange for a while, sort of guilty, knowing that I'd killed someone, but at the same time totally thrilled that I'd done it, and done it well. I think we've all experienced the same thing, but by the time I'd done my second job, something else seemed to have taken over. It's a bit difficult to explain but I guess it's got something to do with the excitement that builds up inside of you when you have to go into a hostile country where you know they hate your guts and would have absolutely no qualms about blowing your brains out. You get this huge rush of adrenaline through your body. Going in disguise into a heavily guarded area under their very noses and carrying out the operation, assassination or whatever, knowing the serious consequences of what you're doing and coming out again without a scratch, it's unbelievable!' Spot looked thoughtful for a brief moment then continued.

'The bit I really enjoy is the unknown, the element of surprise, especially when they think it's impossible to break their security, you know. To get to our destination and find that it's not exactly like the photos we've seen, having to change our plans there and then. It's having the ability to work out any problems we may encounter, right under their very noses, to make what seems impossible, possible: that's what gives me a kick. The things you'll learn will never fail you. Do you see?'

I nodded. His enthusiasm was totally infectious.

'You see, we come from the place they least expect, somewhere they'd never dream anyone would even attempt, and because of that it sometimes feels as though we're almost cheating in some way. You could almost feel sorry for the bastards. It's having that edge that gives you a buzz, that and the fact that usually we're already on our way home before they even discover what's happened. There was this one job we did, I can't say where, but we got word back that they were suspicious about the sudden death of a guard and some valuable documents going missing. They weren't certain exactly what had taken place but the word came back via intelligence that someone thought they'd seen something but couldn't be sure. That's when Ken came up with that little saying of his, "There was a man who wasn't there, he wasn't there again today, I wish that man would go away." '

'He said that to me when I first came here,' I said, remembering.

'Well, Geordie, it sort of sums us up, if you know what I mean. It's a bit like the feeling when someone has been in your room: they may not have touched anything but you just know someone has been there, don't you? Or when someone has left the house 10 minutes before you get home: you can tell that they haven't been gone very long.' I nodded, knowing exactly what he meant.

Suddenly he nudged me. 'Hey, Geordie, you know that break you didn't want? Well, I've just spent half an hour explaining things to you, so you've had it whether you wanted it or not.

Come on, let's get on with it!'

And so my training continued with them. It was great, I was learning how to move and think and be completely different. Sometimes I spent a complete week with them returning to camp only for the weekend; then I would be back with them again the following week. Other times I would only train for a couple of days then spend the next two weeks back at camp. They never gave me specific times or dates when I could expect to be picked up and it appeared that nobody in my unit suspected a thing.

Whoever was covering my back was doing a first-class job, but they were undoubtedly helped by the apparent lack of organisation that was prevalent in the army system. Once you were given your orders and instructed to report to another camp, nobody seemed to care much as long as you got back when you were supposed to and that any paperwork you had was all in order.

In the beginning, they would often ask me to do something, watch me then smile or laugh and walk away shaking their heads and I thought that I must be doing it all wrong, or that they were taking the mickey. Puzzled, I collared Chalky.

'What are you all laughing at?' I asked him, looking down at my trousers to see if something was wrong. 'What's so funny?'

'Nothing, Geordie! Slow down a bit that's all, you're putting us to shame!' he said. 'No, honestly, I'm only joking, but you're learning this a hell of a lot quicker than we did!'

'Another 30 or 40 moves and you'll be ready,' Dynamo added.

'Ready for what?' I wanted to know.

'You'll find out soon enough. A job could pop up at any time and we want you ready for that. At the speed you're going, you'll be ready to do some initiative tests pretty soon!'

'Initiative tests? I thought I'd already done one!'

'No, these tests are used to see how quick you're going to be at picking things up, assessing situations, learning river crossings and the like,' he told me.

I was relieved to know that they were merely laughing with genuine surprise at the speed with which I was learning and how quickly I cottoned on to complex things that others would possibly find difficult to fathom. They had no need to encourage me but nevertheless it was great to be praised for once in my life. I was totally surprised at how quickly I was learning the moves and how I could remember with comparative ease what they showed me. Not for the first time, I wondered how anyone could have possibly known that I would have this kind of ability when I had not even known it myself.

Although I found it relatively easy to copy the moves of 'the machine', it was only after a couple of days that there came a moment when it just all clicked into place. Until then, my actions had not seemed to have any real power to them, but then I just felt everything come together, the moves and combinations, the weapons, the boot knives and the sash.

The aim was to turn me into some kind of fighting machine but at first, I just could not understand how these actions could possibly achieve that: they were the most unorthodox movements I had ever seen. I even thought for a while that perhaps they were exaggerating. But after a few sessions, I really began to understand just how 'the machine' worked and what in fact it could achieve.

Eventually the 150 basic blocking and striking motions would build into the 7000 smoothly precise actions Dynamo had mentioned to me. The power I was developing learning the moves was incredible and the way in which I was now able to move was quite unbelievable. They were right, there was no other way of describing it: I was acting like some kind of machine.

Everything was gradually becoming clearer to me and I now knew that I had the ability without using my fists, or indeed any punching or kicking actions, to kill or do some serious damage with relative ease; breaking a man's neck or limbs was simple to do. My actions were so powerful yet required so very little effort and used such small amounts of energy that I was never left exhausted. It was utterly incredible!

To be able to take a few men out without having to resort to gunfire or explosives would have to be done like this. I could not imagine any other way of doing it so successfully. Whoever had designed and worked out this method of combat really knew what it was all about. The whole system was quite ingenious. All of the equipment became an extension of your body, with everything designed to connect and slot together so smoothly like the pieces of a jigsaw, and the boot knives and sash were there to fill in any gaps.

When I started training with the sash, that wonderful piece of equipment, I was utterly amazed at what I could do. Although I had not learnt all of the moves yet and only had turnips in front of me as targets, it was still incredible what I was able to achieve. It fitted in completely with everything I had learned so far and extended my range thereby enabling me to take out anyone I couldn't reach with my hands. I could see the total surprise an attacker would get. They wouldn't stand a chance and I would be able to rip them to pieces in seconds.

The whole system was just so unbelievably cleverly worked out, it was obvious why it had to be kept such a secret, why in fact they operated in the way they did. It was just the kind of knowledge that you did not want to be made known to just anyone. I seriously doubted whether any of the guys I knew, however, could ever be able to pick up anything like these techniques: it had taken most of them weeks just to get to grips with marching up and down.

I thought taking a handgun, rifle or whatever from someone who had no qualms about killing you was pretty clever stuff. But to have the ability to prevent that person from shooting you just by your actions alone, and then to be able to make him do what you wanted him to do by those same actions, that was something else.

Now I could easily prevent a group of attackers from opening fire on me when I took out one of their pals, by moving in such a way that if they did use their guns they would actually end up shooting each other. This was just another aspect of my training, learning the art of how to completely control a situation and any action resulting from it.

It was amazing how the four of us worked together as a group. Having the ability to know where the others were all the time meant that we could each coincide our moves and keep out of the others' way. And, because I had mastered moving my head at one with my body as I turned, I now had the ability to constantly look around me so that I was always aware of the direction an attack might come from. This also enabled me to use my peripheral vision to its maximum efficiency.

I learned how to decide whom I should attack first if surrounded.

By walking backwards into my chosen victim, I would surprise him and encourage him to attack my back, thereby controlling the situation, so that I could then move into the position I needed to be in to attack someone else, or to draw another person into attacking me, using the first person as a shield if necessary. And by doing so, I would always remain in complete control of the whole situation. By constantly moving in this way I was able to monitor 360 degrees around me at any one time. Anyone I touched was taken out, or disabled, thus eliminating the risk of having them attack me again. Anyone out of my direct reach could be taken care of by using the sash.

It was a marvellous system, as skilful and as complex as a chess game.

7. Ready for action

Once I became proficient with the combat moves of the machine they began to instruct me in the specialised ways of retrieving lines, using a variety of different types of arrowheads in order to cross ravines and seemingly impassable rivers.

During one of these sessions, Dynamo decided that the time had also come for me to carry out some initiative tests.

'OK, something has come up, Geordie, and you've got to grips with the machine and the weapon training a lost faster that we expected. It's just as well; as we've said before we never know when we might be called on to do a job and we need to be at full strength; there are just a few more things we have to show you.

'As you know, we always choose difficult crossing areas where we know no one without our skills and knowledge would be able to follow us across. Do you remember when I mentioned to you a while ago that we would be putting you through some initiative tests to see how quick you're going to be at learning river crossings and the like?' I nodded.

'Well, we're going to do some today. You see, Geordie, it's one thing to learn the moves of the machine but we also need to know how you're thinking, so this is what I want you to do,' he told me, grinning. 'But if you don't do this in less than half an hour, you won't get any tea for the rest of the day.'

'Come on,' I laughed, knowing that he was teasing me about the amount of tea that I drank and that I was always ready for a cuppa. 'What do you want me to do?'

He pointed to the other end of the building. 'Look over there. Do you see that egg on top of that piece of wood?'

'Yes, sure!' About 40 feet away from me, a short piece of wood about one and a half inches thick and about six inches long stood on its edge with an egg precariously balanced on top of it. It was obvious that the slightest movement would cause the egg to fall and break.

'OK. Well, wait here for a moment.' I did as he asked and stood looking at the egg wondering just what he had in mind, thinking it must be some kind of a joke. Dynamo came back carrying a ball of string together with a dog-clip and a small piece of wood.

'Don't move, Geordie,' he said, and taking the piece of wood scratched a circle around me in the dirt. 'The object of the exercise is to take the egg off the top of that piece of wood, without break-ing it of course, and get it back here within this circle. At no time must the egg touch the ground, you mustn't move out of the circle at all and no one has to help you in any way. Here's a ball of string and a dog clip. I'll give you five minutes to pick up anything else you can find lying around which might be of use to you. Do you understand?'

'This isn't some kind of wind-up, is it?'

'No, it's not! This is serious, old boy, and your time starts now!'

There wasn't very much lying around the area except for the old oil tin that we used as a dustbin and inside it all I found was a cardboard box, which had been torn, squashed and thrown away. Better than nothing, I thought, although I had no idea at that stage what possible use it could be, but there was nothing else around. No sooner had I picked it up than Dynamo said, 'That's it, time's up. Get in the circle.'

'You've got to be joking,' I said. 'I've only got this piece of card-board.'

'And a ball of string and a dog-clip, what more do you need?' he said, still laughing.

'I take it you've done this?'

'Yeah, of course, we all have,' he grinned. 'Right, I'm going to give you three-quarters of an hour, starting now.'

I sat down. Well, if they can do it so can I, I thought. I must have sat there for about 10 minutes trying to work it out, looking at the structure of the building to see what I could use. I knew how to get the string down there and back but the one thing they had not shown me was how to pick a damn egg up without breaking it.

Then suddenly it came to me. I was fairly certain that by re-shaping the cardboard back into a box and using the string and dog-clip, I would be able to do it. Using my boot knife I cut one long slit lengthwise in the bottom of the box and two shorter slits, one at either end of this, creating two flaps. Attaching the dog-clip to the string, I threw this over the girder directly above the egg. Then by manipulating the string as I had been shown I was able to bring the dog-clip back to me.

By piercing four small holes in the top of the box, I could feed a second piece of string through these, then tie the dog-clip to it and to the top of the box in order to add weight to it. I then manoeu-vred the box by using the two lengths of string until it was suspended about two inches directly above the egg. I let the box down over the egg; the added weight of the dog-clip on top of the box pushed it down over it. This forced the egg between the two flaps cut into the bottom, which closed behind the egg once it was inside, trapping it there.

All that remained was to draw the box back towards me. I thought I had blown it when the piece of wood fell over and the egg disappeared. I fully expected to find it smashed or, at the very least cracked, but, much to my colleagues' astonishment and mine, I accomplished the whole task in just over half an hour.

'Brilliant, Geordie,' Chalky exclaimed, as they all clapped.

'We've all done it, but none of us came up with that idea,' Spot said.

'Does that mean I get a cup of tea, then?'

Dynamo laughed. 'That was the easy one, lad, try this. Stay where you are in that circle and don't move.' He walked down to the other end of the room and placed a small table where the piece of wood and egg had been, then came back to me and handed me a brick wrapped inside a piece of sacking.

'OK. Tie that tight underneath the table. When you've accom-plished it there must be nothing, no string or anything else, connecting you to either it or the table. You've got the same length of time as before and when you've done this one you can have your tea.' He paused briefly and grinned. 'Then you've only got three more to do.'

I could see what he meant about the first one being the easiest! They told me that the tasks they set me were designed to test my powers of assessment, initiative, speed of thought and actual thought processes. A right mouthful, I thought.

I had to think in a way I had never previously done, look at each task differently and carefully weigh up all of the possibilities from every angle. I had never been asked to do anything like this before but the first task had already whetted my appetite and I found myself really enjoying it. Each task was progressively more difficult than the previous one but I found that once I got my brain running along the right lines, they actually became easier for me to do. But one in particular was a real brainteaser and gave me a pain in the head thinking about it.

I might have known that when Dynamo had so readily offered me a drink of tea there would be a catch. He placed my cup on a flat piece of wood roughly 18 inches square and about 45 feet away from me. 'If you want it before it gets cold, get it back to you in that circle without spilling it. It has to stay on the piece of wood and mustn't touch the ground,' he called to me from the other end of the room.

At first I was stumped, and stood where I was in the circle racking my brain. But when he walked back to where I stood and handed me two wire coat hangers, I knew exactly what to do.

The tests had been difficult, but I felt as though I had used my brain properly for the first time and was really chuffed that I accomplished them all that afternoon. I felt a great sense of achievement.

'Well done, lad,' Chalky said, slapping me on the back.

'Clever,' Spot said slowly, stringing the word out.

'To be honest, I'm gobsmacked at the way you've just tackled those tests. It's quite amazing and that's not bull. That type of quick-thinking and assessment is vital to us, and judging by what we've seen so far, it's obvious that you've just got the kind of natural ability to learn this type of thing very quickly,' Dynamo told me.

I was pleased to know that they thought I was doing well, although a little embarrassed at their comments. But to receive that kind of praise from these incredibly clever guys was to me quite amazing. Their keen, intelligent minds were always on the go, always querying and wanting to know 'how'? Everything they did was, to my mind, done in a clever or trick way: even mundane, ordinary things, whether it was getting out of a vehicle, going up stairs, or even picking up a pencil. They seemed to use all of these everyday things to some effect.

'We need to get you trained up in the use of all the equipment so we're taking you up into the hills tomorrow,' Dynamo went on.

'Great!' I told him. 'I've really been looking forward to training with that gear now I've a good idea what it's used for.'

'We've got quite a lot to show you, Geordie,' Chalky said. 'The main problem is that we can only stay in that area for a couple of days at a time. British troops regularly patrol around up there and bumping into any of them would be a tragedy. We've had a few narrow escapes in the past.'

'What do you mean, what happened?'

'Well, I know they're our lads but nevertheless no one has to find out what we do.'

'Do you mean that we would have to...?' I said in astonishment.

'Yes,' Spot interrupted quickly before I could finish. 'We'd have no option; you see, we would look like terrorists to them and they might not ask any questions but just start shooting. We simply can't take the chance of them opening fire on us.'

'Obviously we've got to avoid that situation at all costs,' Dynamo pointed out. 'Remember, we don't exist. We simply can't afford to let anyone know of our existence, especially our lot. Besides, as Chalky said, we've had one or two close shaves with them before.'

'So let's just hope we don't bump into any of them, for all our sakes, eh?' Chalky said quietly. 'The main reason I brought the subject up is that we have to do the river crossings near the foot of the hills as it is the only place where the rivers are anywhere near wide and deep enough for our purposes. There isn't anything really suitable on the island so we have to make do with what is available.'

'Oh, Geordie, do me a favour will you?' Dynamo asked. 'Nip outside and move the jeep around the back.' I went to do as he asked and was just about to climb into the driver's seat when there was a sudden noise from above and Chalky came sliding down the roof and grabbed a hold of me, yanking me away from the jeep.

'Sorry about this, Geordie,' he said apologetically. 'But I've got into the habit of doing it whenever I get out. You can't trust these local bastards to keep their hands off anything, you know.'

And with that, he bent over and removed his boot knife from where he had wedged it under the driver's seat, blade pointing upwards and just touching the underside of the pad. Anyone plonking themselves down on the seat would have been in for a very rude awakening!

We spent four days up and around the Troodos Mountains living rough. They taught me a variety of survival techniques, and we practised abseiling and crossing rivers, or ravines, using all of the strange-looking arrowheads and equipment I had often wondered about. There were about seven or eight different types of arrowheads and what they could do was ingenious to say the least.

No wonder they wanted to keep it all a secret, I thought, as the uses of the various arrowheads were explained to me. Suddenly the reason for their odd shapes began to make sense to me at last. It was fascinating and I was like a kid with a new toy.

As we moved around the area they selected a number of different sites in order to demonstrate the equipment and for me to familiarise myself with it.

'As we've explained before,' Chalky said, 'these bits of equipment are what help us to carry out the seemingly impossible and to get in and out via the most unexpected routes. Let me explain what each of these arrowheads is called and what they're used for.' He picked one up and gave it to me.

'This one is called a single shot pickup. It's used to carry a light line across a river or from one building to another, where there is only one secure point, which enables us to then get a heavier line across with only one shot. These two work together,' he said picking up two different ones. 'This one is a stub end and this is a pickup, then there is another one here called a gripper. The purpose of all of them is the same as the single shot pickup, that is to carry a light line across an obstacle which then enables the heavy line to follow.'

It was all very clever stuff. Most of it they had devised and invented themselves.

'The reason we have so many different types is so that we can assess each different situation, then, by using the relevant piece of equipment, get the lines across no matter what the terrain is like,' Spot explained. 'By using these arrowheads in conjunction with either a bow or crossbow depending on the distance, and by attaching ourselves onto the heavy line using our pulley wheels, we can cross a huge variety of obstacles and distances very quickly, without getting our feet wet.'

Although the training was as hard and intense as ever, I was in my element and thoroughly enjoyed every aspect of it. By now I was raring to go and could not wait to put it all together, and eventually into practice.

The following week I spent back at camp but, as Dynamo had warned that an operation could come up at any time, I thought it would not be long before I was picked up again. I was right: on the following Monday Chalky was waiting on the road for me.

And now, as the battered old American jeep bounced along the scorched and dusty track dragging behind it a billowing trail of choking white dust, he turned to me grinning from ear to ear.

'This could be your lucky day, lad,' he shouted above the noise of the engine. 'You've been waiting to see the machine in action. Well, now you're going to get the chance. I think this is what you've been waiting for.'

'Why, what's happened? What's the job?' I shouted back, desperately trying to cling on to my seat as we rattled over the rough terrain. Chalky did not reply immediately as just then, one of the front wheels hit a large stone in the pot-holed track with a bone-jarring crash. The jeep rocked violently, almost overturning. I was thrown hard against the steel frame of what had once been the windscreen and almost over it onto the bonnet. Chalky laughed as he regained control of the vehicle and I fell back into my seat, rubbing my bruised ribs. He obviously thought this was great fun.

'What's the job?' he repeated, mimicking my Geordie accent. 'You're beginning to sound like one of the lads already. Hang on a few minutes. You'll find out soon enough when we get to the hut,' he yelled, still laughing.

About 10 minutes later he brought the jeep to a screeching, shuddering halt outside the dilapidated training hut then dismounted in his usual fashion onto the bonnet.

'What's the big idea?' I asked. 'How come you're always telling me how invaluable I am to you and yet you've just about killed us getting here?'

Chalky just laughed. 'There's no time to hang about, Geordie, there's work to be done. Besides we can't afford to be spotted by any British troops patrolling this area.'

There was a sudden thud at the rear of the jeep and I felt the pressure of cold metal on the back of my neck as a familiar voice quietly said, 'Gotcha!' close to my ear. I turned around to see Dynamo's grinning face. He was pointing a .303 rifle straight at me.

'Where did you come from and how did you suddenly appear like that?' I asked. I had heard nothing of his approach and could not see anywhere in the near vicinity where he might have been concealed.

'Just making sure no one was following,' he said, winking at me. 'But one day I'll find it impossible to do this to you.' Then he jumped off the jeep and followed Chalky into the building. I wondered if he had been up in the hills watching our approach, but as he was wearing his CTC, he could have been hiding anywhere. I pushed the thought aside for the moment and smiling, despite my sore ribs, I went inside too.

'Close that bloody door will you?' Spot shouted, complaining about the dust storm that the jeep's arrival had created and which had swirled inside the building each time the door was opened. To my surprise, Ken was sitting at the table with Spot. I had not seen him since the night I went through the 'One Step Beyond' some four months before. Chalky had told me that Ken brought our orders and supplied transport and whatever else we needed.

'Hi there, Geordie, come on in!' he said. 'Nice to see you again. Right, now we're all here let's get on with it. I've got a little job for you lads.'

Spot winked and smiled at me as Chalky and Dynamo joined him and Ken at the table. Dynamo shoved a chair my way with his foot and nudged me as I sat down next to him. 'Now we'll have some fun, eh Geordie?' he said rubbing his hands.

Chalky must have seen my surprise. 'That's right, Geordie, fun.

When you've been on a couple of these operations you'll know exactly what we mean,' he said.

I helped myself to a couple of sandwiches from a plate Spot handed round and poured out a cup of tea. Although I was now one of the team, I got the impression that the operation, whatever it was, had been planned before I arrived and they were merely going over it once again for my benefit, in order to make me aware of the details.

'Right, lads,' Ken began. 'There are a bunch of guys up in the mountains that we believe are responsible for running most of the guns to various parts of the island. As you know, in the past their chief method of attack has been by means of hit and run tactics using guns or home-made bombs and incendiary devices against their targets: mainly British servicemen and installations. You've probably heard about the incidents involving the deaths of British servicemen and some of their families.'

I had certainly heard rumours around my camp about the murders of several British servicemen, including a sergeant shot in front of his little boy in Nicosia. And it now appeared that the terrorists were targeting the families too. Rumours were spreading about another incident involving a sergeant's wife who had been killed while out shopping with her daughter. Most of these apparently random terrorist attacks took place in broad daylight; they were intended to demoralise the British troops garrisoned on Cyprus and thereby maintain an atmosphere of crisis. However, the army verified none of this, in case British soldiers went on the rampage taking revenge on the locals.

'Intelligence informs us,' Ken went on, 'that the number of terrorists is on the increase and there are now believed to be over 200 activists, not to mention EOKA sympathisers, on the island, many of whom are hiding and being trained up in the Troodos mountains.'

'Surely there are enough troops on the island to take care of that?' Chalky asked.

'Well, the army have increased the number of their patrols in the area and have stepped up the road blocks,' Ken went on. 'In general, they don't do too bad a job in keeping a lid on things under the circumstances, but there just aren't enough of them and, to a great extent, their hands are tied, which is where we come in. But I think the main problem is that the troops underestimate most of these people and the level of support they have.

'The crux of the matter is that these bastards appear to be changing their tactics. Our information is that the Greeks expect the island to be invaded at any time by the Turks and are preparing themselves for an attack. Intelligence believes that they are now being supplied with much more sophisticated weapons. Just what these are and where they're coming from we're not quite sure, but it seems a pretty safe bet that they've now managed to get their hands on grenades and mines, that sort of stuff. We've been given a pretty good indication of the area where these guys are holed up and that's the reason we're going in. Our job is to find out exactly what weapons they have got and destroy them. Besides,' he chuckled, 'it's Geordie's birthday later this month: it might be a good idea for him to get some practice in by having a little party up in the Troodos and let him have the chance to show what he can do!'

The table was covered with maps and papers and Ken pointed to a spot on one of them. 'Our reports indicate that these bastards are hiding out in these caves around here. They keep changing their location but there have been signs of activity in this area within the last 24 hours. We believe they are regularly taking truckloads of guns and explosives up into this area, probably smuggled in from mainland Greece,' Ken said. 'OK. Any questions?'

Yeah, loads, I thought, but not wanting to show my ignorance and inexperience I kept quiet. Although I wasn't scared, I felt a little apprehensive because it was my first operation. But, with the training I had been given, I felt very confident and was raring to go. I just knew I could do it!

'What sort of opposition are we going to be up against?' Dynamo asked. 'Can you give us any idea of numbers?'

'Intelligence informs us that they are a group of about 10 or 12. You'll have no backup from the rest of the team: there'll only be the four of you.'

'Well, let's hope that Intelligence have got it right,' Chalky muttered.

'Oh, and keep a tight rein on Geordie, lads,' Ken laughed, winking at them. 'We don't want him to get carried away and kill some local farmers, now do we?' he added.

We spent some time discussing the equipment, route and transport we would take and decided upon only the bare essentials.

'The idea is to hit them hard, get in and out as quickly as possible,' Dynamo stated.

Ken nodded. 'That's right. This area is unknown to us, so it's pointless making too many plans. Just look on it as an extra bit of training. OK, then guys, I'll leave you to it. Catch you later.' And with that, he left.

Each of us had a locker in the building and from the variety of equipment we had stored, selected only those items we needed for this operation. We knew the type of terrain and didn't want to be weighed down with unnecessary gear. We each took out ropes, harnesses, pistols, ammo, boot knives, dog-clips and a new CTC, together with our MK1s, sashes, a canteen of fresh water and dry biscuits, which we called 'dog biscuits'.

As this was to be a totally clandestine, unofficial operation, there was to be absolutely no indication that any of us were British servicemen. Besides, if the unthinkable happened and we were caught, the British army would deny all knowledge of us anyway.

I changed out of my army uniform of shorts and khaki shirt into clothes similar to those always worn by the others: a white shirt, jeans, an old army tunic and American-style laced-up boots, which we wore rather than standard army issue boots. These American-style combat boots had softer soles and were longer in the leg than the ones we were ordinarily issued, making them ideal for concealing boot knives. Finally, around my waist I fastened the belt-like weapon we called the sash, the most lethal piece of equipment we carried.

As I was collecting my gear, I once again wondered about the organisation of all of this. How did all this stuff actually get here and who looked after it when we were gone? It seemed to me that the lockers were possibly removed from the building whenever we left it. They were always in a slightly different location each time I returned. Although the training area was in the middle of nowhere, there was always the possibility of some locals or even an army patrol stumbling across it. Removing our gear would certainly help to avoid detection.

We each placed our equipment into identical canvas holdalls, which we put ready for when we left, together with a map of the area. As we would leave at 0100 hours, we rested up for the remainder of the day and evening.

When it was time to go, we threw our bags into the back of the jeep and set off. There was a fine drizzle falling and it was freezing cold in the open vehicle. Ken had given us the co-ordinates of the area the terrorists were reported to be in, and as we travelled, the others chatted together and cracked jokes as they discussed the job and the route we needed to take. I said little during the journey. I wasn't frightened or nervous, just a little anxious about what might happen. But I had every confidence in my colleagues, who had a lot more experience. I knew that I would not be here with them if they didn't think I was totally ready for it.

There was a 10 pm curfew on the island and we had to be careful to avoid army roadblocks or any form of confrontation with British troops, who would probably view us as terrorists. In order to do this we had to take little-used narrow, winding tracks; these could be just as hazardous as the main routes, as we had no way of knowing whether we might bump into a group of terrorists using them for the same reason we were.

It was very dark on the steep mountain tracks and we had to drive relatively slowly since we couldn't use the jeep's headlights for fear of being spotted either by terrorists or troops. But every so often, the moon shone through a break in the heavy cloud and we caught glimpses of the sheer drop down the mountainside only inches away from the jeep's wheels as we gradually climbed higher and higher.

The brief spells of moonlight were very bright and it was just possible to make out the fresh tracks of a bigger vehicle where it had dislodged several large stones and part of the road on its way up the narrow, winding track. Dynamo began to travel a little faster along the tortuous track ahead of us. He seemed totally oblivious to the dangers of the narrow trail that was now partially obscured by a swirling patchy mist. Eventually, the fine drizzle turned into a heavier, steady downfall.

'Oh, great!' Chalky said. 'That's all we need. Those tracks will be gone soon.'

'It doesn't matter. This has to be them, no one else would be daft enough to come up here; the army certainly wouldn't risk it!' Dynamo pointed out, peering ahead of him.

Spot was sitting in the rear next to me. 'How do you feel, Geordie?' he asked.

I turned and grinned at him, water dripping off the end of my nose. He looked and sounded so calm and relaxed, in fact they all did. I was cold and soaked to the skin, but adrenaline was pumping through every inch of my body and I was trying very hard not to show just how 'keyed up' I was. I knew that my actions today would no doubt result in someone's death, the first death I would be responsible for. But I was ready.

'I'm OK, Spot,' I replied. 'Just fine!'

I just wanted to get on with it, to really prove to these guys that there were right to have chosen me, to show them that I really was one of them, part of the team, and ready for action.

8. Operation Pinprick

It was a couple of weeks after my first operation up in the Troodos Mountains and just before my 19th birthday, November 1958. I was training with Dynamo when Ken suddenly arrived. I hoped that his arrival meant there was another job for us. Dynamo and I broke off our training and followed him into the 'office' area.

'Well, Geordie, it's your birthday soon so we've decided to give you a few weeks off,' he said, to my total surprise. 'We'll see you after Christmas, sometime in the New Year, unless something happens in the meantime and you're needed.'

I tried not to show how bitterly disappointed I was. I thought that he had come to brief us for our next operation but this was a bolt out of the blue. Six weeks without training, without seeing Dynamo, Chalky and Spot, six weeks to the New Year, six whole weeks of being stuck around the camp doing routine work. I was utterly deflated.

Back at camp work mainly revolved around preparations for Christmas, when a pantomime and variety show were to be put on by the lads. As I crossed the parade ground one morning, I met Sergeant Lupton.

'Well, Urwin, I'm certainly looking forward to seeing this act of yours,' he said as he walked past.

'Eh! Act, what act, sarge?' I said, gawping at him. I didn't have a clue what he was on about.

'The one you're doing for the Christmas concert. You've got your name down for it!' he said, over his shoulder. Immediately I knew who had dropped me in it: my so-called pal, Dave Buckfield. He and Bill were always volunteering me for something or other, putting my name down for all kinds of things: table tennis, darts etc. I was good at both but, unfortunately, could not take it too far. In the army, if you were good at something like that, it always meant taking part in some kind of league against other camps and I could not get involved in anything like that, which would mean being tied up on certain dates with matches etc. I had to be available for The Sixteen whenever they needed me.

God knows what I would have to come up with now for this little caper Bill and Dave had involved me in.

As the days passed, more and more people began to ask me what I was going to do. I had all kinds of ideas but none of them seemed right. Then one night I went to the pictures with a couple of the lads. Before the main film, they showed a newsreel where a bloke had lain on a bed of nails with a paving slab on his chest while another guy smashed it with a sledgehammer. My mates were impressed.

'It's a con,' I told them. 'There's a knack to it. It's not that difficult to do if you know how.'

'If it's so easy, why don't you do it for your act, then?' Bill said.

'OK, then, I will,' I replied, taking up his challenge, relieved to have something to do at last. It took some time to get enough six-inch nails to make my 'bed', and over the next few weeks, I scrounged around for as many as I could find. They weren't easy to come by and I had all the guys searching about for me and bringing them back from other camps. I practised my act and press-ganged a reluctant Bill into being my 'assistant', although on the one occasion he attempted to lie on the 'bed' when there weren't enough nails in it and he ended up with a sore and bleeding backside.

On Christmas Day, I got ready to perform my act in full for the first time. Bill and I had not been able to practise the slab-breaking bit before as we had only been able to get our hands on one paving stone, nicked from another camp, and obviously did not want to use it. We tied towels around our heads for a bit of an oriental feel. When it was our turn, I asked for two strong men from the audience to lift the slab onto a towel covering my chest as I lay on the bed of nails. As the two volunteers came forward, Bill pranced about the stage like a magician's assistant, pointing to what I was doing until I grabbed him and shoved a large sledgehammer into his hands.

'Here,' I told him. 'Get on with it.' He suddenly became concerned that, not having done it before, he might injure me.

'Ow 'ard do I 'ave t'it it?' he said, with a worried expression. 'I might cave your bloody chest in!'

By now, I was holding the large, heavy slab on top of me.

'Just get on with it, hit it as hard as you can, right in the middle, and watch my flaming fingers,' I told him as he stood with the hammer hovering above me amid loud shouts and jeers from the audience.

'Just belt it!'

'Go on, hit it!'

'Bash the bloody thing!'

'Smash his chest in!'

Bill crashed the hammer down onto the paving slab, which instantly broke into four or five pieces. The audience roared their approval and he began prancing around again holding the hammer above his head. We were a success and, more importantly, I came through it unscathed!

In early January, much to my relief, my team-mates started to pick me up for training again. For some reason, our training had now intensified and I was with them on a much more regular basis, every other week in fact. I asked Dynamo what it was all about.

'Well, it's a while since we last saw you, Geordie. We don't want you to get rusty, now do we,' he said and took a swipe at me. I countered his move and he went on.

'Cyprus is off the map, now, Geordie. The government's about to give them what they want so we can concentrate on doing the jobs we're trained for. Not spending our time chasing these daft sods around the mountains.'

I swivelled my body and countered another of his moves. 'By the way, what you said to me about me signing on for three years, you did say I would get two weeks' home leave, didn't you?'

'Of course,' he replied. ' But you'd better discuss all of that with Ken.'

For months, I had thought long and hard about this, ever since it had first been mentioned to me during my initiation. I was still torn and not really able to make a firm decision. During these last few weeks away from them, I realised just how much I wanted to remain a part of the group, to keep on training and carrying out operations. The simple fact was it was in my blood now. I could not get away from it.

And yet I desperately wanted to see my mother again, not just because I missed her but also to let her see that she had been right to encourage me to do my national service. I wanted her to see how much I had changed, how I had grown up, gained confidence and lost my stammer. I wanted her to be proud of me. I wished with all my heart that I could tell her about the group. I knew just how proud she would be that I had been so specially chosen: she had always told me that I was special, that I would never end up like my father, but of course, most mothers think that about their kids. Obviously, I would never be able to tell her or indeed anyone about The Sixteen. I was also unsure how she would react to me signing up for such a long period.

But, on the other hand, for the first time in my life I felt that I had met real men, not loudmouthed boastful drunkards but men who trusted in my judgement and whom I trusted implicitly. For all that I had spent a lot of time with the lads back at camp since we had come here, it was these guys who were the first real mates I had ever had. They had given me an unshakeable belief and faith in myself and my abilities. They had shown me how to achieve my full potential and, as desperate as I was to see my mother again, I was equally desperate to carry on working with them.

I just couldn't decide what to do; I was almost halfway through my national service and would be sent home and demobbed at the end of the year. I knew that I would have to make my mind up quickly and decided to speak to Ken about it as soon as the opportunity arose.

For a couple of weeks nothing much happened; I trained one week and spent the next back at camp. The following Monday I assembled on the parade ground with everyone else and after roll call we were assigned our duties for the coming week. The sergeant called out half a dozen names, including mine, for a works party, which meant I could be sent anywhere on the island.

A corporal was assigned to our group, and when we were dismissed off the parade ground, I went over to him to find out where we were being sent.

'We're all going to a camp near to Famagusta, but you'll be on your own at an ordnance depot at Dhekélia, Geordie,' he said. 'They want you to drive a forklift truck or something, some cushy number. We'll drop you off as near to the depot as we can.'

Bill was also in the group and we sat next to one another on the truck taking us off to the other camps. 'How the ' ell did you get a cushy number like that, you jammy sod?' he asked. "s all right for some. You must have pals in high places,' he joked, totally unaware of how close to the truth he was.

'Oh yeah, like last week you mean, stuck in that sweaty cookhouse? I must have lost half a stone in weight and peeled 20 in spuds. Call that cushy do you?' I joked back.

We drove along the main coastal route through Limassol and Larnaca, passing a couple of army checkpoints along the way. After about three-quarters of an hour the truck came to a halt near to a road junction. The corporal jumped out of the cab and shouted my name.

'Urwin, out! This is where we leave you,' he said, handing me some papers. 'Here's your orders. Report to the officer at that gatehouse.' He pointed towards the nearby ordnance depot then he climbed back in the truck. 'And don't forget, we'll be here to pick you up at this spot 1700 hours on Friday,' he yelled as it drove off.

'I'll try t' get round t' see you through t' week,' Bill shouted at me. 'Righto,' I yelled back with a wave, and then began to walk towards the camp. I could see a jeep parked nearby on my left; as I walked along it suddenly pulled up alongside me and there sat Chalky, grinning.

'Hop in, Geordie.'

'Thank goodness for that,' I sighed as I sat down beside him and we roared off in a cloud of dust.

'What's the matter, did you think we weren't coming back for you?' Chalky yelled above the noise of the engine.

'Well, not so soon,' I shouted back.

'What's up, have you had a hard time?' he laughed.

'You can laugh,' I said. ' But I've been stuck in the flaming cook-house all last week cleaning pans!'

'So what! You must have been getting the best of the grub, eh?'

'What about these orders then? I'm supposed to be driving a forklift truck at that camp back there,' I said waving the sheaf of papers the corporal had given me.

'They haven't got any such orders and they aren't expecting you, so forget about it, and don't ask how, because even I don't know that.'

'But there's a pal of mine coming to look for me during the week,' I told him, remembering about Bill.

'Well, he won't find you, will he? Anyway he won't get in the camp if he doesn't have a pass so stop worrying about it.'

As usual we were flying along the road at breakneck speed, bouncing and jolting over every rock and stone. 'You didn't tell me what happened to those puppies. I bet they caused you some problems, didn't they?' Chalky shouted changing the subject.

'I gave them to one of the officers I'm a bit pally with, Lieutenant Stevens. He's a bit of a dog lover and said he'd try to find them good homes. I had a job convincing him that I'd found them near the camp though, but I think he believed me in the end. Anyway, he's taken them to other camps to be trained as mascots or something.'

We were yelling at one another in order to be heard above the racket of the engine, and it was difficult to have a proper conversation. As usual we were flying along narrow twisting tracks in order to avoid travelling on the main roads, and I was beginning to get the feeling that we were going around in circles, but I knew that eventually we would end up at that old hangar. We came to a small river and Chalky slowed down only a fraction before driving straight across it and travelling on for about another half an hour.

Each time I was taken to the training area I arrived by a different route. I always had the feeling that we were being observed, but I never saw anyone, and, although I was not aware of Chalky giving any kind of signal, as I suspected he had done in the past, I was fairly certain that other members of The Sixteen were nearby guarding the place until we left.

My team-mates always seemed to be very relaxed, but I knew that security around the training area had to be tight. Despite the fact that they smiled and cracked jokes a lot, I knew that this was something they were deadly serious about. They needed to be. We could not afford to have anyone, terrorists or British troops, find us there. I had brought the subject of security up only once before when Dynamo, in an unusual moment of seriousness for him, had let it slip that their security was the best there was, but then he quickly changed the subject and it was never mentioned again.

The landscape began to look familiar as we neared the mountains and suddenly there it was, roughly four to five hundred yards in the distance, the old hangar. Well, that was what I called it but it was really too small to have held anything other than perhaps a couple of light aircraft. We drove in through the gateway or what remained of a metal barred gate, which was now mainly broken and rusting. As usual, there were no obvious signs of security in place, just the feeling that someone was closely watching us as we pulled up outside the old tin hut.

Chalky pushed the old creaky door open and following him in I saw my other team-mates sitting around a dirty old table that was covered with bits of paper, maps and photographs. Dynamo turned towards me, smiling.

'Here's Geordie. I'll bet he can help us to solve our little problem.'

'You must joking,' I said. 'I thought I was here to learn off you lot.'

Chalky nudged me. 'That's why you're with us, young man. You were good at stuff like this during your training, so I'm sure you'll be able to help us to come up with an answer now.'

After my first operation, and my blunder with the rope that had almost resulted in my death, I had wondered whether they might think I was not up to it and reconsider my being part of the group. I really felt that I had let them down badly, but they never referred to it; it just wasn't important to them. Besides, going over past events simply was not their way of doing things. They did not waste time; that was then and this was now. Their attitudes towards me had not changed. If anything, I now felt more a part of the team than ever before.

'Well, what's the problem?' I asked.

'Our problem is in Beirut,' Chalky replied. 'For the last two hours we've been trying to find a way to eliminate the target and get away without anybody knowing'.

Spot shook his head. 'Beirut, of all places. They couldn't have picked a friendlier place if they'd tried.'

'What's the target and where's Beirut?' I had heard of the place but was not quite sure where it was.

'The target is a man and Beirut is in Lebanon, Geordie,' Spot explained.

'Well, I've heard a lot about the place, but I never thought I'd be going. How are we going to get there?'

Dynamo nudged me in the ribs. 'Don't worry about it, Geordie, it's all been taken care of. A hack is picking us up before daylight tomorrow.'

'A hack, what's a hack?

'You've heard of helicopters, haven't you? Well, these heli-copters are used for reconnaissance and search and rescue missions. They' re known as hacks by the guys who use them,' he explained. 'Short for "hackney"; you know, like the London taxis.'

'A helicopter?' I said, astounded. ' I've seen pictures of them but that's all.'

'Well, you'll be flying in one tomorrow,' Chalky chipped in. 'For obvious reasons, he can't take us all the way. We're going to have to be dropped into a small fishing boat and travel the rest of the way by sea. The trouble with that is we've only used the helicopter on two previous occasions and on the last one we had to abseil out of it, which gave us a few problems.'

'That's right,' Spot agreed. 'We hadn't realised that we were going to have to do that, so we'd nothing rigged up inside the hack to make it possible to abseil out of it. We had to fasten our ropes to the floor and when we dropped out of the door the flaming thing was all over the place. They're pretty unstable things: unless of course it's just the way Ken flies them. Anyway, we found that the best way to do it was to leave from both sides at the same time.'

Chalky interrupted him. 'Don't forget, Spot, Ken said that brackets have been fastened above the doors so we should be able to exit standing up, which will make it a hell of a lot easier. We'll go through the procedure later on, Geordie. It isn't difficult but you'll need to familiarise yourself with it. We'll fasten the abseil lines before we leave.'

'The boat will put us ashore about nine miles north of Beirut, very near to a small village. Apparently, there are usually a lot of small fishing boats in the area around that time of day, so we won't look out of place,' Chalky continued.

I was really excited at the thought of a helicopter trip. 'How on earth did you manage to get hold of a helicopter, hack that is?' I asked him. He put his finger to his lips, winked and smiled. 'Ssshh!' was all he said.

'I know, I know. I shouldn't ask.'

'That's right. You' re learning.'

Spot was looking at some papers on the table. ' We've been informed that our target operates from a government building, an office block, which is well guarded. There doesn't appear to be an easy way to get him inside the building,' he said. 'We've looked at the whole set-up and the only alternative is to get him when he comes out for his lunch. We've been informed that he eats every day with some colleagues in a small café nearby, but there's always a military escort of at least two accompanying him. So, we should-n't have any problems in recognising him. What we have to do is find a way of disposing of him without drawing any attention to ourselves.'

'Our intelligence informs us that the target is to move out of the country very soon,' Chalky explained. 'We understand that there is something big going to take place in the area; we don't know exactly what it is yet, but we must take him out before then. We aren't entirely sure of when he is moving but we do know that he is definitely going to be there for a few more days at least,' he added.

Dynamo handed out some photographs showing our target, the office block, street and café.

'Apparently his sleeping quarters are changed at regular inter-vals, but the change follows no set pattern, so it's difficult to pinpoint where he'll be at night. The only thing he does consis-tently is to have his lunch between 1200 and 1400 hours with a military escort to the café and back,' he said. 'Of course, there are a hundred things that could prevent him from doing this. He could be in meetings, be too busy or even ill; he might not even go to his usual place but that's a chance we'll have to take. However, lunch seems to be the one thing he does regularly, and he has to be taken out at some point.'

'Well, we've got less than 20 hours to come up with something to solve the problem and only one chance to take him out,' Chalky pointed out. 'Believe me, guys, this isn't going to be easy. This place is in the centre of the city, it's going to be very crowded and crawling with armed troops; just getting to this building alone is going to be tricky. If we're spotted these people will try to tear us to pieces; don't forget that it's not so long since our lot gave half of their country to the Israelis. So if we don't get it right, we won't be back in time for supper,' he joked. 'Now, if anybody has any bright ideas, we could do with them ASAP.'

Spot nudged my arm. 'Come on then, Geordie, fire away. We leave here at four in the morning and need to be in the vicinity of that building by 1100 hours so we have time to walk around and familiarise ourselves with the general area.'

'Do you really think I'm up to doing a job like this so soon after the last one? It' s only been a few weeks. Has it got to be tomorrow?'

'Don't knock yourself, Geordie,' Spot said, winking at me. 'You're not alone, you're part of a four-man team and besides you're the quickest learner I've come across.'

'Anyway, we don't have an option,' Dynamo explained. 'The trip from here to Lebanon is already set up because that's when the helicopter is available and we've only got it for two or three hours tomorrow. Fancy a cuppa, Geordie?'

For several hours we sat around the table drinking tea and eating sandwiches, laughing and joking with good-natured banter as we discussed the various ideas each of us came up with, some totally serious, some deliberately daft. I really enjoyed being in their company; they involved me totally and listened to all of my opinions and ideas as we weighed up the viability of each suggestion and the possibility of taking the guy out without being detected.

For once in my life, someone was actually listening to me as if what I said counted, that it really mattered. It was a great feeling even though I could hardly believe it and, more importantly, it made me really feel part of the team. I felt inspired, despite having the definite impression that they had already worked something out and were merely trying to encourage me to think, leading me in a certain direction, in order to see what I would come up with.

'There's got to be a way to do this without causing any commotion,' Chalky said. 'So to simply break his neck or knife him is out of the question really. And it's going to be difficult to rig something up to blow him away, as our information is that there are two cafés he uses regularly, one on either side of the street, plus several more in the area. Anyway, an explosion would simply alert the whole place and it would be all too easy for them to seal the area off and make it difficult for us to get back out.'

'Besides that, we don't want to be seen carrying anything which might draw attention to us. Don't forget it'll be broad daylight and we'll need to blend in with the locals, so the less we carry the better,' Spot added.

'Yes, that's right,' Chalky agreed. 'Anyway, as you know, Geordie, we prefer to stay away from that sort of gung-ho operation if we can help it: it's never that accurate and usually ends up with innocents, like kids, getting hit. And I do have a conscience,' he continued. 'Besides, we like the personal touch; it's much neater and less hazardous. Carrying explosives can be rather uncomfortable and anyway the reason we are being sent in is because this kind of thing is what we do best. Any idiot can do a "crash-bang-wallop" job.'

As usual Dynamo was bursting with energy and raring to go. 'This guy is proving to be a bloody nuisance. Why don't we just hijack a bus and run the bastard over?' he joked. 'Seriously though, what about trying to poison him? Drop something into his cup while he's sitting having lunch in the café or rig something up to scratch or jab him on the skin?'

This seemed to be the best solution so far and for some time we considered the options, the various poisons available that could be put on a needle or into a syringe.

'The trouble with that, Dynamo, is his clothing. It could act as a barrier and wipe the poison off a needle, plus if it's a delayed reaction, how will we know whether it' s worked or not? I don't really think it's feasible, do you?' Chalky commented.

For several hours, we continued to discuss the possibility of using poisoned needles or syringes, as we scrutinised a full-size chart of the human anatomy hanging on a nearby wall. During my training with them, I studied the human structure in considerable depth and had learned how it worked, how its organs, muscles, arteries and nervous system interconnected. I had to know all of its vital points and weakest areas and how the skeleton formed the framework with which everything else linked. Now, looking at the wall chart, an idea began to form in my mind but the fact that it would have to be carried out with such incredible pinpoint accuracy made me reluctant to tell them. I didn't think they would go for it.

'What would happen if the needle was just long enough to puncture his heart?' I said slowly. 'If it was long enough and coated with poison, then even if the poison didn't work I'm sure the needle entering his heart would do the trick.'

Dynamo looked at me for a moment, then got up from the table and went over to the chart on the wall.

'Well, what do you think?' I asked dubiously, as Chalky and Spot sat smiling at me for a moment longer then walked over to join him.

They stood talking quietly to one another for about five minutes then all three of them came back to the table, sat down and stared at me. Dynamo leaned back in his chair, folded his arms and said evenly: 'Brilliant! How are you going to do it? How are you going to execute this?'

For the first time in ages, I almost stammered. 'I haven't the faintest idea. Does it have to be me?'

'Why not, it's your idea,' he replied calmly.

Spot was still grinning at me. ' You're a bit of a dark horse, aren't you?' he said. 'You know exactly what will happen if you puncture the heart. You've been doing your homework, haven't you?

'This is brilliant, Geordie,' Chalky said quietly. 'But it's got to work first time. The needle will need to pierce the sac around the heart, which will then fill up with blood. It takes a little time for the blood pressure to build up, but once it has done it will look just like a heart attack. There should be no visible signs or any marks on him apart perhaps from a small red dot on his chest where the needle has broken the skin.' He paused for a moment before continuing. 'And, more importantly, it might just give us the time we need to get clear.'

'How would you propose to do it?' Spot asked.

'Well, I've given it a bit of thought and it's obvious that the trick will be in getting close enough to him. If I can do it quickly enough, and providing I don't hit his ribs, he shouldn't feel a thing other than me bumping into him.' I explained. 'By the way, do we have any idea of the kind of thing he usually wears? We'll need to know.'

Spot rummaged around on the table and picked up a photograph of the target, which he handed to me. The man in the picture was a tall Caucasian, about 40 to 45 years old, dressed in a light coloured suit, shirt and panama hat.

'Our intelligence informs us that so far he's been seen mainly wearing a white or sometimes a grey lightweight suit with white shirt underneath. But I'm afraid we won't know that for definite until the day,' Spot told me.

'This guy looks white. Is he?' I asked.

'Yes, he is. He hasn't been in the country long enough to get very tanned, so it'll make him stand out more. There's no room for error.'

I was pretty confident that I could do it using the movements of the machine. After all that was what the machine was all about, the ability to repeat the same action and hit the same spot with deadly accuracy over and over again, specifically designed to ensure that we could inflict maximum damage with minimum risk of detection.

'I'll have to make sure I don't hit one his shirt buttons,' I pointed out.

'Or his ribs,' Chalky added. 'Otherwise he'll be jumping around in agony.'

'At what point do we do this: when he first leaves the building, when he's at the café or when he's returning?' Dynamo asked, thoughtfully.

'I don't think we'll know that until we get there; we'll just have to play it by ear,' Spot replied. 'But if we try to get him before he gets to the café and for some reason it doesn't come off and we can't manage it, then we may have a second chance when he's had his lunch and goes back to work. I think the best thing we can do now is to help Geordie practise and perfect the manoeuvre.'

'I think it will have to be from the front in the solar plexus, just between the ribs. We can't get him from the side and I don't think that it will be possible to take him from behind, either. Besides, his shirt will be a lot thinner than his jacket.' I said. ' We're going to need a needle about five or six inches long, made of hardened steel with a T-piece wooden handle on it. And I'll need a dummy to practise on.'

Chalky laughed and pointed at Dynamo. 'There's the ideal specimen. He'll make a jolly good dummy; he's definitely the right man for the job.'

Dynamo jumped to his feet laughing, 'Watch it, you, men have died for less than that. Right then, Geordie, I'm the target. Chalky, Spot, you're the guards.'

'What happens if there are more than two guards, Dynamo? What happens if we don't get the chance, or it doesn't work?' I asked. I didn't want to let them down and was naturally a bit apprehensive about the responsibility I was being given.

'Our information is that he usually has two guys with him. If he has more than that we'll just have to deal with it on the day and, more importantly, we'll just have to make sure it does work,' he replied emphatically.

We began to practise the manoeuvre, putting the 'guards' into various positions around the target, in front, to either side then at the rear. By using the movements of the machine, I was able to ensure that I hit Dynamo in exactly the same spot each time, no matter what position he was in or where the guards were.

We tried to come up with every possible scenario and, after several hours of practice, believed that we had covered every eventuality. The only way I was going to be able to manage it would be to pretend to bump into the target. Somehow I would just have to find a way of making it look accidental on the day. I spent a further couple of hours practising on a dummy, ensuring that I hit the exact same target area, over and over again, while the others tried to come up with alternatives. The main problem was that we didn't readily have access to the types of poison we needed at such short notice. To my amazement, as the day wore on it seemed increasingly obvious that my idea was going to be the only viable option for carrying out the operation without having to fight our way out.

'They'd think I was a right nutter if I told them about attempting this back at the camp; I'd probably be discharged for being mentally ill!' I sniggered to Dynamo. 'I can understand what you were saying to me about going back and telling them the truth about what I've been doing. Who in their right minds would believe this?'

'Well, you'd better believe it because if it doesn't work we'll end up having a fight on our hands. So you'd better get it right, Geordie; we're depending on you, old boy.' Dynamo winked, and grinned back at me.

'Oh, that's great,' I said, laughing. 'I've done one operation and suddenly I'm the expert.'

'Well, none of us have exactly done this one before, but there's a first time for everything, mate, and this is yours.'

'If I get the chance to bump into this guy, what can I say to him, Dynamo? How the hell do I say "sorry" in Lebanese?'

'You'll have to know a few more words than that. We're going to have maybe a couple of hours to wait for this guy so you're probably going to have to do a bit of shopping! We'll have to teach you to say "how much is that", "thank you very much" and most importantly "can you show me where Woolworth's is"?' He sniggered.

Dynamo was fluent in several languages including Arabic and he spent the next couple of hours trying to get me to say the phrases he felt I would need. He kept laughing at my attempts, most of which sounded like someone either being sick or spitting. As he instructed me, I continued to practise on the dummy using a long, stiff hair from a yard brush as a needle. Spot had gone off in the jeep sometime earlier and it was late when he arrived back, just as we finished.

'How's this, Geordie?' he said, producing a very strong piece of wire about eight inches long that looked like the spoke of a bicycle wheel (although I was fairly sure that it was not; it was too strong).

'Any good?'

'Yes, that's perfect. All I've got to do is shorten it and put a point on the end. Where did you get this from?'

'Don't ask.' He grinned and tapped the side of his nose with his finger as he walked over to the side of the hut and picked up a sweeping brush. 'You want a handle for it, don't you? Here, take a bit off the end of this brush!' he said, throwing it to me.

We cut off about two inches from the brush shank, thinned it down a bit and put a hole in its centre to fix the sharpened 'needle' into. I needed a safe place to carry it, so I made a small hole in my sash where the buckle was and slipped the needle just inside at my waist front. The small piece of wood slipped easily into my pocket.

It was getting late and we needed to rest up before setting off. My head was buzzing as I lay down to try to sleep. I closed my eyes and went through the motions of bumping into the target and eventually dozed off, with Dynamo's foreign phrases repeating again and again in my head.

We slept from about 2330 hours. We had to be up at 0200 the next morning and ready to leave by 0230 when the hack was due to arrive.

9. A death in the market place

As usual, we travelled looking as much like the locals as possible, dressed in jeans, a shirt and boots. I also wore an old combat-style jerkin. The only things we carried apart from our sashes were our boot knives.

'Here, Geordie, you come from Newcastle!' Dynamo said, mimicking my accent as he threw what looked like a black and white checked tablecloth towards me. It was a large fringed scarf, of the type worn by men in the Lebanon, which would help to cover up the best part of my face.

'Before we go anywhere we'll have to get to work on blue eyes here!' he said to the others. I had noticed when I arrived the previous day that they had all allowed a few days' beard to grow and looked a bit scruffy, obviously in readiness for this mission, whereas I was clean-shaven. This, of course, was a requirement of the regular army where special permission had to be obtained in order to grow a beard, but already they looked pretty much like natives and by comparison, I thought I looked like a mannequin in a tailor's shop window.

They quickly set to work changing my appearance. Although I was fairly deeply tanned by this time, they darkened my skin even more by applying some kind of cream in order to make me look as though I had a 'blue' beard or five o'clock shadow. This cream resembled the 'gun blue' I had used on shotgun barrels at home. Another cream mixed with a black powder was applied to my hair, which made it very black and shiny and made my scalp incredibly itchy. Spot told me that all of this would wash off fairly easily and I noticed that when I scratched my scalp the colour rubbed off onto my fingers.

'Make sure you don't get wet, Geordie, we don't want your make-up to run, now do we?' Chalky joked.

By 0215, we were all ready, fully kitted out with our weapons, rope harnesses and dog-clips attached. Spot glanced at his watch and went outside to watch for the hack. At about 0225, we heard the noise of it approaching, but as it was dark we couldn't see anything yet. Chalky, Dynamo and I quickly followed Spot outside taking the hurricane lamps from inside the hut to put out in a square as a landing guide.

Suddenly, the helicopter seemed to be right on top of us; its black outline looked huge to me as it hovered deafeningly above us for a brief moment. The downdraught from its blades sent choking clouds of dust flying, which knocked over the hurricane lamps.

As he prepared to land the pilot switched on a spotlight and, blinded by both it and the thick swirling dust, we stumbled around grabbing up the lamps then quickly extinguished them before throwing them into the hut. I could barely see a thing and the noise was unbelievable.

Bent double, I dashed forward to the helicopter and scrambled on board just as the thing started to leave the ground. The noise was deafening. I saw the shadowy figure of Chalky standing in the opposite doorway as I scrambled in on my hands and knees, just as the helicopter began to rise and move forward all at the same time. Caught off balance I fell onto some controls in between the two front seats. The next moment two hands grabbed my shoulders and pulled me backward onto the seat behind and Chalky yelled into my right ear.

'Buckle up, Geordie,' he shouted, gesturing towards the seat belt. Spot was sitting on my left, and he and Chalky hooked our ropes above the doors onto the newly fixed brackets mentioned earlier, ready to throw them out later. They piled the remaining coils onto the floor in front of them where they held them in place with their feet.

The doors had been removed, presumably in an attempt to make access easier and to lighten the load, so we were open to the elements. Inside it was dark, and quite a squeeze with the five of us. The back had been removed from one of the front seats and Dynamo sat on this next to Ken, whom I now recognised sitting in the pilot's seat.

Inside the noise was deafening and although I immediately put my hands over my ears, they hurt from the racket. Spot nudged my left arm and handed me a headset similar to one that he was now wearing and indicated that I should put it on. When I removed my hands from my ears for just the brief seconds it took me to put on the headphones, the noise was horrendous. Even with the headset on it was impossible to make out anything above the engine's racket.

We seemed to level off quickly and, as I regained my balance, I looked out through the open doorway and tried to get my bearings but saw only the outlines of treetops directly beneath us before Ken switched the spotlight off. In the far distance I could just make out a couple of small lights from houses but I was totally disorientated and didn't know which direction we were heading in.

I could see very little in the cockpit, as it was only dimly lit by a couple of indicator lights on the control panel. The dark outlines of the others were just visible as they fumbled about with the ropes on the floor.

We flew along only feet above the ground, twisting and turning to avoid detection, and I guessed that our speed must be about 80 miles an hour. We had only travelled for a few minutes when Ken switched the spotlight back on briefly. Suddenly we went into a steep dive as though we were about to crash, and in the powerful spotlight beam I could see the scene below us: a cliff edge and beach, with small white waves breaking on it.

Ken switched the spotlight off again and we headed straight out across the waves into the inky blackness. It was worse than a fairground rollercoaster ride; my stomach was heaving and at times, I felt as though I was being pushed through the floor.

At first we flew very low over the sea; the sky had just enough light in it for me to make out the waves below. A cold wind blew in through the open doorways and right through the cockpit. Then suddenly the helicopter began to climb and as it levelled off again Ken indicated that we needed to keep our eyes open. He was talking over the headset but I still couldn't hear a thing for the racket. Chalky lifted one of my earpieces and shouted at me to watch for a red light.

About ten minutes later Dynamo pointed to something at the 10 o'clock position. Ken looked in the direction he indicated then swung the hack over and, lining up with the now visible red light, headed in that direction. The red dot bobbed about in the distance as we headed towards it; it was the light of the small fishing boat waiting for us. As we drew nearer, the light began to flash off and on and Ken gave us the thumbs up signal to let us know that the boat had seen us, and immediately dropped the aircraft down again to about 30 to 40 feet above the sea. Then he gave us another thumbs up signal to indicate that we were just above the boat and turned the spotlight on again as Chalky and Spot moved into position one at either doorway.

They each threw out a rope and fastened on their dog-clips before swinging out into the openings where they stood for a moment with the tips of their toes on the edges of the doorways, looking beneath them. Suddenly they both dropped out of sight and the hack rocked violently from side to side. I sat holding the rope until it went slack and I knew it was my turn.

Dynamo moved into place in the opposite doorway as I put two wraps around my dog-clip and stepped out into the opening. Looking down, I could see a small boat bobbing around all over the place about 30 feet below. The helicopter swung backwards and forwards above it as Ken struggled to hold it steady and keep it lined up above the boat, but as Dynamo and I moved, our shifting weight inside the helicopter caused it to sway drastically.

For a brief moment Dynamo stood in the doorway opposite, then he disappeared. I immediately followed him and as I began hurtling downwards toward the boat, I realised I should have had three wraps on the rope instead of two. I had some difficulty in stopping my descent, which I just managed to do about four feet above the water just as Dynamo landed straight into the boat just ahead of me. But I was swinging about all over the place. The little boat was bobbing around like a cork on the choppy sea, which was being made worse by the helicopter's downdraught. As it rose beneath me, my legs crashed into its small cabin. I let go of the rope and fell heavily onto the deck hitting the wooden engine cover as I landed in a heap. The helicopter immediately turned away from us, back towards Cyprus, with our abseil ropes dragging through the sea beneath it. Once the spotlight went out the hack disappeared from view.

I lay on the wet heaving deck, my ribs aching from where they had made contact with the engine cover as Chalky and Spot came over to help me up. They were laughing as much as I was. A wonderful smell of frying bacon wafted out from the tiny cabin.

'My name's Lynch,' said the guy in charge of the boat, sticking his head out of the cabin door. 'You're just in time for a bacon sandwich.'

How he managed to cook in that tiny confined space with the boat rocking violently I have no idea, but manage it he did and produced a wonderful bacon sandwich and steaming cup of tea. I warmed my freezing hands around the hot mug and looked up at Chalky sitting opposite me.

'How did he get here?' I said, nodding towards Lynch.

'He's one of us and that's all you need to know, Geordie,' Chalky replied and winked at me. 'Naturally, nobody picks us up but us.'

'Well, I'm certainly not going to ask how he got his nickname.'

Lynch came out of the cabin again. 'We're about 30 miles from the mainland, so make yourselves comfortable.'

He has got to be joking, I thought, looking around the deck of the tiny craft. There were pieces of net and bits of cork lying about but all I could find to sit on was something that resembled an old lobster pot, while the others made themselves as comfortable as they could on top of the engine cover. The sea was quite rough and the little boat was being tossed about quite a lot, which after the bacon sandwiches made us all feel a bit queasy but no one was actually seasick.

After we had been travelling for about an hour and a half, the sky began to lighten and in the distance, we saw a few small fishing boats. As we proceeded, more came into view. Lynch paused as he came out of the cabin carrying another cup of tea for me and looked over at them for a moment.

'Part of the local fishing fleet,' he observed before adding, 'We've still got about another six miles to go before we reach the mainland.'

As we made our way towards the shore we saw more and more of the small fishing boats, all of them heading out to sea. We appeared to be the only ones going towards the shore.

'This must look a bit fishy, don't you think, us going the wrong way?' Spot sniggered. 'Won't they be a bit suspicious of what we're up to?'

'No, don't worry: some of them fish all night and are usually on their way back in at this time of the morning,' Lynch told him, confidently.

The sun was higher now, warming the early morning air and glinting brightly off the water ahead of us. Gradually the coastline emerged from the early morning haze and we began to make out a number of bays and small coves. About a mile offshore, Lynch passed Dynamo a pair of binoculars.

'We've been lucky so far. I haven't seen the patrol boat in the area,' he said as Dynamo scanned the shoreline.

'Bloody hell, have you seen this lot, its like flamin' Morecambe Bay over there!' he exclaimed. 'There's a lot of people moving about and the port area is pretty busy. I thought it might be quieter this early in the morning.'

'Here, give me a look.' Chalky motioned for Dynamo to pass him the binoculars. 'You're right, this could cause a bit of a problem.'

'Don't worry,' Lynch said calmly. 'There's another cove we can go into around that headland about quarter of a mile to the north of the village; there is an old jetty there too. We should be out of sight from everybody in there but you'll have to take a chance and make a jump for it onto the jetty. I don't want to get in too close and beach this thing.'

Chalky and Spot took it in turns to watch through the binoculars as we drew closer to the shore then suddenly Spot nudged him.

'Here, Chalky, take a look at this. I can see at least four blokes lounging about on that jetty with weapons. Two of the swine look as though they've got rifles, and the others are carrying Sten guns. Look!' He passed the binoculars to Chalky and turned to Dynamo.

'I don't understand why they should be there. It's difficult to make out from here if they're soldiers or not, but it looks as if they could be wearing some type of uniform like khaki jackets,' he said as Chalky then passed the binoculars along to me.

I was surprised to see that the village was quite busy. Like Dynamo, I thought there wouldn't be many people about at this time of the morning. It was larger than I expected too, with a lot of small boats dotted around the harbour area and a couple of large cargo boats tied up alongside the jetty.

Lynch had changed our course and we headed past the village on our starboard side towards the small bay to the north. 'That should give ideal cover,' he said, pointing to the sandy embankment surrounding the bay. 'No one should see you getting ashore from this position.'

The remains of a jetty stuck out about 30 to 40 yards from the beach. It was an old wooden construction, broken down and in a bit of a state. As we got closer, we could see that it had not been used for some time and was literally falling to bits. Lynch threw four bundles of fish onto the deck, half a dozen in each bundle tied together with string. Chalky picked them up and held them out in front of him, wrinkling his nose. 'And just what exactly are we supposed to do with these?' he said. 'I hope this isn't lunch.'

Lynch grinned at him. 'Try to look like fishermen.'

'Well, we're obviously not very successful ones judging by the age of this lot, are we?' Chalky joked back, looking at the fish he was still holding up in disgust. 'Where are our rods, then?'

Lynch just laughed and steered the boat in as close as possible to the jetty. 'I'll be back here 1700 hours this evening about 200 yards off this point, so don't be late and keep me waiting, there's good chaps. If you aren't here then, I'll be back at 2300 and again at 0500 and so on; you know the drill.'

Chalky threw the fish onto what looked like a sound piece of the jetty then jumped off the boat as it moved alongside. I followed closely behind him, but as I landed on the rotten timbers they gave way beneath us with a loud crash and I began to slip backwards into the water. Chalky grabbed me and hauled me up beside him.

'I hope no one heard that,' he muttered. 'Bit early for a bath, isn't it Geordie?'

By now, Spot and Dynamo had also jumped off the boat and landed without any problems further along the jetty. They both ran up the slight embankment and looked over the top as Lynch headed the boat back out to sea.

'See you later,' he shouted and sped off.

'It's OK, we're in the clear,' Dynamo said. 'Nobody from the village could have heard the racket Geordie made, it's too far away.'

'It's not my flippin' fault that the rotten jetty's falling to bits,' I said indignantly, kicking out at a decayed bit of timber nearby.

From our position, we could see most of the nearby village. It was fairly compact with a main street running through the middle of it. We sat there for about 10 minutes taking in the layout of the place and checking to make sure we were not going to bump into any trouble. Although it was still early and the place seemed pretty quiet and peaceful, there were a lot of people moving about. It was particularly busy by the main jetty where workmen were unloading a couple of large vessels and reloading the cargo onto a nearby truck. The guys with the guns we saw earlier were nowhere in sight.

'OK, let's get on with it,' Chalky said, taking a map out of his back pocket and laying it on the ground. He glanced at his watch. 'Right, it's 0655. We're here and the border with Syria is over that way roughly where those mountains are.' He pointed to his left. 'We've got about nine miles to go, south of where we are now, following that road on the other side of the village.' Following where he pointed, we saw far in the distance to the east a range of snow-capped purple-grey mountains, outlined in the early morning sun.

'The situation is this: we've got bags of time so we don't have to rush anything, and this village doesn't look as though it's going to cause any problems. I think those guys with the rifles might just be acting as local policemen; I don't think they're going to be a problem to us. So we'll break up into pairs; what do you reckon? Geordie and I will go through the centre of the village, you two go around the outside and we'll both meet here where the side street meets up with the main road leading to Beirut,' he said, pointing to a spot on the map.

'That shouldn't cause us any problems; it's only a small place,' Spot said.

Dynamo nodded. 'You and Geordie go ahead and we'll catch up

with you in a few minutes, it'll look less suspicious that way and we won't draw attention to ourselves.'

For all we had bags of time, Chalky immediately stood up and set off down the embankment. 'Come on then, Geordie,' he called back to me over his shoulder.

We entered the village along what appeared to be the main street and passed some of the old people we had observed from the embankment, but none of them took any notice of us. The whole place was a complete shambles, with boxes and litter lying all over the place. For all it was still early there was quite a bit of activity going on and a lot of people sitting around outside some of the buildings. These might have been shops or cafés but they all looked to be either shuttered or boarded up. Most of the buildings were single storey concrete looking affairs but there were a few relatively large constructions of two or three floors.

It was not a very large place, only about half a mile long, and we walked through it quickly, passing several side streets lined with square-looking houses and buildings and a few stationary old cars. As we neared the pre-arranged meeting place, we saw Spot and Dynamo coming towards the same junction from our left.

'What a dump,' Dynamo said as they caught up with us. 'How can anyone live in a place like that? The poor sods haven't got much, have they?'

'Whose bright idea was it to carry these stinking things?' Spot said in disgust, throwing the fish he was carrying into a nearby gutter.

'Phooh, yeah, you're right,' Chalky said and we dumped ours too. 'I think Lynch was having a bit of a laugh there.'

We headed south along the fairly wide main road. In lots of places the concrete was cracked and holed and it was badly in need of repair. We saw very little traffic. Just a few pickups and the odd car or truck went by and guy on a bike, but he just kept his head down and pedalled on.

As we walked, we discussed our contingency arrangements should I fail to take the target out as planned. Obviously, we would need to go ahead and take the target out together with his two guards, as they posed the most immediate threat, and then make our escape in any ensuing confusion. We would then head towards the busy port area, pretending to attempt to escape by boat, but would actually double back to the crowded main area of the city where we could lie low until dark. The military would probably continue to look in the area we first headed for and not expect to find us back in the city centre. Dressed as we were like the locals, we would be able to blend in more there than if we headed straight out onto the open road.

Obviously, such a delay would mean that transport was imperative for us to make an escape. In order to do this, our best option would then be to head out towards the main road and try to get a military vehicle and some uniforms to help us get out of the city and back to the village; military vehicles would not generally be stopped at roadblocks or checkpoints. However, we didn't plan in too much detail. If we needed to change our original idea we would simply play it by ear, making use of whatever was available around us at the time.

We walked for about four miles with the sea on our right. Although still early in the day, it was already very hot and sweat was pouring from us. Hearing a truck approach us from behind, just as we began to climb up a steep hill, we kept our heads down until it passed by and continued on its way. It was an old vehicle and as it reached the brow of the hill, it began to struggle and gradually slowed down until it was barely moving. As we had kept up a steady walking pace after it passed us, we were actually beginning to overtake it. Just then, another truck appeared over the brow of the hill travelling in the opposite direction, loaded with workmen and armed troops. Chalky, who was leading the way, quickly indicated to us to fall back behind the slow truck and use it for cover. It didn't look as though the old truck was going to make it so I kept my head down and started to give it a push and the other three joined in. By this time, the truck with the troops had driven by without giving us a second glance and headed off towards the village we had just walked from.

The slow vehicle was loaded down with crates of fruit and apples and as it eventually climbed over the brow of the hill Dynamo jumped onto the back, smashed open one of the crates and threw each of us an apple. 'Here's lunch, lads,' he said, laughing.

The truck began to pick up speed as he jumped off and the

driver beeped his horn in acknowledgement of our help. Dynamo waved back at him a half-eaten apple in his hand. Suddenly the truck stopped, the passenger door opened and a man climbed out. Immediately we stuffed the apples up our shirtfronts like naughty schoolboys as the man called out something in Arabic. Dynamo walked towards him and they had a brief conversation before the guy got back in the truck and it drove off.

Dynamo turned to us with a huge grin on his face and bit into his apple. 'I thought we might have a spot of bother there for nicking the old boy's apples but he very kindly offered us a lift into town, chaps, which was jolly decent of him, don't you think? Naturally I had to decline his offer,' he said, as we all burst into helpless laughter.

From the top of the hill, we could see the skyline of Beirut in the distance, about five miles away, its buildings outlined against the sea where a couple of large ships were heading towards the coast. We sat for a few moments eating our apples, watching the distant city. It looked massive to me, the biggest place I had seen in my life so far. I could not believe that we were actually going to walk right into this place and kill someone in broad daylight.

The outlines of the buildings were totally strange to me with round roofs and towers and funny spires unlike anything I had seen before. Dynamo told me they were called mosques and minarets.

It was blisteringly hot under the cloudless sky. The road was dry and stony and our feet kicked up little clouds of dust as we walked; our boots and trouser legs were caked with the sand and dirt. Just past an old burnt out rusting car, a stream of water ran down towards the road. It probably should have gone underneath it through a nearby pipe, but this was badly cracked and broken and instead the water ran right across the road. It was probably a sewer and it stank. The stench was indescribable. It was covered with swarms of flies and insects, which flew up into the air as we ran past with our hands covering our mouths, noses and eyes.

'Filthy bastards,' Chalky said. 'God knows what's lurking and fermenting in that lot.'

Dynamo turned to me again. 'By the way, Geordie, have you got that needle handy?'

'Yeah, just a second.' I looked at my sash and pushed the buckle up but couldn't find the spot where I had hidden the wire. 'Bloody hell, I think I've lost it! I can't feel it!' I said frantically feeling along the bottom.

'Hang on, Geordie,' Chalky said, running his hand around my back underneath the sash. 'I think I've found it; it's worked its way around to the back. Just a moment,' he said.

He tried to push the needle back towards the front of my sash but it seemed to be stuck so he took out his boot knife and put a small nick into the belt to get at it and ease it out. 'Right, we're laughing. I've got it. We don't need to call the operation off,' he joked and slapped me on the back.

I was so relieved. I thought that it might have dropped out when I fell onto the boat. Taking the small piece of wood out of my pocket, I fixed the needle to it and, holding the wooden handle in my hand, I hid it up my shirtsleeve.

We had now reached the outskirts of Beirut; the place was a total shambles, like a shanty town. Gradually the buildings began to increase but they were mainly ramshackle affairs and badly in need of repair. The streets were full of old cars that had been stripped and burnt out. I looked around me in amazement. Little kids ran around half-clothed with nothing on their feet and women, mainly dressed in traditional clothes with their heads covered, carried large cardboard boxes and loads balanced on top of their heads. Some of the older men wore long traditional garments and most of them wore some kind of headgear but, in general, they were dressed in more Western-style clothes, suits or shirts and trousers. They didn't seem to be doing very much, just sitting around.

Groups of young men hung about on every street corner, almost all of them carrying weapons of some sort, mainly pistols, but we saw others with Sten guns and old .303 Lee Enfield rifles. They were dressed in various types of pseudo-army gear and appeared to be stopping people, searching cars and vehicles.

'Best to get off the main streets now, I think,' Chalky said. He turned down a stinking, filthy alleyway and we began to criss-cross through a maze of back streets and alleyways, working our way towards our target area using a map of the city Chalky carried, which he told me they had been studying for over a week. Lines of drab washing hung everywhere, litter and rubbish were piled up in corners with mangy dogs or cats rummaging through it. There seemed to be very little vegetation anywhere. The buildings were close together, tall blocks of flats with washing, clothes and rugs hanging from every balcony. Just about every street had water gushing down it; the pipes must have been in a terrible state. People bustled around, there were vehicles of every description, and the din was deafening.

Most of the shops were windowless with just long tables inside and at the front. Many of these had cloth-covered bundles of meat laid on them and strangely shaped and coloured polony-type sausages hung from the ceilings. Other shops had tables on which stood pottery, lamps, bottles or small rugs. The air was filled with strong, strange, mostly nauseating smells: unusual foods being cooked, the stench of decaying sewage and poor drainage, all of these mixed together with exhaust fumes. We walked through it all, completely unnoticed. It felt so weird.

Gradually the streets began to widen and the tall buildings, many of them now obviously office blocks, were clearly in a better state of repair. As we neared the main area of the city, the crush of people grew ever greater, the noise even louder and over everything hung an almost tangible feeling of tension. None of these people looked happy; none of them smiled.

Chalky indicated for us to group casually together outside a shop selling tobacco and cigarettes. 'We're almost at our target area: the building he works in is around here somewhere; I'm sure it's at the end of this street,' he said in a low voice. 'I think it would be better if we split up into twos and worked our way down either side of the road.'

Spot nudged my arm. I followed him around the corner into a wide busy street. 'Geordie, what do you feel like?' he asked quietly.

'I feel a bit strange but pretty excited,' I whispered back. 'What an awful miserable place, though, and I thought Byker was a dump.'

'And this is the posh bit,' he grinned.

We pushed our way through the crowds, trying to keep up with Dynamo and Chalky on the other side of the road, without looking conspicuous. About halfway down the street Dynamo waved us over.

'This is it, lads,' he said confidently, checking his watch. 'We're early, so Chalky and I will check this place out, you two go that way and check the area out, see if there is any transport about we might be able to use. If all hell breaks loose we might need some quickly. Don't go too far away, though. We'll meet back here in half an hour at 1100.'

Spot and I walked back to the other side of the street and looked around for a while. We needed to familiarise ourselves with the immediate area as part of our contingency plan, should I fail. We checked up some of the narrow side streets to see if they could be used as exits in case something went wrong. There were cars and trucks everywhere but most of them were ancient.

'There's plenty of old bangers around, Spot, but I can't see us speeding off in any of them.'

'We could probably run faster than most of these,' he agreed.

Returning to the main street, we saw four or five young guys coming straight towards us. Each of them was armed with a semi-automatic rifle hanging from a shoulder strap and they all carried a pistol in a holster at their waists. We both stopped and turned to look into the nearby shops. The guys stared blankly at us then walked straight past, their guns pointed down, their fingers in the straps. Spot and I looked at one another and grinned, then made our way to meet up with Dynamo and Chalky as arranged.

'This is definitely it,' Dynamo said quietly. 'The café is about 300 yards down the street from his office building.'

'I'll tell you what,' I said. 'We spotted a shop selling rugs about 100 yards before you get to the café on the same side. I'll hang around there and hope he crosses the road before then. If he doesn't I'll just have to get him later when he comes back.'

'He could be in there for ages,' Spot pointed out.

'Well, I'll just have to wait and hope he doesn't take too long for his lunch break.'

'I'll stand nearer the building and signal to you when he comes out, Geordie,' Dynamo said. 'Chalky, you stand across the road in front of me, and Spot can wait near the café. I'll follow him when he comes out.'

Dynamo went over to the building and Chalky moved off to the other side of the street as arranged, while Spot and I began walking along the street toward the café. The whole area was packed with people, the majority of them in traditional clothes, especially the women, but to my surprise, there also appeared to be a lot of foreigners in the area, tourists I supposed. The majority of the younger men were dressed like us so we blended in relatively easily. Swarms of scruffy little kids hung around the tourists, begging.

We reached the carpet shop and Spot continued to walk on towards the café while I stopped. I could see Chalky still walking down the other side of the street. The idea was that as the guy got closer to me the others would also move nearer just in case something went wrong and I needed backup.

I joined the crowd of people looking at the carpets that the shop owner had stacked around his shop and laid out on a table in front of it. I was dripping with sweat as I concentrated hard on the rugs in front of me, pretending that I was interested in buying one while actually looking over towards Dynamo waiting for his signal. My mind was racing as I tried to work out a way in which to distract the target while I jabbed him.

The owner of the shop was a toothless old guy, dressed traditionally, his skin deeply wrinkled and creased. He was babbling away at me, trying to get my attention but as I couldn't understand a word of what he said and didn't want him to get a good look at my face in case he saw my blue eyes, I just kept shaking my head and waving him away with my hand.

I was growing impatient and looked at my watch. It was 1245: only minutes had gone by but it felt like hours to me. Where is this guy, I thought, why the hell has he not come out yet?

The needle up my shirtsleeve was jabbing me in the arm and, although I wasn't nervous, I just wanted to get this over with and get out of the place. I was still sweating profusely and unconsciously wiped my hand across my forehead to remove some of the drips of perspiration. The old man kept on staring and jabbering away to me, pointing at his rugs and I now had the added problem of one of the beggar kids clinging to my trouser leg and shaking it to get my attention. I tried to push him away but he

147

was a persistent little blighter. It was a nightmare. Eventually the kid realised he was getting nowhere with me and to my relief, transferred his attention to a woman tourist standing next to me.

Feeling something sticky on my fingertips, I looked down and saw to my horror the dark stain of my make-up and I realised that it must have come off when I wiped my forehead. There was a mirror behind the shopkeeper and I tried to look into it to see how much damage I had done but the old guy kept getting in the way as he yammered on at me. I could see only a small light smudge, barely visible. Phew! I quickly rubbed my fingers across it to re-cover any paler skin showing through, smiled at the old guy and moved a few yards away, all the time glancing across at Dynamo.

However, as I looked back at the nearby rugs an idea began to formulate in my mind. I went back to the shop and began to pick them up. I realised that I could use one of them to 'accidentally' bump into the target and to cover up my action with the needle. I selected one about three feet long and not too heavy: it would be ideal. I had difficulty in hanging on to it as the old guy kept trying to take it from me to open it up and show me what it looked like and a woman tourist wanted to pick it up to buy.

Just then, I glanced across at Dynamo and saw him give me the thumbs up signal: the target was out of the building at last and on the move. I stood on my tiptoes trying to see above the crush of people in the street and quickly spotted him. His armed escorts were slightly ahead of him, pushing people out of his way as he strode arrogantly through the crowds, dressed as we expected in a lightweight pale suit and wearing a white panama hat. He was scowling and looked in a foul mood.

Suddenly he stepped out into the middle of the street and began to cross it leaving his two guards to catch him up, which meant that they were now behind him. Brilliant, I thought, he is coming straight for me. I could see Dynamo also slightly behind him; everything seemed to be going to plan. Then, just as suddenly as he had crossed the street, the man changed direction again, turned up a side street and disappeared from view, closely followed by his escorts.

I threw the rug back onto the table and quickly began to walk towards the alleyway he went into. The plan would have to change. I was about 15 yards away from the alleyway when one of the guards came back out of the side street quickly followed by the target and the other soldier and began to walk towards me. I immediately doubled back towards the carpet shop and grabbed up the rug.

The first guard was shoving people out of the way again and the target was very near. The old man was jabbering at me and I reached into my pocket and threw all of the Lebanese money I had been given at him, hoping it was enough to shut him up. It went everywhere and he began to scramble about collecting it up.

The first guard pushed past me and I swung around to my right in between him and the target and pushed the rug up into the man's face. Dropping his cigarette, he shot both of his hands up in front of him to get rid of the obstruction. Using the machine action that I had practised so many times, in a flash I pierced his chest. But I didn't feel a thing and thought I must have missed him: the guy only stopped briefly, then pushed the carpet out of his face and strode off. Immediately, the guard behind him shoved me out of the way into the street and moved off too.

I looked down at the needle but couldn't see anything on it. I saw Dynamo on the other side of the street staring over at me with both arms raised as though to say, 'Well, what happened?' I shrugged my shoulders. I knew I hit the guy in the right place but he was still walking towards the café.

I turned to see what was happening but the street was crowded and I couldn't see very much. The old guy was rabbiting away at me again, trying to give me some money: I had obviously paid him too much for the rug. I shook my head and pushed his hand away. I still could not see what was going on, so I stood on a pile of his rugs to look over the top of the people in the street. I could now see the target's white hat as he reached the café.

Then suddenly he disappeared. I heard a loud crash as he fell. It had worked.

There was a huge commotion around the café, as everyone in the street seemed to dash over to it all at once. I turned to Dynamo and gave him the thumbs up signal as the old guy yammered at me yet again pointing to his rugs, which I thought was a bit rich when I had just overpaid him for one of the crummy things.

149

I quickly moved away, still carrying the small rug, and began to walk across to the other side of the road towards Dynamo, when I spotted the little beggar kid sitting on the edge of the curb. I needed to dump the rug, so I shoved it into his arms as I passed. At first, he looked stunned, and then he stood up and began to struggle off with it. He was a skinny, little thing and the carpet was taller than he was. It probably weighed twice as much as him too.

Dynamo slapped me on the back, a huge grin on his face. 'You did it. Well done lad! You certainly hit the target. But I don't think you should have been so generous. That poor little sod will probably get into trouble for nicking that rug!' he laughed. 'Come on let's go. Where's Spot?' he asked Chalky who had just arrived behind me.

'What on earth were you doing with that carpet, Geordie,' Chalky wanted to know.

'Let's get away from here and I'll tell you on the way,' I said by way of an answer; I just wanted to get out of the place as quickly as possible. 'Where is Spot?'

'He's still over there beside the café, isn't he?' Chalky said turning to look down the street just as Spot came dashing over to us.

'You got him, Geordie, brilliant!' he burst out.

'Where the hell have you been?' Dynamo asked.

'You should have seen it,' Spot said excitedly. 'At first the guy seemed perfectly OK and I thought you hadn't done it, Geordie, and then he just dropped like a sack of potatoes over this table and chairs. Completely ruined a perfectly good meal, too.'

'Come on, let's get away from here before anyone notices us.' Dynamo warned and moved off towards a nearby alleyway. 'It'd be daft to be spotted now, wouldn't it?'

We got off the main street as quickly as we could but looking back down the alley, I saw crowds of people milling around the café and the little kid still struggling with the carpet. We followed the narrow alleyway Dynamo had turned into, then Chalky checked his map and we retraced our steps to the outskirts of the city before heading out towards the road back to the village. For some time we kept looking behind us to see whether we were being pursued, but there were no signs of anyone following us.

When we reached the top of the hill where we had helped to push the truck, we paused briefly and looked down towards the city. Although the road was very busy now with traffic in both directions, everything appeared to be normal.

As we walked along, they bombarded me with questions, wanting to know every detail of what I had done, laughing and joking at my explanations. It felt great. Even though we were desperately thirsty and hungry, we were all elated and the walk back to the village did not seem to take very long at all. No one took the slightest notice of us on the busy road and we ignored them: we just couldn't give a damn.

Around 1430, we reached the outskirts of the village and discovered a tap against a wall. There were some kids playing nearby but they weren't interested in us and just kept on with their game.

'Stand back, lads,' Dynamo said, grinning. 'Let the man with the carpet have a drink first, he deserves it.' The water from the tap was warm and probably contaminated but I didn't care: my mouth was parched dry and it tasted wonderful.

Skirting around the outside of the village we made our way back to the embankment to wait for Lynch. We had almost two hours to kill until he was due so we lay on the sand in the scorching heat and rested, taking it in turns to keep a lookout. Suddenly Spot hissed a warning.

'Take cover, lads, there's a patrol boat coming.'

We immediately dived over to the other side of the embankment well out of sight of the passing old torpedo boat. We watched as it sped past just in front of Lynch heading towards the cove. He quickly pulled alongside the remains of the jetty as we ran along it and jumped on board.

'I can see that everything went to plan, otherwise you wouldn't all be here in one piece, would you?' he cracked. 'Hey, where are my fish?'

'Never mind that, where's that bloody frying pan of yours?' Dynamo spoke for all us. 'We're starving!'

'Forget the frying pan for a moment; let's get well away from here,' Lynch said as he revved the engine and we immediately shot away from the jetty and headed straight out to sea. 'I've been watching those patrol boats all afternoon and they've been passing here fairly regularly. I think the only reason they didn't stop me just then was because I was on my own, but if they see you lot it might be another matter. Did you see what they are using?' he asked. 'Old British torpedo boats, so let's get out of here!'

The return trip to Cyprus seemed to take ages; there was no speedy helicopter this time. We ate for what seemed like hours, huge amounts of sausages and beans, bacon sandwiches and cup after cup of tea. By the time we'd finished, we all felt quite seasick again. Night fell and we lay exhausted in the bottom of the boat as it motored relentlessly on and we eventually arrived back at Cyprus around midnight.

Lynch dropped us off at Dhekélia in Larnaca Bay and then disappeared with the boat while we sat for an hour waiting for Ken to pick us up. Although the boat journey had been long, we were early in getting back, he informed us when he eventually arrived. Well, you could have fooled me, I thought, that bloody journey seemed to be never-ending.

The five of us squashed uncomfortably into the jeep and Ken sped back to the hangar. We were all very tired. All we wanted was to get some sleep, so we didn't talk much. Ken told us that British troops were hot in the area, and we had to be careful, but mainly we sat in silence.

'I trust everything went to plan?' was all he said as he dropped us off.

'Smooth as a baby's bum,' Spot replied, grinning broadly.

After a good night's sleep, we started training at about 0900 hours the following day and Ken arrived an hour later. We discussed the operation in detail with him and Dynamo explained how we carried it out.

'Well done, Geordie,' Ken said, shaking my hand. 'Our intelligence information certainly proved to be right about you! I've got a sneaking feeling that you'll soon be teaching them,' he said, nodding his head towards my team-mates.

The rest of that week I spent training and practising with them. Then on Friday Chalky dropped me back at the ordnance depot at Dhekélia in plenty of time to be picked up by the working party's truck and taken back to camp. When the truck arrived Bill was there sitting at the back.

'Where the 'ell 'ave you been? I came looking for you, you bastard!' he said by way of a greeting.

'I've been making a few quid playing darts. Besides those slave-drivers in there had me working late,' I told him, hoping he would accept my explanation and leave it at that.

'Huh, nice of you t' think of me!' he grumbled. 'Dun't matter, they wouldn't let me into t'camp anyway. I see Grivas Bodily Harm's been at it again!' he said, using the British troops' nickname for the head of the EOKA terrorists and, thankfully, changing the subject.

10. Briefing for Cairo

The jeep skidded to a stop outside the hut and Chalky dismounted onto the bonnet in his usual fashion. He had picked me up earlier, just outside Limassol, where I was dropped by the working party's truck as usual. I was supposed to be on detachment at the nearby camp. I followed him inside and up the stairs to the 'office' where Dynamo was sitting, relaxing and drinking tea. As I entered, Spot appeared as if from nowhere and came in behind us wearing a CTC.

'Hi Geordie,' they said almost in unison and Dynamo gave me a small wave of acknowledgement.

'You're all looking a bit rough this morning; what's happened to your razors?'

They all had a few days' beard growth and, as it was unlike them to look scruffy unless there was a job on, I guessed that this must be the case.

'Ken was here earlier; he'll be back later with the hack,' Chalky said and I knew that I was right.

'What's up?' I asked.

'Well, Geordie, old boy, I think you're really going to enjoy the little excursion we've got lined up for today. In fact, I think we should all have a smashing day out,' he said, grinning broadly.

'That's right. You'll have a great time,' Spot added. 'Come on, sit down, have some tea and we'll tell you all about it.'

The office was fairly gloomy. Its only source of light came from a small broken window in the gable end of the building where the strong sunlight lit up a small area of the floor. We moved the small table and our chairs into the light and sat around it with our tea and biscuits.

A couple of large maps covered the table top and hung down the sides; one was of Cyprus, Lebanon and Israel, the other a detailed map of Egypt. I noticed several red dots on the map of Lebanon and Israel. 'What are they?' I asked.

'They mark the sites of fuel dumps. If one is discovered or missed, the next location can be used,' Spot told me.

As usual Dynamo was full of beans and bursting with energy. 'We're going to take you to see the pyramids, Geordie. Our target is in Cairo,' he explained. Now I saw what they meant by having a great time!

'Flippin' heck! You've got to be kidding me,' I blurted out. 'Cairo? What are we going to do in Cairo and how are we going to get there?' I just couldn't believe it.

'That's the reason we need to know where the fuel dumps are, the hack will have to refuel from one of them en-route.'

Although I was excited about going on another mission with them, Cairo was a long way off and I was a little apprehensive. It must have shown on my face as Spot immediately picked it up.

'Don't worry, Geordie. We'll be with you all the way. We're only going to pop over to Cairo tomorrow to knock off this bloke called Nasser,' he laughed.

The significance of what he said did not quite sink in immediately. I had never heard of the man and so, as far as I was concerned, he was just another target. Besides, I was so taken up with what I had recently learned and the professionalism of my colleagues that, as long as I was with them, I would have gone anywhere. Then Spot explained to me just exactly who the target was.

So that was the job, Colonel Gamal Abdel Nasser. Only the President of Egypt! The plan was to go right into the heart of Cairo the next day and take out Colonel Nasser. Just like that. He had to be the most guarded man in Egypt.

'Our information is that the Colonel will be visiting a certain headquarters or garrison in Cairo tomorrow and is expected to leave late in the evening,' Chalky said, handing me some of the black and white aerial photographs of the building that lay on the table.

I studied them closely. To me the place looked impregnable.

Situated in the middle of a heavily populated area made up of narrow streets, it was surrounded by two high wire fences of at least 13 feet, which could be alarmed, and guarded by both Arab and Soviet troops.

I looked up from the photographs at my three mates in amazement. I could not believe what they were actually contemplating. I knew about Suez and that British, French and Israeli forces had recently attacked Egypt, and Cairo in particular and, obviously, these people hated our guts. The audacity of planning to go into the heart of their capital to assassinate their President took my breath away.

However, from the training I had been through with them and our previous missions, I knew without doubt that if it could be done, we were the only people who could do it.

'Piece of cake, eh Geordie?' Chalky winked. I smiled back at him, unable to speak for a moment. I couldn't help but wonder if this was where I might end up in an Egyptian jail or be found lying dead in the streets. I shook myself mentally: I should not be thinking like that at all; they had taught me to think differently, to be positive, but I supposed that it would take time until I was as relaxed about things as they were. It had gone through my mind on more than one occasion to wonder about whose place I had recently taken and just what exactly had happened to him. It was a question I had never asked and they had never explained it to me. I was not about to ask them now.

The rest of that day and late into the night we spent planning: discussing and deciding routes, what gear we would take, how we should dress and how best to conceal our weapons. To the uninitiated, it would seem an unimaginable and impossible task for four men armed with sashes, knives, a couple of crossbows, ropes, pickups and MK1s to walk into a well-armed, heavily guarded garrison and carry out this mission.

As ever, no one was obviously in charge. That just was not how we worked: everyone's thoughts and ideas were given equal consideration and discussed in full. Although I was the most junior member of the team in age and experience I was never made to feel that my input was any less valid than theirs, just the opposite, although it was clear to me that they had already been over the details several times before I arrived.

As we collected our gear together I realised that, although I was proficient with all of it by then, I had only used most of it in training exercises, never as yet on a real job, unlike them.

'Is this it?' I asked Spot, indicating the small amount of equipment we were packing.

'Well,' he replied, ' if we want to blend in and look like the locals we have to carry as little gear as possible; you know, it's not going to be that much different from Beirut; it's just a few extra miles that's all. We've got quite a way to go from our drop-off point to the target, about 80 miles, so we need to be inconspicuous, try and look like workmen or something like that.'

'We know that it's quite a while since the last raids,' Chalky added, 'but they're pretty slow at doing things out there so there's still a lot of road repairs going on in this area. We should be able to get away with carrying something that looks like work gear in a couple of bags: anything more than that might draw attention to us.'

'Eighty miles! How long have we got to do that in?'

'Fourteen hours from the drop-off point. But don't worry, if it comes to it we can always catch a bus!' Dynamo laughed. 'Even if we've got to nick someone's camel we'll get there in time. Besides, there's always some form of transport lying about.'

'The most difficult part will be getting from here to our drop-off point without being seen,' Chalky pointed out. 'The hack will drop us roughly 15 to 20 miles north-north-west of Port Said in a swampy area just west of the river, then return to pick us up early the following morning. That's if we make it and get back there again, of course. So we'll need to sort out some form of transport when we get there, otherwise we won't get back in time to be picked up at 0930. It's going to be a pretty hairy run for Ken, trying to stay low enough to be undetected by their radar, but we'll have surprise on our side.'

'Won't the area be busy at that time in the morning?' I asked.

'Probably, but that's exactly why they won't take much notice of us; why should they? Besides, by the time they get around to doing something about it we'll be back into Israeli air space,' Spot said. 'Ken will be arriving at 0500 hours with the hack. We'll be pushing it to its capacity on this trip, so it's been modified for us, a bit like a newer model if you like, but to save on fuel we have to carry as little weight as possible.'

'The fuel capacity of the Sycamore is only about 89 gallons, which will take us roughly 268 miles; the overall trip will be over 500. If everything goes to plan, we're to be dropped at a deserted part of the Egyptian coast at approximately 1000 hours, after first refuelling here,' Chalky said, pointing to one of the red dots on the map. 'It's in a pretty remote location on the Israeli border. In order to take us a few extra miles the hack's been fitted with another tank, in addition to its two ordinary ones; just a precaution in case our designated fuel dump's been discovered.'

'So what happens if we have a problem on the way and have to ditch it?' I asked.

'Don't worry, it's not the first time we've done a journey like this and we've never had any real problems so far, but if we do, things are in hand.' Chalky cheerfully informed me.

I wondered if by that he meant the whole of The Sixteen would be standing by to help. So far I had not met any of them other than my three team-mates, Ken and Lynch, but I was really looking forward to the day when I did. Ken had told me that eventually I would meet them all and I wondered if this might be that occasion. But then if it was it would probably mean that we had run into some problems.

Although I felt very much a part of the team, and was certainly as well trained and skilful as my team-mates by now, I still felt new and that I had an awful lot to learn about them. I knew they were extremely careful with what they told me and that most of the information I was given was strictly on a need to know basis, concerning only the current operation.

It was obvious that they knew a great deal more about one another, and the rest of the group, as I had overheard them discussing previous missions from time to time, but when I tried to find out more they just told me to forget it. I don't think that this was due to any lack of trust on their part, just the way in which they operated, but often I felt at a bit of a disadvantage.

As we didn't want to carry too much gear or arouse suspicion, we decided that we probably would not need to wear jackets or coats. If it did get cold we would just have to improvise along the way. So, in order to look more like ordinary workmen, we merely wore white shirts, cotton trousers and boots, which made it slightly more difficult to carry concealed weapons. However, we decided on each of us carrying our MK1s and 50 rounds of ammo as well as our sashes and boot knives.

We also carried two battered canvas bags between the four of us which each held a 120 foot rope, a light line, pick-ups, ten pulley wheels, a folding crossbow, eight assorted arrows with different specialist heads plus a new CTC each and whatever ammo we were unable to conceal about us. We also had a water canister and some 'dog biscuits' each.

Our preparations for the job went on until late that night, after we had assembled and checked our gear. Once we were completely sure that we had prepared everything we needed for the trip, and were satisfied that we had studied every detail of the target area, we discussed our contingency plan should anything go wrong. If for some reason we were delayed by a couple of hours, we would miss our designated pick-up time and would need to remain inconspicuous for several hours until the next pre-arranged time at around 1600 hours.

For all that we had spent the better part of a day and night discussing the job, and my head was full of details, I had no difficulty sleeping that night nor did any of the others. We woke early the following morning and as we ate breakfast, I helped Spot prepare some sandwiches and fruit to eat on the journey, as we knew there would be no time to eat when we got to Egypt.

As soon as we were ready, I was impatient and eager to be on our way. It felt as though we'd been sitting waiting for hours when suddenly the whole building shook, as the hack flew overhead and the dust storm it stirred up flew through every crack and crevice in the old building. Choking and barely able to see, we grabbed our bags and rushed outside just as it landed about 20 yards from the hut.

To our surprise the props immediately began to slow down, then Ken jumped out and ushered us back inside and up into the office.

'Nasser's changed his plans,' he said. 'He's moved out of the area. But there's another job: you need to take care of someone else instead. Fortunately he's in the same building, otherwise the whole operation would have been aborted. Our information is that he's a senior foreign military adviser but the security around him won't be so hot. The building and its surroundings are those in the photographs you've seen; the target has changed, but the plans are roughly the same.'

Ken produced two large black and white photographs plus a smaller one of the target himself for us to study. Dynamo took this, put a slit into the waistband of his trousers and hid it inside. We left the two larger photographs on the table, time was of the essence now, and we had to get to the fuel dump before 0800 hours. The place would be cleaned up after we left and, as usual, there would be no trace of anyone ever having been there. I still had no idea who did this, but I suspected that it could only be other members of The Sixteen.

Grabbing our gear once more, we dashed outside and followed Ken towards the dirty grey helicopter. It was the first time I had seen it in daylight and I was surprised at its strange shape, which made it look as though its back was broken. Its entire insignia had been obscured.

Ken already had it started up and just as we threw in our gear and scrambled on board, the thing began to leave the ground. It was very cramped with our bags and I clambered into the front and sat down. The next thing I knew was a tap on my shoulder and turning around I saw Dynamo, clinging on to the outside of the helicopter, indicating that I should move into the back. I was immediately pulled over the back of the seat by Chalky and Spot and forced into the middle of them. Dynamo swung inside, climbed into the front and sat next to Ken as if hanging onto the outside of a helicopter almost 100 feet from the ground was an everyday occurrence for him. Seconds later, we shot away across the top of the old hangar and began hurtling towards the sea at rooftop height, twisting and turning to avoid detection.

The first part of the flight took us approximately 250 miles to find the refuelling dump near to the Israeli border. Even though we were wearing headsets, conversation was impossible due to the high noise level and we mainly communicated by using hand signals and lip reading.

In order to avoid detection by radar, Ken flew low over the sea, practically skimming the waves. Unlike my first helicopter flight, this time I was able to see all around us. It was great fun.

After a couple of hours, we ate some of the food we had prepared earlier and shortly after, Ken held up his hand and indicated 10 minutes to the fuel dump. We could see the Israeli coastline ahead of us and passed over several small fishing boats below.

The fuel was located in an area of small hills only about 100 yards off the beach, where we landed near to a marshy, reeded area. Ken took some bearings off local landmarks to locate exactly where the fuel was buried. After we removed some sand and soil, we found it, about a foot below the surface, several 50-gallon drums stored inside a large wooden box. Also inside the box was a hand pump for extracting the fuel.

Just as we were lifting the planks of wood covering the drums, a jet fighter approached from the north to roughly within a mile of us. My heart was in my mouth: in this part of the country, a Meteor could only be an Israeli plane and I was sure that he must have seen us.

'Look out lads, a plane!' I shouted to the others and immediately began to run away from the helicopter and the fuel towards some nearby bushes, which I dived into for cover. My mouth was dry as I crouched waiting for the inevitable, but there was no loud burst of gunfire; nothing happened; everything was quiet.

When I looked up again I saw the others staring at the now disappearing plane, which for no apparent reason had suddenly veered off to the west. They all seemed totally unconcerned and strolled back to the fuel dump.

'Well, you certainly flew into action pretty damn quickly then, Geordie,' Spot said, laughing. 'You can come out now, he's gone.'

Sheepishly I emerged from behind the bushes feeling a complete prat. But, after prolonging my embarrassment for several minutes, they eventually admitted that they had all run for cover too and had followed me for a short distance before realising that the fighter had changed course. I got the definite impression that they were not a bit surprised when it had; it was almost as if they had expected it to happen.

We quickly set to, refuelling the hack; personally, I couldn't get the blasted thing filled up quickly enough. Once we had finished refuelling we re-covered the remaining drums, making sure that the surrounding area showed no trace that we had been there. The downdraught from the helicopter would blow enough sand and soil around to take care of any signs that it had landed.

We now flew very low over the sea, almost touching the waves. Sea spray covered the windscreen at times and Ken had to use the wipers to clear his view. At one point, the spray hit the carburettor air intake beneath the hack and it began to splutter. It was bouncing around all over the place and rattled so much that I expected it to ditch into the sea at any moment, but as usual, the others were totally unconcerned. We kept out about five miles from the mainland for most of the remainder of the journey and, every so often, we would catch glimpses of the shoreline in the distance.

All of a sudden, we heard a loud flapping noise coming from the outside of the helicopter. Oh, God, this is it, I thought, sure that we were about to go down. Then, to my complete amazement Dynamo decided to investigate. He climbed out onto the side of the helicopter and vanished out of sight for a few seconds. I had no idea what he found to hold onto or how he managed to hold on to it, as we were travelling at about 90 miles an hour and the hack was constantly bumping and swaying about. None of the others turned a hair. They didn't seem concerned about him at all.

The loud noise abruptly stopped and Dynamo appeared again, smiling. In his hand, he carried a large broken leather strap, which he held up in front of us then threw it into the sea before casually sitting down again as though nothing had happened.

We had been travelling for quite some time when Ken indicated that we should get ready as we had less than 40 miles to go. A few minutes later, I spotted a small lighthouse in the distance and nudged Spot and Chalky.

We were to land at a point about 20 miles north-north-west of Port Said and roughly 85 miles north of Cairo. The lighthouse I had just seen was a few miles west of Port Said. The mainland was getting closer and closer and we were now only minutes away from the drop-off point near to one of the main rivers of the Nile delta.

The hack hovered for a short while as Ken searched around for a safe place to set us down, dropping to only feet above the marshy ground. We jumped out into a couple of inches of water and the instant our feet hit the ground the helicopter veered away and disappeared into the distance. As soon as it had gone, we took our bearings and began to walk in a south-easterly direction, but had not travelled far when Dynamo suddenly shouted 'Take cover!'

We hit the deck as a MiG 15 suddenly appeared out of nowhere and flew past us before disappearing in the same direction as the helicopter.

'You don' t think Ken's been picked up by their radar do you?' I asked, concerned that he might be shot down. I didn't think that the plane had seen us, as it was travelling far too fast and we were passing through an area of tall reeds which reached to our shoulders.

'Don't worry about Ken, Geordie, he's a hell of a pilot,' Dynamo assured me, sensing my anxiety. 'He knows this area like the back of his hand; he'll be in Israeli airspace before they get anywhere near him. Besides, we'll be picked up no matter what: Ken is covered.'

I didn't ask what he meant by this; I was learning not to ask questions.

Soon the marshy ground began to harden beneath our feet and the reeds thinned out. It was mid-morning and the air was scorching, hot and sticky; there was a strong smell of sewage in the area and millions of flies buzzed everywhere. We made our way southeast from the drop-off point towards some small hills in the distance; the whole area appeared to be uninhabited.

Never in my wildest dreams had I ever imagined anything like this would happen to me. I was just 19, this was my third mission and already I could feel the adrenaline starting to flow. I was really looking forward to this.

11. The journey

I checked my watch: it was just after noon. We had been walking for about two hours and were drenched in perspiration. I calculated that we must have travelled about nine miles from the drop-off point and ahead of us was more of the same dry, hilly landscape covered in rough scrub.

'Where's that damn river, Chalky?' I said, brushing the sweat from my eyes.

'It's got to be just over that hill ahead of us, Geordie. We should meet it just below a place called Dumyat and if my calculations are right it's just ahead of us.'

'I hope you're right. I'm melting away here,' Spot said, wiping his sleeve across his face.

By now the heat was unbearable. I hoped that once we got near to the river it might be a bit cooler. Swarms of flies and insects constantly buzzed around us; they were driving me nuts.

We walked on towards the hill and began to climb but as we neared the top Chalky signed to us to stop and listen. So far, we had seen no one, but now we could clearly hear voices in the distance and the sound of vehicles, so we crept to the top and cautiously looked over.

Spread out below us was the biggest, widest river I had ever seen. It was so unexpected that it took me totally by surprise. As it stretched away from us into the distance, the golden sun beating down on its surface made it look like a long, twisting, silvery snake. Its banks were covered with green trees and reeds for as far as we could see and a wide strip of lush, fertile land spread out from either side until it ran into the desert beyond. Dozens of small boats were sailing along it in both directions. It was the most beautiful and peaceful sight.

For a stretch of about quarter of a mile, it formed a series of small coves before reaching a large level area adjacent to a nearby road, where the bank straightened out. The road ran very close to the river at this point and about quarter of a mile away we could see a large group of men working on it.

A column of dust in the distance caught Chalky's attention and he took out his binoculars to scan the area. 'I wonder what's going on over there.'

'Let's have a look,' Dynamo said, taking the binoculars from him. 'Yes, I see what you mean. I count three truckloads of soldiers and workmen, I think. I can't quite make out what's going on but it looks as if they're repairing that road and the soldiers seem to be stopping and searching cars.'

'That's all we bloody need.' Spot took the binoculars Dynamo passed to him. 'Look at that as well: beyond those trees the road is only about 200 yards from the river and there aren't any trees or reeds just there.'

There were dozens of armed soldiers in the area and several military vehicles manoeuvring and turning very close to the riverbank on the level ground. We could clearly see that they were stopping vehicles and searching them. Obviously, we had to avoid them at all costs, we could not afford to be stopped or held up at this point. Although we tried to look as much like the locals as possible, in order to blend in, our disguises would not pass any type of close inspection.

Dynamo glanced at his watch. 'We've got 10 hours to find the target. We'll have to make a move before someone spots us. Come on, let's get down to that riverbank as quickly as possible.'

It seemed that the only way to bypass the soldiers was by following the riverbank, about 500 yards away. The embankment leading down to the river was covered with reeds and scrub, which eventually petered out just before the level area near to the road works. There was no cover at all at this point and it was so open there would be no way to pass without being seen by the soldiers or workmen. We just didn't have time to wait until nightfall; we had to do something now and quick. It looked impossible.

In one of the coves we could just make out the remains of a small jetty and, using the reeds and scrub on the embankment as cover, we cautiously made our way down to it. The reeds were tall and thick and we sat in among them to examine an old map we had brought with us, to try to work out how we could get past this area.

'While we're looking at the map, one of us should go and watch the troop movements and see how close they come to the embankment,' Spot said. 'There might be a way we can get past them without being seen.'

Dynamo nodded in agreement. 'It looks as though we're just going to have to take a chance and walk past the place and hope that no one tries to stop us.'

We couldn't see any activity on the river so Chalky crept up through the reeds to the top of the embankment. Suddenly he came dashing back.

'Take cover, lads,' he hissed. 'There's no way we are going to get past that lot, the soldiers are sitting just yards from the river, but I've just seen the top of a sail. I think there's a boat coming around that bend any minute now.'

We couldn't see the boat from where we were hiding in the reeds, but moments later it rounded the bend in the river and seemed to head straight for us. I could see four people on board: one was standing on the deck holding a pushbike while a couple of them lowered the large single sail. Another guy was using the oar at the stern. He turned the boat around and sculled it into the cove backwards bringing it in close to the shore, heading towards the small jetty just yards away from us to drop off the man with the pushbike.

The guy holding the bike handed it to one of the others on board as he climbed over the side onto the jetty; then it was handed back to him and he began to make his way with some difficulty up the embankment through the rushes, pushing his bike before him.

'Why don't we "borrow" that boat?' I whispered to Dynamo.

'That's exactly what we're going to do,' he replied, quietly. 'We don't have any other option. No one will see us from here, it's too sheltered.'

'We'd better hurry. Look, they're leaving,' Chalky said. Dynamo turned to him and spoke quietly out of the corner of his mouth.

'I don't think they're going to offer us a lift, do you? I'll follow the guy with the bike and make sure he doesn't come back. You lot go and get that boat.'

As the man with the bike moved out of sight, Dynamo followed him up the embankment and we pushed through the reeds onto the jetty, then casually started walking out towards the boat not wanting to panic the crew, who had just started paddling away from the shore. Chalky called out something in Arabic to get their attention; otherwise, they would have been out of reach by the time we got to the end of the jetty. Whatever he said seemed to work. They looked rather surprised to see us there but they stopped paddling to let him approach. Chalky kept talking to them as he got nearer to the edge of the jetty.

The 20 foot long boat was now just close enough to the shore for us to reach it with a running jump. The men on the boat watched us closely as we moved towards them, then suddenly one panicked and shouted a warning to the others as he rushed to the stern and tried to push it away from the jetty. The other two men ran towards the front as Chalky and Spot landed on board in quick succession.

The old jetty was awkward to run along and the boat was now about six feet away. I used one of the wooden supports to help launch myself towards the side of it, but as I pushed off it gave way with a loud crack. The guy at the back had picked something up off the deck and was about to try to hit Spot, but he immediately spun around as I landed with one foot on the boat while the other bashed into its side. The guy raised his arm to strike me just as I managed to get my other foot onto the side of the boat and I stood up balancing on the edge. Using a blocking, locking grip, I was able to use him to pull myself aboard but I overbalanced and fell into him, which in turn forced the guy to fall backwards and he hit his head on the other side of the boat. As he attempted to get up, I swiftly broke his neck.

Looking up, I saw that the other two boatmen were already dead, lying crumpled on the deck. One of them had his hands clutched to his stomach where blood was pouring from a knife wound and covering the sail he lay on.

Dynamo had been watching the guy with the bicycle to make sure that he didn't see or hear anything or try to come back to the boat, but he was now standing on the jetty waiting to be picked up. Using the oar at the rear of the boat as a rudder, I sculled it back in to the riverbank. As he jumped on board, Dynamo looked about.

'No problems, lads. Right, let's get rid of them quick,' he said, and began to pull a long, white, smock-type garment off one of the dead men. But it was saturated with blood and he changed his mind.

Meanwhile Spot and Chalky had weighed down two of the bodies with some heavy metal objects they had found lying on the deck before dumping them overboard. There were two soft splashes and both bodies immediately disappeared under the muddy dark brown surface.

'I'll try to get this damn sail to work, Geordie, if you can dump that one over the side; and don't forget to weigh it down,' Chalky said as he set about sorting out the tangled jumble of ropes on the deck. I searched about and found a small length of chain, which I tied around the dead man's chest. The aft of the boat was still fairly close to the jetty as I dropped the body over it feet first, but when it hit the water the chain fell down around the legs and the top half of the body floated up, his smock had filled with air and his arm kept bobbing up to the surface. I sculled the boat nearer to the riverbank and discovered that the body had landed on a sub-merged ledge and lay in only about three feet of water. I grabbed at the arm, wrapped another piece of chain around the wrist and then watched as the body sank and disappeared.

'Don't worry about it too much, Geordie, the crocs will get them anyway,' Chalky calmly informed me.

'Crocs, what crocs? You're kidding me aren't you?' I had no idea that there were crocodiles in this part of the world. But he just grinned and carried on sorting out the sail.

The others were looking around the boat and acting as though nothing had happened, so I sat down in the aft with the oar in my hand and began to use it as a rudder trying to look relaxed too. Spot discovered a couple of white smocks similar to the one

Dynamo had tried to pull off the dead guy. These were worn by many of the locals in this area. He tried them both but they were far too small so he threw one to Dynamo then the other to me. They were a tight fit but eventually we managed to squeeze into them just as we rounded the bend and came into full view of a group of soldiers on the bank.

Chalky noticed them first. 'Geordie, get us away from the bank, we're getting very close and one of them is sitting watching us. We don't want any confrontation with these guys, we haven't got the time,' he whispered urgently.

About five soldiers were lounging against a truck; then one of them got up from where he had been sitting on the running board and began to stroll towards the edge of the river. He had his thumb in the strap of a sub machine gun that was hanging upside down on his right shoulder, and a cigarette in his other hand.

The sails were not responding the way we expected them to and, for all there was only a light wind, we were being driven in even closer to the bank. I tried to steer away from the shore, almost smashing the bloody oar with the effort, but nothing seemed to happen and I could feel that the currents here were obviously very strong.

'Come on you guys, hurry up and do something with that bloody sail, I'm losing control and the wind is pushing us further into the side,' I urged them quietly.

By now the soldier had walked right to the edge of the river-bank and stood watching, staring at us suspiciously. We were only about 50 yards away from the embankment and I felt that any moment now the guy was going to say or do something so, as we didn't want to draw any further attention to ourselves, I sat back smiling at him while Chalky fiddled about with the damn sail. It looked as though we were definitely going to hit the embankment.

Dynamo spoke to me softly. 'Listen, if we crash into the bank I'll see if I can keep this guy talking while you make your way around to the other blokes by the truck; you know what to do. I think we'll be able to take all of them out without anyone from the road seeing us, it looks as though they're at least 500 yards away and that truck should block their view anyway. But we'll need to get as close to these guys as we possibly can. It shouldn't be a problem, they can see we aren't armed. Leave our weapons in the bags, we don't need them, just sit and relax, we don't want to give him any excuse to open fire on us. We won't be able to use our sashes because of these damn smocks, so we need to be really close, OK. You know the routine.'

As he spoke, Chalky suddenly managed to loosen something on the sail, which immediately filled out and the boat slowly began to change direction. Just then, the engine started up on the truck and the driver began to shout something to the soldier on the embankment. He drew on his cigarette then flicked it into the river before turning away and walking back towards the truck. Then he stopped and looked back at us over his shoulder for a moment. His pals on the truck started shouting at him but he seemed reluctant to leave. The driver leant out and shouted too and he quickly went back to the truck and jumped onto it. As they drove off, we could see him standing in the back still staring at us.

'Bloody hell! That was close. Trying to get us killed, Geordie?' Chalky laughed.

'It had to be the currents. Look, we're moving away from the embankment now but the sail doesn't seem to have changed position very much,' I explained. 'What took you so long with it?'

'Stupid buggers, they had their rope in a flaming granny knot.'

The deck of the boat was covered with fishing lines and nets and I couldn't help thinking that those guys were not soldiers, just simple fisherman whose boat we wanted. It just didn't seem right that we killed them simply because they were in our way. They would have had no idea just what they were up against. If they had been armed soldiers or terrorists who didn't care whom they killed, like in the Troodos Mountains, I would have had no qualms about killing them.

We were all fairly quiet as the boat began to move slowly down the river. Because we were so very alike, and because of our training and the way we worked so closely together, I felt that we practically had the ability to read one another's minds, and I could sense that we all felt the same about killing these people.

Spot was rummaging around and searching the front of the boat, when suddenly he stopped and pulled out a canvas bag. Turning to face me, he held up a Sten gun and service revolver.

'Look at this, it's a bloody good job we got the bastards before they got to these. The swine had enough weapons here to start their own private little war,' he said, kicking the bag. 'And we thought they were just simple fishermen.'

I sat back and felt much better when he said that. The atmosphere on the boat immediately changed. Chalky turned towards me.

'We can't afford to take any chances with these people. They feel that they've been betrayed by the British and they hate our guts.'

We settled down and travelled unhindered for approximately seven miles. It was slightly cooler on the river, but still blisteringly hot. Spot had picked up a fish knife from the deck and was cleaning it on his trouser leg.

'You know, one of those swine tried to stick this in me,' he said indignantly. They all treated it so casually, as though they were out for a Sunday afternoon trip. Dynamo was so relaxed that he actually waved at people on other boats in the distance; it was just as well that they couldn't see him properly.

'What a bunch of miserable sods,' he said, as none of the locals waved back.

'Stop messing about, you'll draw attention to us. Look, we're going nowhere fast in this bloody thing,' Chalky said, looking about him. 'Let's take it in there and sink it.' He pointed at a small, nearby cove. The boat had served its purpose and got us past the danger area but the damned thing was travelling much too slowly. We had to be in Cairo by no later than 2300 hours and it was now around 1430.

Our information was that our target often worked late and slept on the same floor as he worked; he was expected to leave his office between 2200 and 2230. If we wanted to get to him on time, we would have to ditch the boat now and find some quicker form of transport.

We were approaching an area where several streams met the river and could see in the distance that it was becoming busier and there was now a lot more activity ahead of us.

As we began to pull into the cove we quickly pulled the sail down. We could not take the risk that this might stick up out of the water and draw the attention of someone on the riverbank. I sculled the boat further into the cove as the others tried to undo the mast but they had problems with a large wooden pin at the bottom of it. Dynamo searched around for a few moments before finding a three-foot long steel bar with a ring on the end of it. Using this he began to hack away at the pin. Suddenly the whole lot came down on top of us and almost capsized the boat.

'That's the way it's done, lads,' Dynamo laughed. He barely gave us time to get near the bank before he started to punch holes in the bottom of the boat with the steel bar.

'Hang on, we're not going to make it if you keep doing that,' I shouted at him, laughing and sculling like hell to try to get the boat to the shore as water began to lap around our feet. My arms were just about dropping off as the boat crashed into the side of the embankment and we all fell about laughing. Dynamo was jumping about the boat bashing holes into the bottom of it, the water now up to his knees. He looked like a mad monk in his white smock and each time he tried to punch a hole with the metal bar the steel ring bashed his knuckles.

'What the hell could this bloody useless thing possibly be needed for? I've just about broken my knuckles with it,' he complained. Chalky, Spot and I stood on the riverbank doubled up with laughter as he pranced about in a demented fashion.

'I don't know what you lot are laughing at, the bottom of this boat is like bloody concrete!' he said, just as the stern started to slowly disappear beneath the surface. He quickly ran to the front with it sinking behind him and jumped off to land beside us on the embankment. The four of us stood for a brief moment watching it slowly disappear, bits of cork popping up to the surface as it did.

'Come on, let's get a move on,' Chalky urged. 'We've got to get out of here and find some transport fast. We're losing too much time.'

With some difficulty, I removed the tight smock, tied it around some bits of rock and threw it into the water. Spot and Dynamo stayed to ensure that all of the boat sank and disappeared, while Chalky and I picked up the canvas bags and made our way about 100 yards along the riverbank to check that it was clear. There were clumps of small bushes and trees on the steep embankment, which provided us with some cover as we headed towards a slight bend in the river where we came across a stream of sorts running down the embankment. The water was dirty grey in colour and as we got closer, we could see that it had cement in it.

Silently Chalky and I crept up the embankment in case there was anyone at the top and carefully peered over. A large cement mixer stood only yards away and nearby was a truck full of workmen who must have just finished for the day. Two of the men were filling buckets with water from a water tank and throwing it into the cement mixer to wash it out; this had created the small stream of dirty water we had seen. The men in the truck were shouting at them, presumably to hurry them up. We ducked back below the edge of the embankment.

'It's a bloody good job we didn't get here sooner, or we could have walked right into this lot,' Chalky whispered. 'You'd better go back and warn the other two.'

I swiftly slid back down the embankment leaving him on his own at the top with our bags, keeping an eye on the workmen. Spot was now roughly halfway between the sunken boat and the cement stream; Dynamo was a few yards behind trying to pull his smock off. I gave them the signal to take cover and they both dived into the reeds on the embankment while I quickly scrambled back up to where I had left Chalky. Just as I reached him the two men threw their buckets into the cement mixer then ran towards the waiting truck and climbed aboard as it began to move off.

Turning around I slid back down the hill and gave the 'OK' and 'all clear' signals to Spot and Dynamo then went back again to where Chalky now stood. Picking up our bags, we began to make our way along the top of the embankment to where we thought the other two would appear.

'That's a bloody shame, we could've used that truck,' Chalky said.

'There's 20 men on the back of it!' I exclaimed.

'So...?' He grinned at me. At that moment, we heard the sound of another truck approaching from the same direction as the other one and Spot came out of the reeds a few yards ahead of us; we quickly ran towards him.

'Where's Dynamo?' Chalky asked as the three of us took cover in the scrub.

'Just ahead of us,' Spot replied.

It looked as though the truck was going to drive on and, as it passed, I looked out through the bushes and could just make out that it was an army vehicle with a driver and two other soldiers in the back. At this point, Dynamo came crashing out of the bushes bent double as he struggled to pull the smock over his head; it was too small and was stuck on his arms. It appeared as if he had not heard the truck drive past. Just then, it stopped and reversed to within a few yards of him. Dynamo froze for a moment and from where we were, it seemed likely that he was looking through the neck of the smock to see what was going on. We realised that he had heard the truck and come out of the shrubs on purpose; there was no way he would have just come out into the open with that stupid thing stuck over his head.

'Hang back a bit,' Spot whispered to Chalky and, leaving our bags with him, we broke cover and began to make our way towards Dynamo. The two soldiers had now jumped off the back of the truck and were casually walking towards him too, as the driver climbed out of the cab and followed them. They were obviously army personnel but it was hard to believe they were soldiers, as they looked so scruffy. Two of them wore berets and the other had on some type of Arab head-dress.

One of the men continued to walk towards Dynamo, smiling at his struggle with the smock and calling out in Arabic, although I had no idea what he was saying. The other two changed direction when they saw Spot and me emerge from the reeds and began to walk towards us. Chalky stayed behind as Spot had suggested, hiding in the reeds with the two bags. Spot and I slowly began to move apart in case we had to use our sashes. These were the only weapons we could use right now, as gunfire would have alerted anyone nearby.

Eventually, Dynamo yanked the smock over his head, straightening up as he dropped it on the ground and grinning at the soldier no more than three feet from him. He touched his left inside elbow joint with his right hand, which was the signal to take these guys out, and we immediately released the safety catches on our sash buckles. We knew then that Dynamo would have already taken the catch off his buckle under the cover of the smock. The soldier stopped smiling and quickly turned to shout a warning to his comrades, while at the same time going for his revolver.

Dynamo reacted instantly and hit his buckle. With a whistling sound the spring on his sash released the weapon so fast and with such power that the man would not have seen a thing. Dynamo's first swing severed two of the man's fingers, which went flying through the air together with the gun he had been holding, and then hitting him again on the back swing he took a big chunk out of the man's leg.

Almost simultaneously, Spot and I released our sashes and took out the remaining two soldiers, who to begin with were distracted then rooted to the spot by the swiftness and ferocity of Dynamo's attack on their colleague.

This was the first time I had actually hit someone with the sash and on my initial swing, the metal edge buried itself deeply into my target's neck. Bleeding profusely, the man reached up with both hands to grab it just as I managed to tug it free. His fingers were ripped to shreds by a series of small spiked studs set into the surface of the belt near the buckle as it eventually came loose.

Twisting from right to left, I swung the sash across my body in order to bounce it off my left arm and to propel it forward with extra momentum on the return swing. I aimed for the soldier's head just above his right ear, the sash made contact with him and with a crack his skull split open. He went down at once, blood squirting profusely from the deep gaping wound.

As I looked around I could see that Spot had killed the other guy with one blow and the guy was lying in a pool of blood with part of his jaw missing. I seemed to have put a lot more effort into using the sash than the more experienced guys who made it look so easy! The soldiers must have got the shock of their lives having approached what appeared to be three unarmed men.

Chalky emerged from the reeds and came over to us. 'I'll take care of the truck and get it out of sight while you clean this mess up,' he said. The guy Dynamo hit was now rolling around the ground screaming in agony. Dynamo grabbed hold of him and dragged him into the reeds.

'Geordie, get a hold of this guy and keep him quiet. We need to get the others out of sight. Here, use this.' He picked up his discarded smock and threw it towards me and I immediately stuffed part of it into the terrified man's mouth to stop him from yelling. Grabbing the collar of the soldier Spot killed, Dynamo dragged the body towards the top of the embankment.

'We'll need their tunics and berets,' he said, sitting the body up against his knees and yanking off the jacket. While I was struggling with the hostage in the reeds and trying to prevent him from squealing, Spot went over to the guy I killed who was lying on his face and pulled at the dead man's jacket which made the arms to come up above the head. Blood was still oozing from the man's wounds and the collar and lapel of his jacket were saturated.

'You certainly made sure of this one, Geordie, old boy,' Spot pointed out. 'There's blood all over the front of this tunic. Never mind, I don't suppose it'll be noticeable from a distance. But I'm not wearing it. It's your kill and your jacket.'

Dynamo had thrown the other man's tunic and beret towards the edge of the reeds where Chalky had hidden our bags and now started to drag the body down the embankment. The ground was wet and slippy and the body began to slide, moving faster than he could keep up with. Tripping up, he also began to slide and almost fell into the river, finally ending up with the inert body on top of him. Laughing, he pushed the dead man to one side.

'You nearly got me, you bastard! You never give up, do you?' he said, then ran back up the embankment and grabbed the injured man.

'Geordie, go and see if you can find something to dig a hole for these guys. I'll look after chummy here,' he told me. 'Keep your eyes open, there could be more of these swine about.'

As I moved off towards the cement mixer, Spot spoke to him in a low voice. 'We could be in a hell of a mess, here, Dynamo. There's bound to be a search party sent out to look for these guys when they don't turn up.'

'That's why I didn't get rid of him straight away, I want to know where they're going and what time they were expected,' Dynamo explained. As I turned, I noticed a pistol lying on the ground. It was a British service revolver. A finger lay nearby. Oh God, I thought, no wonder the guy is in agony.

I quickly ran back along the top of the embankment to where the men had been working and looked around. A broken shovel had been thrown under the cement mixer; it was covered with dried cement and most of the handle was missing, but it would do.

Spot and Dynamo were in the bushes kneeling over the soldier and talking to him in Arabic when I got back. Chalky had returned from where he had hidden the truck behind a small group of nearby trees just off the road and was dragging the other body down the embankment. He called up to me.

'Oh you've found something, good! Come down here. It's out of the way but it'll be easier to bury them, the ground's softer than up there.'

I joined him at the river's edge where we dug three shallow graves in the soft mud; we couldn't just dump the bodies into the river as we had nothing to weigh them down with and they might pop up somewhere. As I started to make my way back up the embankment Spot and Dynamo were dragging the now inert body of the third soldier down by his feet. They had obviously got as much information from him as they could before taking him out. We simply could not afford any loose ends.

'Geordie, do me a favour, will you. There should be a revolver and a couple of fingers lying around up there somewhere: see if you can find them,' Dynamo said as he passed me. I went back to the spot where I saw the gun and finger earlier and picked them up, but could not find the other finger anywhere. Back down the embankment they were burying the last guy. I wrapped the gun and his finger in the smock I had previously stuffed in his mouth and threw them into the river.

'Right, let's get out of here,' Spot said. 'We should make good time now we've got a truck. That guy told us they were heading to another camp about 80 miles north-east of here. If he was telling the truth, it's going to be a while before anyone realises that they're missing.'

From the information he and Dynamo had managed to get out of the soldier, we knew that they were not expected back at their camp until the following day; if the information was reliable. It meant that we had the truck until daybreak the following morning and by then we should be long gone, if luck was on our side.

Checking the truck out, we discovered four 5-gallon drums in the back so we topped up the tank. We didn't want to take any chances with the fuel. Luckily the tank was already pretty full, which meant that we should have enough to be able to use the truck to get back to our pick-up point.

Dynamo, Spot and I put on the three tunics, which were similar to my own khaki uniform; however, they were all a bit on the small side, uncomfortable and tight. Nevertheless, we managed to squeeze into them. None of us wanted to try wearing the head-dress but Dynamo and Spot were now both wearing the berets. As there was only room for three in the cab, someone was going to have to ride on the back of the truck.

'You look the most like an Arab, Spot,' Dynamo said. 'It'll have to be you. Besides, your beret fits! I'll drive.' He jumped into the driver's seat. 'Come on, you lot, get in, we haven't got all day.'

We were making good time. We had roughly five hours and about 60 miles to go but we still had to find the garrison building. Dynamo put his foot down and we shot off.

Spot leant over the cab and poked his head through the gun turret.

'Take it easy, old boy,' he said. 'Have you seen the time? We need to get there for nightfall.'

'Yes, you're right. That should give us ample time to locate the garrison,' Dynamo said and slowed to a steadier speed.

We could see a long way into the distance along the mainly deserted road. Most of the activity seemed to be on the other side of the river, in small boats. As we drove along Chalky and I searched the cab for anything that might come in useful and he discovered a brand new oil filter still in its box under his seat.

'That's bound to come in handy,' he said and stuck it into his holdall.

'What the hell are you going to use that for?' I asked him.

'It's brand new. We could use it as a silencer for our pistols.'

I looked at him and shook my head in disbelief, thinking he was winding me up.

'Yeah, that's right, Geordie,' Dynamo said to my amazement just as Spot stuck his head through the gun turret in the top of the cab.

'Watch out lads, this could be trouble: there's a truck full of troops heading straight towards us!' he said. We had been travelling for approximately an hour and had just climbed a slight rise. Spot being higher than us on the back could obviously see further along the road. We didn't know what to expect, but the truck merely drove straight past us, the driver flashing his lights in acknowledgement.

A couple of miles further along the road and the city skyline became clearly visible on the horizon. I thought that Beirut looked big, but it was nothing compared to this place: it looked massive. The outlines of the taller buildings and minarets were strange and wonderful shapes. We passed an old guy walking along the road towards the city. He was dressed in long dark traditional-style clothes leading a string of several heavily laden camels, the weirdest creatures I had ever seen. It was like something out of a fairy tale.

The traffic on the road increased now and everything, whether it was a truck, car, bus, scooter, bike or cart was laden with either goods, packs or people. The whole place was crawling with troops and civilians; people were everywhere you looked; it was just like a hornet's nest. The smell was horrendous, a mixture of poor drainage and sewers, rotting vegetation, strange foods and camel dung.

On the outskirts, as in Beirut, a lot of the place looked to have been thrown together but as we drove further many of the streets widened and were lined with well-built and balconied buildings, many of them ornately decorated.

Chalky and I had been studying a map along the way and had marked a bridge across the river that we needed to locate. Once over this we should only be about half a mile away from our target. Our other landmark was a huge mosque, the Citadel, which was surrounded by a high wall and looked like a fort or castle.

'We have to find a place to leave the truck as close to the target area as possible. I've got a sneaking feeling that we'll be leaving in a hurry,' Dynamo wryly commented. 'We could have half of the Egyptian army chasing us, so we need to get out of the city as quickly as possible. Is there anywhere near the target area where we could leave it?'

We were caught up in the heavy city traffic now and travelling fairly slowly along a wide road running parallel to the river. No one took any notice of us, as we were just one among dozens of army lorries around.

'This map isn't much help,' Chalky grumbled. 'But there's a lot of side streets around that area and a few of them seem to lead directly to a square which looks as if it's only maybe 200 yards away from the target area. The bridge we need to find can't be more than half a mile away now.'

'Where's the square once we get over the bridge?' Dynamo asked.

'Once over the other side, we need to turn right and drive for about quarter of a mile further into the city,' Chalky answered. 'When we get that far I'll direct you: there's too many side streets and judging by what I've seen so far, I don't think some of them will be able to take the width of this truck, so we'll have to play it by ear.'

The streets were now very heavily congested and we were almost at a standstill, with some sort of hold-up further ahead of us. The smell of exhaust fumes was stifling and everywhere was noise and commotion: vehicle engines, honking horns and the babble of thousands of people.

'Must be rush hour,' Chalky commented.

'Do you see all of those army lorries on the other side of the river?' Dynamo asked. 'They all seem to be heading in the same direction you reckon we need to take, Chalky. Maybe we should follow them and see where they go?'

'You're right, that square is over that way and the garrison is somewhere close by.'

'What else do we have on the target?' I asked them.

'We're never told exactly who the target is or what he does, and we don't want to know just as long as we have a photograph so we know what he looks like. But my guess is that he's a senior Soviet military adviser or an aide assisting the Egyptian government. So he's got a lot on his plate,' Chalky told me. 'He must be under a lot of pressure. We've been told he works very late so let's hope he sticks to his routine. But it doesn't matter if he's a bus conductor. He's got to go.'

'He'll be under high security,' Dynamo added, 'but most of that should be around the grounds of the building. I imagine that he'll feel pretty safe up on the top floor and won't be expecting anything. Judging by the photographs we've seen, getting into the building without being detected could be a bit of a swine, never mind getting out, and we need to find a way of doing it without alerting this lot!' Dynamo gestured towards the mass of vehicles in front of us, which included several army lorries. 'Obviously we have to get in and out without making a sound, so don't forget that oil filter, Chalky, we might just need it.'

We crawled forwards for roughly 10 minutes when Spot stuck his head through the opening again. 'Hey, you lot! Look over there up this side street, there just ahead behind that building: it's the bridge, lads.'

Just ahead of us about 300 yards away was the bridge we were looking for.

'That's the one,' Chalky said, checking the map.

As we slowly approached it, we noticed some kind of activity on the other side where a group of soldiers were struggling to push a truck out of the way to the side of the road. Suddenly, one of them began to walk directly towards us, waving his arms and looking straight into the cab.

'Oh hell, he's coming straight to my side of the truck! That's all we need, I can't speak a word of Arabic. Shall I just throw the body in the river?' I joked quietly to Chalky.

He nudged me in the ribs. 'Shh, don't say a word.'

I just sat there staring at the soldier who, when he got no response from me, made his way to the driver's side of the truck. From ahead of us one of his mates shouted something over to him and he climbed onto the running board to look down the road in the direction of the obstruction.

Dynamo fastened the top of the tunic he was wearing to avoid the soldier spotting his white shirt underneath. 'Pretend you're a workman,' he whispered to Chalky who was sitting in the middle and the only one not wearing an army-style tunic.

'How the hell do you pretend to be a workman?' Chalky hissed back. 'What happens if someone twigs? They can't be that stupid, surely? One of them must notice something's not quite right.

What with Geordie and his blue eyes and blood on his jacket and me dressed like this, I should have been the one in the back of the truck.'

'Yeah, probably. Remember those workmen getting on the back of army trucks when we were in the boat? Well, if they do notice something there's going to be an awful lot of bodies floating down the river,' Dynamo sniggered. He wound the window down and stuck his head out, which prevented the soldier from seeing right into the cab and noticing our trousers or the bloodstained tunic I was wearing.

Just then, the guy ducked his head down next to the window and pointing ahead of him, shouted something to Dynamo, who replied in Arabic and began to move the truck forward. When we crossed the bridge and reached the broken-down truck the soldier jumped off the running board and waved us on.

The noisy streets were busy with groups of armed troops and people everywhere but nobody seemed to take any notice of us. We drove along wide tree-lined avenues, edged with large white buildings and the occasional minaret for roughly quarter of a mile.

'We can't be more than a few hundred yards from where we need to be,' Chalky pointed out. 'Look, you can just see the top of the Citadel over there. We need to turn right somewhere around here. Dynamo, see if you can get down one of these side streets; they should lead us to the square I was on about.'

'Where's the Citadel? I can't see it,' I asked him, looking about me.

'Why don't you ask that old bloke over there?' Dynamo joked, pointing to an obviously blind old beggar sitting on the pavement. Chalky and I cracked up.

'Geordie, see if "The Sheikh" is still on the back, we haven't heard from him for ages,' Chalky said, almost helpless with laughter.

'Hey, less of the cheek, you swine!' came a voice from above us and I looked up to see Spot peering through the opening. 'That was a bit close back there on the bridge, wasn't it?'

'You've been quiet, I thought we'd lost you,' I said.

'I've been standing here trying to look like a workman!' he replied.

'You stupid sod, you're the one supposed to be looking like an

Arab soldier, that's why you've got the beret and the tunic,' Chalky said, gasping for air and holding his stomach.

'I could have been standing here looking like a bleedin' Japanese Kamikaze pilot and these daft sods wouldn't have noticed, old boy.'

'Come on, we've got to be serious here,' Dynamo said, wiping away tears of laughter. 'I'll have to find somewhere to dump this truck soon, the light's starting to go. We've got bags of time so let's have a good look around.'

He turned right down a narrow side street which, after about 50 yards, opened up into a fairly large square filled with army trucks and civilian vehicles lined up in rows.

'This is a bit of luck. You were right about the square, Chalky, but this is a bonus. It'll be like hiding a tree in the woods,' Dynamo said as he drove into the square.

Most of the brightly lit buildings around the square appeared to be cafés and bars with tables and chairs on the pavements in front, crowded with civilians and soldiers. Music was playing loudly. About 100 yards away, two soldiers armed with sub-machine guns were strolling along a row of parked vehicles, talking to one another with their backs to us. As we drove into the square, they stopped and briefly looked back towards us, then carried on walking and continued their conversation. They didn't seem to be interested in us at all. We drove past the first two trucks in the row then Dynamo noticed a gap between them and stopped.

'We couldn't ask for a better place to leave it,' he said. 'It looks as though these two guys are going to take care of it for us until we get back.'

Spot jumped off the back of truck as I got out and began to wave Dynamo into the space as he reversed. The lighting was very poor where the trucks were parked and it was so dark he could barely see me. I put my hand up to stop him coming further, but he didn't notice and reversed a few inches more, nudging the truck behind just hard enough to break its tail lights.

Chalky stuck his head around the corner of one of the parked trucks to see if the two soldiers had noticed but they were still standing talking to one another and obviously hadn't heard a thing, probably because of the loud music. He came around to the back of our truck.

'Don't worry, Geordie, I don't think we'll have to pay for them,' he said, nodding towards the broken lights.

'It's lucky for us those two didn't hear anything.'

'Lucky for them, you mean,' he replied, smiling. 'Be a shame to die over a couple of tail lights. Anyway, we've nowhere to dump the bodies.'

The confidence and assurance of my pals was astounding. They treated it as though it was just a pleasant day out! And yet there was no hint of boasting. They were simply the very best at what they did and they knew it.

12. Suicide in Cairo

Chalky and I grabbed the bags and led the way back towards the narrow street that had brought us into the square. About halfway along it, we turned off right up a smaller alleyway.

'We shouldn't have far to go to the target,' Dynamo commented, then he suddenly stopped walking. 'Hell, I've left the damn keys in the ignition. I'll have to go back for them.'

'That's handy! I'll nip back and get them before someone nicks it. Wait here.' Spot turned around and headed back towards the square. We waited only a few minutes before he returned.

'Any problems?' Dynamo asked.

'No, the two soldiers had gone.'

Just at that moment, a door nearby burst open and a stream of light flooded the alley, blinding us. Several men came out of the doorway into the alley, jabbering away to one another, and turned our way. Quickly we pretended to be standing having a conversation. Luckily they took no notice and just passed by us without a second glance.

We set off again down the dingy, narrow street; we needed to get back to the main road to get our bearings. Every now and then, someone would walk past, often glancing at us as they did, but nobody stopped or spoke to us. I supposed that we really looked the part. Besides, the street lighting was virtually non-existent so it was pretty dark, which helped. As we walked along we could hear voices from inside the various buildings we passed, most of which appeared to be family homes. Strange varieties of strong, spicy, cooking smells mingled with other unfamiliar smells in the streets. At the end of the lane, we saw a large building that looked derelict, possibly as the result of bombing.

'I know where we are; we need to turn left here to get back to the main road,' Dynamo pointed out. We did as he suggested and immediately saw the main road directly ahead of us as we walked along the side of the derelict building. Chalky was slightly in the lead and turned the corner of the building first before we reached it. Instantly he ducked back to prevent us following him.

'I think we've found it, lads. There's a place about 30 yards away surrounded by a huge fence with barbed wire on the top. I'm sure this is the building we're looking for. Have a look, Dynamo: do you think this is it?' he said quietly.

Dynamo stuck his head around the corner, and then quickly came back to us. 'Stay here. I'll go and have a closer look to make sure.' He went around the corner and we waited for several minutes but there was no sign of him.

'Where the hell has he gone?' Chalky said. 'It wouldn't surprise me if he's gone and done the job on his own; it would be just like him.'

He and I peered around the corner, while Spot watched our backs. Dynamo was nowhere to be seen. Then Spot nudged me, and we saw him come dashing around the corner behind us from the rear of the building. He had obviously walked right around the place we were standing next to.

'That's it all right!' he exclaimed. 'I didn't think we were so close, but it's definitely the right place.'

'How do you know?' Spot asked.

'Well, it's hard to say but the Soviet flag flying, and the staff car with Soviet pennants and insignia on it, and Soviet troops guarding the place sort of gave me a clue that this was it,' Dynamo laughed. 'This dump is directly opposite the main garrison building: I had a good look at it as I walked around and it looks as though its been bombed some time ago but most of it's still intact. The main thing is, it's only a few yards away from the perimeter fence around the garrison compound. So all we have to do is find a way through it.

'The compound and building are exactly as we saw in the photographs,' he continued. 'Two 13-foot fences about 15 feet apart surrounding a three-storey building and only one way in that I could see. There are four armed guards, two at the entrance to the building, two at the main gate and there's a dog patrol in between the two fences. So, apart from that it should be a piece of cake.'

'So, what you mean…' Chalky began to say slowly.

'What I mean, Chalky,' Dynamo went on, 'is there's only one way in and that's going to be over the top. It's a good job this place here is empty. I can't understand how they've left it standing; it's a hell of a security risk. It looks to be boarded up and I think that part of the roof is missing.'

'Right then, let's find a way in,' Chalky said, indicating the derelict building behind us.

'We need to get in round the back; the front of the compound is lit up like Blackpool illuminations. Come round this way; I don't think it's overlooked and I think we'll be able to get in through one of the boarded-up windows.' Dynamo said, leading the way.

We made our way to the rear of the building, making sure we were not being watched, and found a window roughly nailed up with a few wooden planks, only yards away from the wire compound fence. But just as we were easing the planks off, the dog patrol inside the two perimeter fences came to the corner of the building and began to walk past. The four of us pressed our backs into the wall of the building as the soldier walked slowly by with the dog on a leash. The dog seemed to sense something and kept looking back over its shoulder towards us but the guy just kept yanking it along.

'Can you believe it?' Chalky whispered. 'What an idiot! I mean, just what is the point of having a dog if you're not going to take any notice of it?'

'It's just as well he didn't,' Spot commented dryly. 'The dopey beggar!'

We started to pull off the boards, but two of them snapped with a loud crack, which I felt certain the guard must have heard. I held my breath but nothing happened and we continued to pull the planks away until we had a hole large enough for us to climb through. Once inside we split up and began searching around, trying to find a way up to the roof.

Opening a door, I discovered a massive pile of masonry and looking up saw that there was a huge hole right through all of the floors. It looked as though a bomb had come right through the roof into the middle of the building. A few beams of light from the neighbouring compound penetrated the broken windows and cracks in the walls but despite this and being able to see right through the building to the sky and stars above, it was very dark inside.

Stumbling around, I discovered the rickety remains of a wooden staircase and began to carefully make my way up it. By the sounds coming from above, I realised that the others had already reached the upper floor. Most of the stair treads were missing and getting up was difficult; there was a large gap near the top and the only way across it was to jump. I landed awkwardly and gripped at the tubular metal banister to steady myself but it instantly came away from the wall and I swung out over into the building over a two storey drop. Peering through the darkness, I could just make out that the banister was hanging on by only one bracket fastened to the crumbling masonry.

I began to pull myself up the banister hoping that the bracket would hold until I reached the top. Spot's face suddenly appeared above me.

'What are hanging around for, Geordie?' he joked, offering me his hand.

'How the hell did you manage to get up there without this happening?'

'We came up by another staircase. I thought you were behind us.'

'What other stairs? You could have told me. Show me the way to the roof, then, you clever sod.'

In the darkness, I could barely see the faces of my mates, even though the sky was clear and the stars were so bright that I felt I could reach up and touch them. The only lighting in the area came from a string of bulbs hanging from a wire over the compound together with two large floodlights, which lit up the front of the garrison building and the main entrance.

From the roof of the building, we could make out the flat rooftop of the garrison building opposite. Below us a number of guards were mainly positioned around the front of the entrance. We knew our target was there as we could see his parked limousine, with its insignia and pennant, a larger version of which was raised on the side of the building alongside the Egyptian flag.

In our briefing we were given full details of the layout of the building. The only thing we were not sure about was exactly which office our target would be working from, although we did know it was on the third floor.

We were lucky that the building we were in was now derelict. It was a godsend. Obviously, we had been informed that the building was there next to the compound, but we were not aware until we arrived that it was empty and the state it was in. It was going to make our operation considerably easier, as we could work from the roof undetected. All we had to do now was to get a rope from the roof across two fences that were about 30 feet below us, and onto the adjacent building approximately 45 feet away.

Below us, we saw that the perimeter fences had barbed wire running along the top of them. They appeared to be roughly 13 feet high and 15 feet apart. One of these looked as though it might be electrified or alarmed in some way, as we could see small white bobbins on its main struts. We needed to ensure that our ropes did not touch these fences. There was no room for error: if anything dropped onto them, it would immediately give our cover away.

A low parapet approximately two feet high ran around the opposite rooftop. A telegraph pole was fastened to this and the side of the building roughly 10 feet in from the edge nearest to us, with roughly eight feet of it sticking up above roof level. It had a large bobbin on the top, which appeared to be carrying the main electric supply; below this was a crosspiece carrying dozens of telephone wires that ran across to a similar telegraph pole attached to the building we were on. About four feet beneath the crosspiece we could just make out what appeared to be a further metal bar about 15 inches long that stuck out at a right angle on the roof side of the pole. We would be able to utilise this, if it proved to be strong enough.

The low parapet was capped with concrete slabs, which we worked out were roughly three feet long by one and a half inches thick. By using the rough sizing of these concrete slabs as a guide, we were able to make an estimate of the distance up to the telegraph pole along the side of the building. This gave us a pretty good idea what length of light line we would need to attach to the arrow we would use in order to eventually get a rope over from one rooftop to the other

Spot selected a crossbow and arrow from one of the canvas bags. The arrow had three small fins and one large one, in order to stop it twisting in the air, and carried with it two very strong, thin, light lines, which were different colours so that we could differentiate between the two. We needed the arrow from the crossbow to drop over the metal bar and stop before it hit the roof. This we called a single-shot pick-up, and it would enable us to get the light line over the metal bar. Then when we attached the heavy rope to this, it would also take it over the metal bar and bring it back to us thus forming a loop.

Spot took a three-inch side-casting reel and attached this to his waist. He would normally leave the line on the reel so that when he fired the crossbow it would not become entangled. But, in this instance, because he did not want the arrow to hit the roof when it went over the metal bar so that we could retrieve it, he had to work out the distance between himself and the telegraph pole. He tied up the remaining line so that it would not travel any further than the distance he had measured. If he were accurate, this would enable the arrow to stop just before it hit the roof, which would allow the pick-up on the end of the arrow to be manipulated in order to recover the light line and bring it back to us.

I held my breath as Spot took aim at the crosspiece of the telegraph pole. It was festooned with wires and I knew that the success of his shot was absolutely critical. It was much darker now, making it difficult to even see the small target; if the arrow fell short it would dangle over the street, possibly making a noise by clattering against something, and alert the guards below. If it passed too far over the target and hit the roof it could also make a noise or become snagged.

He took aim, and steadied himself but just as he was about to fire, Chalky tapped him on the shoulder and pointed below. The soldier with the guard dog had suddenly appeared around the corner of the building and was passing beneath us.

Spot quietly waited until the pair of them had walked by, before rapidly taking aim once again and firing. As usual, he lived up to his name and scored a direct hit first time. The flying arrow was silently checked by its securing lines and dropped just over the crosspiece. The arrow now dangled from one line. Spot pulled the lower line, which allowed the pick-up to collect the upper line, bringing the arrow and upper line back to him. By making the light line go around the metal bar and return to him, it formed a loop.

Securing our heavier rope onto the light line, we pulled this over the bar and back towards us again, so that it now took the place of the light line. By attaching a dog-clip to the end of the rope we were able to form a slipknot around the metal bar. Then we attached the rope to the telegraph pole on our building, and tightened it by means of small pulley wheels in order to stop it stretching or sagging beneath our weight as we crossed.

Removing our sashes, we took our rope sitting harnesses from the holdalls and put them on around our legs and waists. Now we could attach a pulley wheel onto the rope for extra safety and start to cross the gap between the two buildings without being seen or heard. Spot, being the lightest, went over first. He unhooked the line from the metal bar and wrapped it around the telegraph pole in order to make it more secure, then checked behind the building to make sure that no patrols were passing before signalling that it was clear for the rest of us to cross. Dynamo, and then I, followed him over. From setting the rope up to getting the three of us across had taken less than 15 minutes.

By the time I arrived on the garrison rooftop, Dynamo had already begun to remove some old bits of canvas and wood from a broken skylight, or possibly a trapdoor, which had been boarded up. He cautiously lifted one corner and we peered through the small opening. Two guards were standing talking to one another by some stairs at the end of a corridor directly below. Silently replacing the cover, Dynamo swiftly went to the edge of the roof and signalled to Chalky that there was a problem, in order to stop him from coming over

'Two guards,' he hissed, holding up two fingers and pointing over to the skylight.

Chalky held up his hand and whispered back: 'Five minutes.' Then he disappeared inside the derelict building. We waited a few minutes before he reappeared on the opposite roof and quickly began to make his way over to us.

'Where have you been?' I quietly asked him. 'What have you been up to?'

'All in good time, Geordie. Wait a couple of minutes and you'll see. I'll show you how to get rid of them,' he said, nodding towards the skylight.

We silently waited a few more minutes then Spot turned to him. 'Well?'

'Give it time, old boy,' Chalky grinned back.

At that moment, there was a commotion at the front of the building, a lot of shouting and the sound of running feet. Smoke began rising from a small hut in the corner of the compound followed by a series of small explosions. Spot dashed to the edge of the building, looked over briefly, and then strolled back to where we were waiting.

'Your handiwork I presume?' he said evenly to Chalky.

'Small store area, full of paint and paraffin: came in rather handy. Right then, let's get on with the damn job,' Chalky calmly replied.

We felt secure leaving the rope in place at this stage. It ran parallel to the numerous telephone cables and wires from the telegraph pole across to the adjacent building and anyone looking up would not have been able to spot it amongst the masses of wires already attached to the pole.

Dynamo led the way over the roof to the skylight and peered through the hole he'd made earlier again, to see if the guards were still there. But by now they had gone, presumably to see what all the noise was about in the compound.

'It worked. They've gone,' he whispered to Chalky. Squeezing his hand through the hole, he released the bolts holding the skylight in place. Once it was removed, we dropped through the opening and landed onto a large box about seven feet below, before jumping quietly down from this into the corridor. Dynamo immediately took out the small photograph of our target he had hidden in the waistband of his trousers, looked at it briefly, then systematically began to try all the doors leading off the landing. The first couple he tried were locked and as no light shone beneath them, he swiftly moved on. He paused by the following door, listening, and then looked through the keyhole.

'There's someone in here,' he whispered, then turned the handle and took a step into the room. Immediately he backed out again, pulling the door shut behind him, and looked at the photograph in his hand.

'That's him, in there!'

Politely he knocked on the door before re-entering the room with the three of us close behind him and walked straight over to a man sitting behind a large desk. The man looked furious. He stood up and walked towards Dynamo with his hand pointing towards the door, and said something in Arabic, no doubt words to the effect of 'What the hell are you all doing in my office?'

Dynamo replied, also in Arabic, before adding in English, 'Sorry about this, old boy.' Using the machine moves, he knocked the man's outstretched arm out of the way and spun him around. He then delivered two instantaneous blows, his left hand to the back of the guy's head while the base of his right palm hit the guy on the right side of the chin. But just as he was about to break the man's neck, I grabbed his arm and stopped him.

'Don't kill him!'

'Bloody hell, Geordie, what's the matter with you?' he exclaimed in surprise. 'That's what we're here for isn't it?'

'Yes I know, but I think I can do this without having the whole Egyptian army looking for us. I'm fairly certain that I can make it look like suicide. I think I know just how to do it,' I explained. 'If he's got a gun, we can do it.'

I began to search the guy but there was nothing on him.

'He's bound to have one,' Spot said, looking around the room.

'What about this, any good?' Chalky pulled a service revolver out of one of the desk drawers. 'What's on your mind, Geordie?'

'I hope this isn't going to take too long.' Dynamo said, glancing towards the door. 'Do you really think you can do it?'

'Just help me set up some light lines, lads. We'll be out of here in no time!' I said confidently. Immediately on entering the room, I had noticed that it had three barred windows and only one door. I had also noticed that the door had an unusual lock that could only be locked from the inside, as there was no keyhole on the other side. It also had a standard lock lower down the door, with a keyhole either side and two bolts, one at the top and one at the bottom. After quickly examining the type of locks on the door, and seeing that the key in the half-lock had a ring with two other large keys hanging from it, I had come up with an idea.

I knew that by using our light lines, I could lock the door, pull the two bolts across and put the keys back into the guy's pocket from outside of the room! Anyone trying to get in after we had gone would assume that he had locked the door himself from the inside. It would look like suicide. No one would be looking for assassins.

The man was still lying on the floor, unconscious. Dynamo picked him up and sat him upright in his chair with his head slumped forward.

'Right, Chalky, do that trick of yours with the oil filter,' I told him. Chalky wrapped some cloth around his hand and the gun, then placed the oil filter on the end of the barrel, while Dynamo grabbed the man's hair and pulled his head upright. Chalky placed the oil filter hard against the man's right hand temple and squeezed the trigger. The gun made a faint popping sound and part of the left side of the guy's head came away. Blood immediately gushed from the wound, up the wall, over the desk and down onto the floor. Chalky and Dynamo lay him over his desk with his right hand hanging down towards the floor, where Chalky placed the gun beneath his fingers. Spot checked the corridor to make sure no one had heard the sound of the shot, faint though it was.

'It's OK. There's still so much racket going on outside they wouldn't have heard an elephant gun!' he said, coming back into the room.

In the meantime, I had made a small hole into the man's jacket pocket with my boot knife and had begun to rig up most of the lines. Chalky looked at me quizzically for a moment; then, quick on the uptake, he smiled slowly.

'I've got the idea, Geordie. Spot, give me a hand.'

Dynamo watched the corridor while the two of them helped to set it up. We rigged up lines over and under the door and through the keyhole. I now took one line and looped it through the key ring attached to the key in the lock. This made a double line that I ran over the top of the desk, through the tiny hole in the dead man's jacket pocket, back underneath the desk and then underneath the door. I then attached a single line to this where it looped through the key ring and took this over the top of the door.

The next line I wound around the two spare keys hanging from the key ring. Again this made a double line, which I also hung over the top of the door. Chalky wrapped a third and fourth line around the door bolts, one top and one bottom, and took one over the door and the other underneath it while Spot pulled a chair to within two feet of the door. Taking a fifth line, he wrapped this around the top of the chair back and fed both ends through the keyhole. Then I did a similar manoeuvre around the two back legs of the chair, taking these lines underneath the door.

'Right, now let's get out of here into the corridor and I'll close the door behind us.'

'Why have you got the lines going through his pocket?' Dynamo asked, puzzled.

'Because I want to put the keys into his jacket pocket,' I explained.

'Bloody hell, is that really necessary?' he said, raising his eyebrows.

'Look, when I do a job I do it properly. You want it to be convincing, don't you? You want this lot to believe he's just topped himself? Well, watch this!'

Looking underneath the door, I pulled on the line around the chair legs and manoeuvred it to within a foot of the door. Then Spot pulled on the other one around the chair back, which caused it to tip over and lie against the door, and kept pulling it until it wedged underneath the handle. Then we released one end of each line and pulled them both back under the door.

I was holding the line around the spare keys and now I pulled it to use them as leverage to turn the key in the half-lock. Then, by allowing these two keys on the key ring to drop again under their own weight I was able to straighten and square up the key in the lock, retrieving this line over the top of the door.

Pulling on the second line through the guy's pocket, I managed to yank the keys out of the lock. By holding onto the first line over the top of the door, I prevented them from hitting the floor. By manipulating the second line, I manoeuvred the keys across the top of the desk into the man's pocket. Chalky looked through the keyhole and told me when the keys were secure; then I pulled on the first line and let go of the second and brought both of them over the top of the door.

Chalky then yanked on the two remaining lines and locked both the top and bottom bolts. By releasing one end of either line, he retrieved them too.

All of this had taken only a few minutes to set up and it gave the impression that the man had locked and bolted the door from the inside, placed a chair under the door handle, put the keys back into his pocket and then shot himself.

'Well, if that doesn't look like suicide, I can't imagine what would!' Dynamo exclaimed. 'But just to make sure...'

As the rest of us climbed out through the skylight and made our way back across the roof, Dynamo leant back down through the opening and fired a shot into the corridor.

I spun around at the sound. 'What did you do that for?' I asked in surprise.

'Well, we want them to believe that he's just shot himself, don't we, so they need to hear a gunshot. I think that should bring them running.'

Quickly the two of us closed the skylight behind us and pushed the wood and canvas back into place to make it look as though no one had tampered with it; not that they would check it anyway. If they believed the guy had committed suicide there was no reason for them to.

Chalky, Dynamo and I made our way back across the gap between the buildings using the ropes and pulleys and Spot was the last man over.

He unhooked the dog-clip and heavy rope from the telegraph pole and then fastened the rope back around the metal bar, still forming a slipknot by using the dog-clip. Attaching a light line to the dog-clip and using the pulley wheel system again, he made his way back over to us with the other end of the light line attached to him. When he reached us, we released the rope with the pulley wheels from the telegraph pole on our side, which we used to keep our heavy rope taut, and then by pulling on the light line we brought the dog-clip back towards us.

Quickly removing it, I fastened the light line onto the heavy rope where the dog-clip had been and then we retrieved our heavy rope, preventing it from falling down onto the fence below, the same method we had used when we put the rope up. There was no trace of us having been there. Gathering our equipment together, we silently made our way uneventfully back through the derelict building to the street below.

'It's early yet, lads, we've got bags of time. I fancy seeing that big mosque. I didn't get to see it last time I was here,' Dynamo joked.

Chalky grabbed him by the shoulder and gave him a shove. 'Come on, stop messing about; let's get out of this bloody place.'

'Aw, I really fancied seeing that mosque and we've got the time to do it too, thanks to Geordie,' Dynamo continued as we began to make our way back towards the square. 'It's not that far away either.'

Chalky turned to me. 'He's not joking you know, he really means it. Bloody tourist!'

Without further discussion, we quickly retraced our steps back along the side of the building towards the narrow alleyway. As we turned into it, they suddenly began to slap me on the back, grinning and shaking their heads in amazement.

'Jesus, Geordie, how the hell did you come up with that idea?' Dynamo burst out excitedly. 'It was ingenious.'

'Well, I had good teachers, didn't I?' I said, a little embarrassed at the fuss they were making.

'Yeah, but we didn't show you anything like that!' Chalky exclaimed. 'We just showed you a few tricks with bits of string, nothing like that.'

'It was brilliant,' Spot added, thumping me on the shoulder and grinning from ear to ear. 'Absolutely brilliant. And it'll make it a lot easier to get back without a general alert; that's if the truck's still there.'

Chalky turned to Dynamo and gave him a nudge. 'Now we know why the team picked him, eh lads?' he said laughing. 'The man's a bloody genius.'

'Aw, stop it,' I said, blushing and shoving them away. But secretly I was thrilled that I had pleased them so much. They were the only people in the world, other than my mother, whose opinions meant anything to me.

'OK, enough of the carry-on, lads, we're not out of the woods yet,' Spot quietly reminded us as we neared the street that led into the square.

The square was empty of people now. In the background, faint strains of music could just be heard. We quickly made our way over to where we'd left the truck. Now and then a door would open and a shaft of light would fall across the square but no one approached us.

Chalky pointed it out. 'Hey look, lads, it's still there.'

Spot immediately dashed over to the truck and jumped inside. 'One of you buggers can get in the back this time. Do they work nightshift around here, Chalky? You look like a workman, get on the back!'

Chalky grinned and climbed onto the back of the truck.

'Suits me fine. Just take it easy, lads, I want to get some kip,' he said calmly, wrapping a canvas sheet around him.

'The jammy sod! Why didn't I think of that?' Spot exclaimed as I climbed in next to him. 'What's that horrible smell, Geordie? Have you stepped in something a camel left behind?'

'It's this damn jacket, I don't know what the hell they had in the pocket but it stinks. I'm surprised that bloody guard dog didn't smell it when we were behind the building.'

Dynamo tried three or four times to start the engine. 'Oh, hell. That's all we need,' he moaned.

'Does he always have this trouble?' I asked Spot, sniggering. 'If I remember he couldn't start a jeep up in the Troodos Mountains either.' Dynamo nudged me hard in the ribs.

'Can't we just take one of these other trucks?' Spot suggested.

'Come on, you know better than that! Even these silly sods would notice straight away if one of those is missing in the morning and start looking for it. Besides, this one's supposed to be 100 miles north of here.' Just then the engine started. 'Thank goodness for that.' Dynamo heaved a sigh of relief and drove off. 'Right lads, we'll just take it easy and have a nice slow ride back. We've got bags of time now, thanks to the genius,' he said, grinning in my direction.

We drove out of the city along the same route we'd followed entering it, and passed only a few small groups of civilians and armed troops along the way. The broken-down lorry was still at the side of the road by the bridge but the area was quiet now. The traffic was virtually non-existent on our return journey, which was as uneventful as Dynamo had said it would be. About 40 miles outside of Cairo, he pulled over and stopped to check on the fuel and found Chalky sound asleep on the back.

'How the hell can he sleep at a time like this?' Dynamo commented dryly as we lifted the petrol cans off the truck to re-fuel it. We drove almost all the way back to the beach area, passing the point where we had initially commandeered the truck 'without the owner's consent', about two miles before we turned off the main road onto an old track.

Dynamo followed the track for roughly six miles to a desolate swampy area on the bank of the river, an ideal spot to dump the truck. He drove it straight into the reeds and halfway down the embankment towards the river. Jumping out of the cab the three of us went around to the back to wake Chalky. He was still sound asleep wrapped in the canvas sheeting.

'Come on, Sleeping Beauty, the truck's starting to sink into the mud!' Dynamo said, pulling the canvas off the back of the wagon with Chalky still in it.

'Aw, come on, lads, leave me alone, it's lovely and warm in here. OK, OK, I'm coming,' he said as Dynamo yanked hard at the sheeting.

'We want to dump it in the river. Come on, give it a push.'

He climbed back into the cab and released the handbrake. Slowly the heavy vehicle began to roll forwards and then as it suddenly gathered momentum he jumped out again. The four of us stood watching it roll into the water then slowly begin to sink out of sight.

'If it's ever found, they'll probably just think those guys had an accident,' Spot commented.

Dynamo took the canvas sheeting from Chalky and using his boot knife he tore it into four strips and gave a piece to each of us. We faffed about with it, each putting holes into our own piece so we could wrap it round and wear it like a coat, tying it around the waist with bits of string.

Dynamo had put some extra holes in his piece then tied it together with bows, and now he began to mince up and down in front of us like a model.

'Ooh, ooh, I say, boys! What do you think of this, Geordie? Perfect rain gear, eh? When I get back I'll be able to set off a new trend. The 'New Look' by Dynamo.'

'Ooh, it's luvverly!' Chalky said and taking hold of the bottom corners of his piece in either hand, he held it out as he turned and pirouetted around. 'What do you think of mine, dear?'

Spot and I doubled up, and were laughing so hard at the pair of them that we couldn't speak. My face and stomach ached. Eventually wiping the tears from his eyes, Spot managed to talk. 'Come on, you two prima donnas, stop prancing about. Let's get to the pick-up point.'

We took our bearings from the river and in good spirits set off towards the marshy area where we'd landed. We must have walked for about eight or nine miles until it became too dark to see and the ground was becoming wetter and softer.

'Let's find a dry spot and wait here for a while. We don't want to go any further through this muck,' Chalky said, his feet squelching on the marshy ground.

We looked around and found a clump of reeds where the ground was firmer and drier and settled down for the rest of the night. We would have to wait until daylight to find out exactly where we were, but, according to our bearings, we knew we could not be more than half a mile away from our pick-up point.

Once we stopped walking, the cold began to penetrate and we were very glad of the canvas from the truck. We pulled it around us and settled down to wait.

13. The return

It was bitterly cold through the night and I lay awake for much of the time, gazing at the clear sky, watching the stars. But at some point I dozed off into a fitful sleep. A rustling sound in the reeds woke me and I opened my eyes to broad daylight. Glancing at my watch, I saw that that it was half past six, the sun was already high in the sky and the air was hot and humid. Nearby the others were still sleeping and I shook Chalky who was nearest to me by the shoulder. He woke and sat up rubbing his eyes.

'Still here, I see, Geordie? The crocs didn't get you last night then?' he said dryly.

'You're having me on, aren't you?'

'No, seriously, Geordie, there are salt water crocodiles all around this area.' I wondered if that was what the rustling sound in the reeds that woke me had been and quickly looked around.

'Why didn't you say something last night?'

'You wouldn't have got any sleep if I had done, now would you?'

'Yeah, but I might have been asleep "permanently".'

Dynamo and Spot were awake now too.

'We've still got a little way to go to the pick-up point; we might as well head off there now before it gets any hotter,' Spot said, checking our bearings.

As we trudged for a short while through the tall grasses and reeds, parting them before us, we disturbed thousands of flies and mosquitoes and they were becoming a real nuisance as they buzzed around our heads. I kept looking around for any signs of crocodiles but luckily saw nothing. Spot in the lead held up his hand and stopped us.

'The ground's too swampy to go any further.'

He was right. As we walked, the marshy ground had gradually become softer and wetter; my feet were now soaking and once again I was pleased I had coated them in vegetable grease before we left.

'You're right, the hack could get bogged down in this lot. We'd better stay back there where the ground's a bit firmer,' Chalky agreed. We retraced our steps to the small spot where we had spent the night. It was slightly firmer and drier than the surrounding area and, hidden from view by the tall reeds, we sat chatting, eating a few dry 'dog biscuits' washed down with lukewarm water from the canisters we had brought with us.

'Ken should be here any minute,' Chalky said, scanning the horizon with his binoculars.

'Shh, listen!' Dynamo urged. I strained my ears and could just make out the sound of the hack although I still could not see it. 'There, there he is.' Almost as he said the words, we saw the helicopter heading straight towards us from the west. It flew in right over our heads, its downdraught bending and parting the tall reeds and grasses, then abruptly turned and landed just a few yards away. We threw off our makeshift canvas coats and picking up our bags ran straight towards it and jumped in.

'What the hell are you doing over here? You should have been half a mile west of this point,' Ken said. 'You're lucky I found you straight away.'

Before we had time to reply or even sit down the hack was back in the air again and heading straight out towards the sea. Ken turned to look at us and gave us the thumbs up sign. Chalky did the same back to him and shouted, 'Mission accomplished.'

Ken headed 140 miles east, back to the fuel dump, where we refuelled and set off again without a hitch. We then flew north-north-west again, back towards Cyprus where about 20 miles south of the island there was to be a boat waiting to pick us up.

We flew skimming the waves once more for just over an hour. Then Ken pointed ahead. Spot and I immediately picked up our canvas holdalls and strapped them across our backs like rucksacks, putting our arms through the handles and securing them across our chests. Then we fastened two ropes above the doors on either side of the helicopter to balance our weight and at the given signal from Ken abseiled down. The hack sped towards a small boat nearby as Spot and I hung just feet above the sea.

The boat was a blue and green cabin cruiser, which raced along underneath the helicopter in a cloud of white spray and down-draught. Spot and I dropped onto its deck and seconds later the other two came down directly behind us. Immediately the hack turned away eastwards and disappeared.

I didn't recognise the guy on the boat, but it was obvious that the other three knew him well, although no one spoke much as we sped off towards Cyprus. About three-quarters of an hour later, they dropped me off at a quiet beach a few miles outside Dhekélia while they went off with the boat. I had no idea why they did this but obviously they had their reasons. I did not ask and they did not offer an explanation.

'Just walk along the narrow road leading off the beach towards a junction, and then keep out of sight until we arrive with the jeep, Geordie,' Chalky told me. When they collected me I would be taken back to the old hangar. There I could leave the holdall and change back into my regular uniform.

Crossing the beach, I found the dusty track leading from it and made my way along it to the junction where Chalky had told me to wait. I sat by the side of the road. It was late morning now and scorching hot. I was parched and concerned about the effects of dehydration. Ken had given us some sandwiches in the helicopter, but the damn things had been dry and tasteless, leaving me hungry and, above all, thirsty.

The cream they had put on my face and hair to darken them was now uncomfortably itchy, but I couldn't risk scratching in case any of it came off. I was hot, tired and dirty and badly in need of a shave. Not too far from where I sat, I saw a gang of workmen, which seemed to be made up of soldiers and some locals. They appeared to be laying drains or mending the road and behind them stood a refreshment tent.

I suspected that some of the guys might be from 524 Company, but didn't recognise any of them. Although I knew I had been told to stay out of sight, I was so thirsty that I could barely swallow and was beginning to feel light-headed. I hoped that the tent would be empty, as they all seemed to be working on the road. I decided to risk going inside to get something to quench my thirst. Carefully hiding my holdall under a small bush near to the junction, I sneaked around the back of the tent, keeping out of sight of the workmen then pushed open the flaps and walked in.

The tent was fairly large and directly ahead of me was a table with a bottle of clear liquid standing on it, which I presumed was lemonade, together with a couple of glasses and some empty Coke bottles. To my left was a canvas partition that restricted my view of the rest of the tent. I couldn't hear anything due to the racket from a generator standing not far away outside.

I had no money on me and as there didn't appear to be anyone about, I decided to pinch the bottle of clear liquid. As I got near to the table, I looked to my left around the end of the partition and saw several British soldiers dressed in work fatigues standing drinking at a long table which was covered with empty bottles and glasses, as were several other tables nearby. They were inside taking a break and as soon as they became aware of me, the atmosphere instantly changed and became hostile. The general hum of conversation ceased and they all stared in my direction.

One tall, overweight soldier glanced over his shoulder at me then turned around and picked up a bottle from the table. 'What the f...ing hell do you think you're doing, you cheeky bastard? Why are you in here?' he yelled at me aggressively, brandishing the bottle.

In my desperation to get a drink, I had completely forgotten the way I was dressed and how I would look to them! Another two standing at a nearby table began to move towards me, one of them holding a crowbar in a threatening way. I knew these guys were not going to let me out of this tent without serious trouble! They obviously thought that I was a local and as such had no business in a British servicemen's refreshment tent. The recent terrorist activities on the island that had caused the deaths of several British servicemen and civilians, and especially the bombing of a crowded NAAFI, had seriously soured relations between the armed forces and the locals.

Oh hell, I thought, I should not have come in here! I couldn't speak to them to let them know that I was actually British too: it would have simply drawn further attention to me; and how could I explain the way I looked?

Suddenly, matters were taken out of my hands as the tall soldier rushed towards me, the now broken bottle in his outstretched hand. I instantly reacted without thinking. I was still wearing my sash. My hand hit its quick-release and it shot into action, smashing the bottle in his hand and catching his leg on the back swing. He instantly dropped onto one knee groaning, as I spun around and broke every bottle and glass within range on the nearby tables. The guy with the crowbar and his pal immediately backed off with looks of horrified and shocked amazement on their faces. I let the belt recoil back around my waist and secured the safety catch with one touch.

The tall guy on the floor was screaming his head off in agony and I was furious with myself for reacting the way I had against British soldiers. But I felt that I'd had no choice. If I had spoken to them, I would have given the game away. I quickly turned around and left, grabbing the unbroken bottle of clear liquid from the table by the tent flap on my way out.

On reflection, I knew that none of them would have realised exactly what had happened because it had all been over in a flash. The time between my releasing the sash and replacing it had been so brief, I knew that they would only be aware of a swishing noise, followed by bottles and glasses exploding all around them as if by magic: just as it had been for me when I had first seen it used on the turnips. Besides, as most of them had instinctively ducked to shield themselves from flying glass, they wouldn't have a clue how I did it. It would certainly have given them something to talk about later, though.

As I swiftly left the tent, I took a large swig from the bottle I had grabbed. But instead of quenching my thirst, to my horror the clear liquid immediately burned my throat and took my breath away. Ahead of me, I saw the jeep standing waiting at the junction and I ran towards it, collecting my bag from under the bush before I jumped in. When I looked back, no one had followed me out of the tent.

'Jesus, what's in that bloody bottle?' I gasped, spluttering and grabbing at my mouth and throat, which both felt as though they were on fire.

'What the hell's the matter with you, Geordie? What's this?' Spot said, snatching the bottle from me. 'You daft sod, you've just had a swig of 100 per cent proof vodka,' he spluttered and then burst out laughing. 'Now you know what it's like to drink liquid paraffin. How the hell did you get this anyway? You were supposed to stay out of sight, young man,' he said, still laughing as he threw the bottle away.

'I was parched and didn't have any money, there wasn't anyone around so I just grabbed the first thing I saw from that tent over there,' I explained.

I couldn't tell them what had really happened: I was too embarrassed. I had never touched alcohol before and I was now determined more than ever that I would never touch the disgusting, foul stuff again.

The jeep bounced off down the rough track and I began to feel ill. My stomach was burning and I felt very sick. The three of them fell about when I explained that I had thought I was drinking lemonade.

When we arrived back at the hangar, I couldn't get to the water quickly enough.

We put our equipment away and I changed back into my regular tropical uniform after first taking care that I had got rid of all of the make-up I was wearing. Four hours later, after some lunch, I was taken back to where I was due to be picked up by the working party's truck.

I had been away for less than two days and, apart from the usual banter, no one on the truck took the slightest notice of me, let alone suspected that I had just been all the way to Cairo and back.

14. A low profile

After the tension and excitement of our operations, camp life was difficult to take. As in all army camps such as this, soldiers generally endure long periods of relentless boredom, broken only by routine daily tasks. This largely depended on what you were consigned to do. Outside working parties, for instance, mainly consisted of digging latrines, putting up marquees or building roads for other regiments, while those who remained back at camp were generally assigned to tidying the place up or working in the cookhouse, which meant endlessly peeling potatoes or cleaning dixies, the only exceptions being those assigned to guard duty.

Outside working parties would usually have a corporal in charge of them and those who remained in the camp would be under the command of a sergeant. As a result, it was not easy to 'disappear' without someone noticing unless you were sent out of our camp on detachment to another. Due to the nature of our regiment, this often happened, sometimes for a couple of days but often for weeks at a time. Other than being off duty, the time spent travelling between the camps was the only time when a regular soldier would possibly have a period without the presence of someone of rank; when they arrived at their assigned camp once again someone would be in charge of them.

On the occasions when I was sent on detachment, I presumed that this had to be arranged by someone of seniority who could fix it so that the camp I was supposedly assigned to would not be expecting me, thereby making it possible for me to 'disappear'. I believed that these orders would have to come from somewhere to my commanding officer specifically asking for me to be assigned to these detachments, otherwise my camp would naturally send whoever was available, not me specifically. I often wondered what the reaction to this by the officers and NCOs at 524 Company must have been. Having said this, I have seen better-organised building sites than the British army, so it possibly was not so difficult to arrange after all.

I constantly wondered about the logistics of this and felt that there had to be someone at my platoon who ensured my name was regularly put onto the list of offsite workers. It could have been the CO or perhaps he knew nothing about it; maybe a junior officer or even a sergeant compiled the working party rosters. I didn't know whose job it was to organise these lists but I knew that someone had to be given orders regarding my whereabouts. It was the only explanation I could come up with but, obviously, I couldn't ask anyone about this.

I would often look at some guy or other, an officer or NCO, and wonder whether they had something to do with it; if perhaps they were the one who organised it. Two officers in particular were quite pally with me, Captain Myers and Lieutenant Stevens. They, for some reason, always seemed to take a keen interest in what I was doing but then they were also fairly friendly with most of the men, so whether they had any knowledge of what I did or not, I never really knew. Then there was this sergeant called Lupton, who had a peculiar way of walking as if he had springs in his heels. He always seemed to be near the gate whenever I arrived back at camp and always made a point of speaking to me.

'Enjoy yourself, Geordie?' he would ask me. 'Had a good holiday?'

He always seemed to single me out but I think that was just his way of being reasonably friendly towards me. Again he never really gave me any reason to suspect that he knew anything about my whereabouts out of the camp.

Ken had warned me at my initiation into The Sixteen that from that point onwards I should not think too much about the organisation of things, or ask too many questions. He knew that I would be curious and want to find out more, but advised me that it would not be in my best interests to try, that I should just accept the way things were.

At first, I could not fathom why The Sixteen would recruit someone from a general working regiment such as mine rather than from an active regiment. But all I was ever told was that it would have been virtually impossible to organise if I had been in any other. In time, of course, I realised that the way in which my regiment operated totally suited their purposes. But I never found out whether I would have still been recruited if I had been in another outfit or whether they had only looked for likely candidates in regiments like mine.

Another thing that really baffled me was how my death would be explained if I was killed on a mission miles away in another country, or wherever it happened. What explanation could be given if I was supposed to be on detachment at another camp yet that camp had neither documentation nor knowledge of my being assigned to them?

But then, I supposed, someone like me being found out of uniform, miles from my unit, would probably be easy to cover up by claiming that I had gone AWOL and was a deserter. Nobody would suspect anyone from my type of unit as being part of any special force.

Ken was right, I shouldn't think about it too much. It was too mind-boggling, and I was not going to come up with any answers. So eventually I tried to give up thinking about it; it was pointless wasting time trying to fathom it out. It was obvious that the powers that be knew exactly what they were doing and had every angle covered. Even so, it was difficult sometimes not to wonder about it all. They had encouraged me to think differently, for myself, to question everything and to only believe half of what I saw or heard. They had educated me and I had changed drastically as a result. I had grown up and the shy, stammering 18 year old had disappeared along with his innocence. For all I looked much the same physically, inside I was a completely different person and even my strong Geordie accent was quickly disappearing.

It is difficult to explain exactly how I felt when I first got back from Beirut. It had been so exciting and I could not believe what we had just done. As Spot had said, something incredible was happening to me. I believed that nothing was beyond our capabilities: nothing we could not do; no task we could not handle. With my combat skills and all of the other tricks they taught me, I truly believed that nothing could touch me. So, when I returned to camp it felt as though I was walking into a graveyard: everything was so deadly quiet, everyone just lounging around. It was much the same after our Cairo mission, and for several long months afterwards my life settled into periods of mind-numbing boredom at camp or undetected periods of intense training and practising with Dynamo, Chalky and Spot.

I lived for the time I spent with them, and crazy as it may seem, I believe I was becoming addicted to living on the edge. Looking forward to the excitement and adrenaline rush of the risks we took was the only thing that made the long, boring chore of life around the camp in between times bearable.

Although I knew I was now a very different person, I still had to pretend to be unchanged when I was with my pals in 524 Company. I didn't find this too difficult, as I would sometimes be with them for only an hour or so in the evening before they went off for a drink to the NAAFI. However, it was more awkward if I was sent out on detachment with them and was around them for a greater length of time. During these periods, I would often go with them to the NAAFIs at other camps. I often found it difficult to restrain myself if they got into any trouble, which happened quite regularly, as it was generally considered an amusing pastime by other regiments to take the mickey out of the Pioneer Corps.

On one particular occasion, just before my first job up in the Troodos Mountains, a few of us were on detachment working at another camp and decided to visit their NAAFI. This consisted of a large tent about 30 by 70 feet, with a bar, tables and chairs. It was frequented by lower ranks and some lesser NCOs. The bar had a jukebox and besides beer and soft drinks it also sold hot dogs and light snacks. Some of the larger camps had several such marquees.

Generally, people bought their drinks and went outside but on this occasion the tent was especially crammed with upwards of 60 personnel from a number of different units and regiments, including RAF, marines and some Americans. Apparently a few of the records on the jukebox had recently been changed by some Greeks and word had spread around that they had managed to get a copy of a record about the late Buddy Holly. This had been banned by his mother after his fatal plane accident, and naturally, because it was banned, everyone wanted to hear it. The Greek blokes had pressed several numbers on the jukebox so we had to wait until these records played through before the banned record came on.

As usual, I was drinking orange juice, unlike my pals and the majority of those around me. As the evening wore on and the beer flowed, a disagreement broke out between one of my pals and some RAF personnel sitting at a table behind us. It was obvious to me that something was about to happen but, despite my efforts to try to calm the situation down, my pals continued to swap verbal insults with the guys on the other table.

I just wanted to get out of the way and avoid any possible trouble. 'Look, come on you lot, let's take our drinks and go outside,' I said. They were playing dominoes and didn't want to leave.

'No, just stay here, forget about them.'

'Come on, Geordie, have another drink.'

'Aw, don't worry about them; we can handle them.'

'They're just a bunch of pouffy Brylcreem boys, anyway!'

The guys at the other table did not let up either as more people crammed into the hot, smoky marquee.

'Hey, where've you left your f...ing pick and shovel, chunky?'

The insults were coming thick and fast and I knew that things were quickly going to get out of hand. I was trying to concentrate on what my mates were saying to me while at the same time keeping an eye on what was happening at the table behind us. Suddenly, one of the RAF blokes stood up and grabbed a nearby fire extinguisher. As he brandished it above his head, it was obvious to me that he intended to bring it down on the head of my pal who was sitting next to me with his back turned. Swiftly standing up, I disarmed the RAF guy, cracked him across the jaw with the fire extinguisher and let him fall to the floor.

There were several corporals and some sergeants in the tent, and as I didn't want any trouble, I quickly propped the extinguisher against one of the tent poles, grabbed the guy, dragged him back to his table and flung him into his seat.

'And don't you lot get any bright ideas, either,' I said, leaning across the table to warn his mates. 'Otherwise I'll stick my pick right where it hurts!'

I quickly sat down again, hoping that in the smoky crowded tent my actions had been too quick for anyone to see what happened properly. Unfortunately, this was not the case.

'Whoa, what are you on, Geordie? I've never seen you do anything like that; I didn't know you had it in you. Give us a swig of what you're drinking, mate,' the guy sitting next to me said and slapped me on the back.

'I didn't do anything, I just helped him back to his seat,' I said, trying to make light of the situation.

'Helped him back to his seat!' one of my other pals exclaimed. 'Nearly put him through it, you mean.' As he was sitting across the table from me, he had watched the whole incident and immediately began to tell everyone what he had seen.

'He was like a bloody robot. Honestly, you should have seen it,' he went on. 'I've never seen anyone move like that. Show us what you did, Geordie.'

'Don't be daft; stop bloody exaggerating,' I told him. ' I didn't do anything. He was drunk and overbalanced when I made a grab for the extinguisher. He must have hit his head as he fell.'

But the guy was nowhere as near drunk as the others, and was far from convinced by my explanation. He shook his head and kept on saying he had never seen anything like it. Luckily, none of the others had really seen anything; there had been too many people around and all they had been aware of was just a bit of a commotion behind them. Besides, they were so used to my general lack of involvement and avoidance of trouble that they all considered me a bit 'soft'. Unconvinced by the guy across the table's explanation of my involvement, they quickly lost interest in the whole thing and went back to their dominoes and drink.

'Don't be daft. There's no way Geordie could have done that.'

'Nah, he's just a lucky bugger; the other guy was pissed.'

The image that I was so careful to project of myself as being shy and quiet had helped me to bluff my way out of a potentially difficult situation. It also helped a lot that I had always been a bit of a loner, normally keeping myself to myself trying not to attract too much attention. Years of stuttering had seen to that.

The atmosphere in the tent was still pretty tense and it was obvious that it was going to get worse with the amount of beer that was being drunk. Besides, it was stifling, as more and more people shoved their way inside and the air became thick with smoke, and heavy with the smell of beer and perspiration. It was not too difficult now to convince my pals to go outside: it was much too crowded in the marquee. My training taught me that I always needed to be in a position where I could see exactly what was going on all around, so I was glad when they agreed to come with me.

We moved well away from the entrance to the marquee and sat on the ground with our backs against the piles of sandbags surrounding it. Although there was a lot of activity going on around the camp, compared to inside the marquee it was fairly peaceful. The light was just beginning to fade and the air was calm and relatively cool. We sat with our drinks listening to the records playing. Then voices began shouting excitedly, 'This is it, this is it!' Everything went quiet as the long-awaited record began to play.

As the gentle melody began, we settled back to listen to the softly singing voices. The song was full of emotion, in remembrance of the pop stars who had lost their lives on the ill-fated flight: Buddy Holly, the Big Bopper and Ritchie Valens.

Suddenly, the earth vibrated beneath us as the air was filled with a tremendous explosion, and I was flung forward onto my face, sandbags landing on top and all around me, as a huge blast inflated then collapsed the tent. Bodies, limbs, broken furniture and glass flew out, showering down everywhere. For a few seconds everything was still and quiet, then all hell broke loose and the air was filled with the sound of moans, groans and screaming.

I tried to get up but the heavy sandbags pinned me down. My whole body felt numb and I thought I must be injured but could not feel any pain. My mouth and eyes were full of dust and I was finding it hard to breathe. Gradually, I managed to move my head and took a full breath. I could just make out people running around, their voices seeming to come from a long way off. I couldn't hear properly; my ears were still ringing from the noise of the explosion. One at a time, I tentatively began to move each limb and quickly realised that I was not seriously hurt. With difficulty, I managed to push my way out from under the sandbags and struggled to my feet. I looked around me in total disbelief at the devastation; there was blood everywhere like splattered red paint.

Nearby my mates were also struggling to get out from under the heavy sandbags, and I was worried that some of them might be seriously injured. I immediately helped to pull the bags off them and checked that they were all OK. Like me, they were all shocked, and were anxious to find out if I was all right. But, luckily, none of them was hurt.

'Jesus, Geordie, what the hell was that? Are you OK?'

'Yeah, don't worry. I'm all right, I've just got a gob full of dust,' I reassured them.

'God, what a bleedin' racket! What happened?'

'Oh Christ, I'm deaf. I can't hear properly!'

'Bloody hell, it's a good job we came out when we did. Shit, look at that: what a f...ing mess!'

Nearby under the heavy canvas of the demolished marquee, people who could move were trying to find a way out and those who did emerge staggered about dazed and bleeding. By now my ears were beginning to clear and the air was filled with noise. Everywhere people were running around shouting. Red Cross, military police, NCOs : everyone trying to get to the injured people under the canvas. All that remained of the tent were the two end poles where it had once stood; the rest of it lay around in tattered shreds.

I went to help but was ordered away by an MP. He dragged me from the area and told me to go to the guardhouse along with others who were uninjured. There we were all searched and briefly questioned.

'Are you going to hold us here?' I asked one of the MPs.

'Why?'

'Well, we've been here all week on detachment and we're due back at our camp by 2300 hours,' I explained.

'Right. Show us your ID, then you can go. If we need you we'll send for you. Make sure you return immediately to your own units,' he ordered, brusquely.

Rumours were rife about the incident and that two British servicemen had been killed. It was widely believed that Greek terrorists had planted a large bomb in the jukebox and rigged it to go off when the banned record was played. By ensuring that several other records were played first, they had given themselves time to get well away. I had no way of knowing if this was the truth, but it sounded fairly plausible. As usual, to ensure that there were no repercussions and to maintain morale, the whole thing was hushed up by the military, and no official explanation was ever given. But after that, security around the camps was considerably tightened up, and a large number of Greeks working at camps were dismissed.

Another incident when I almost blew my cover had taken place some months earlier, shortly after we first arrived at the camp and I had begun my training with The Sixteen. It was to have a profound effect on one young soldier. I was on guard duty with several other lads and it was my turn for a sleep break. On this particular night, I was woken by the sound of a woman's blood-curdling scream and immediately rushed outside to join the others.

'What the hell was that?'

'I dunno. It came from over there somewhere,' a young soldier named Curran told me, white as a sheet and obviously very scared. He pointed to an area some 700 yards from the camp where there was a small brick building which housed an old generator. At that time, there was no barbed wire perimeter fence, nothing to separate the camp from the surrounding area. I wanted to investigate there and then, but the officer in charge insisted that we waited until first light in case it was a terrorist trap to lure us out of camp in the dark.

As soon as it was daybreak, he assigned a patrol to go out and investigate, which included both Curran and me. Checking carefully for a possible ambush or booby traps, we reached the hut and as we rounded the corner of the small brick building one of the lads in front of me opened the door. He took a step inside then instantly came flying back out.

'Urrgh! Jesus Christ! Bloody hell!' he groaned, and then abruptly pushed us out of his way as he began to retch noisily.

We cautiously peered inside. Sprawled across the top of the old generator was the body of a young Greek woman of about 18. Her throat had been slit to such an extent that her head was all but severed from her body, which was saturated in blood. Her skin had turned from what must have been a dark olive to a sallow, almost yellow colour. The officer in charge immediately yanked us all out and closed the door.

'Get back to camp, you lot,' he ordered. 'This mess'll have to be dealt with by the officers.' Subdued, we returned to the camp. None of us spoke: it had been a pretty horrific sight. Shortly after, the CO, several senior officers and the medical officer arrived to take charge and later that day I heard that people from the nearby village, probably relatives, had arrived to take her body away.

Naturally, the camp was soon buzzing with the news and all of the gory details. The rumour was that she had been killed because she fraternised with British soldiers, who to the Greeks were the enemy. Apparently, she had been seen by some of the locals in the company of British troops and they had meted out their own form of punishment. That was almost certainly the reason for her execution by the terrorists. Whether they brought her there specifically to kill her as a warning to the soldiers, I do not know, but it seemed to me a terrible waste of a young life and an awful thing for her own people to have done.

Even so, the sight of a young woman so brutally murdered did not physically or mentally upset me as it did many of the others who witnessed it. I returned to my tent and went back to sleep without any trouble.

A few weeks later, I was on guard duty with Curran again. He was a small, quiet guy of about 19 who looked as though he should have been working in a tailor's shop. I think the incident must have been preying on his mind over the couple of weeks since it had happened. At the time, though, he had said he was OK.

He seemed a bit quieter than usual but that was all. However, later that night while I was on a rest break, he suffered a form of breakdown, whether as a direct result of seeing that Greek girl or not, I will never know. I had just done two hours on first watch and was lying sound asleep on the top bunk in the guardhouse when suddenly I heard the loud crack of gunfire and all of the guardhouse lights went out. Immediately I dived from the top bunk onto the floor and found two other guys lying beside me.

There was a lot of shouting going on outside and we feared that it might be a terrorist attack. The two guys had their torches and switched them on as the door burst open with a crash and one of the other lads on duty rushed in.

'Where's the officer? Curran's gone crazy,' he yelled. 'It's him that's doing all the firing. There's bullets going all over the place; we can't get near the stupid bastard.'

'The officer's not here yet,' one of the lads replied.

'Well, something's got to be done before somebody gets killed. He's spraying bullets all over the bloody camp.'

'Are you sure it's him?' I asked.

'Yeah, it's him all right; he's gone bleedin' barmy.'

Just then, the gunfire stopped and we all dashed outside, the two with the torches just slightly ahead of me. We got to within a couple of yards of the sandbags, but I could not make Curran out properly. Suddenly he turned around towards us and the torches lit up his face. His eyes were wide and staring and he looked completely dazed. Immediately the bullets began to fly again in our direction, towards the torchlight, whistling over our heads as we dived to the ground. The torches were quickly put out.

'Where the hell did he get all the bullets from?' I asked, unable to understand how he had managed to get so many, as the amount issued to us was strictly controlled. It was dark and there were no lights where Curran was, but I could clearly see the bright flashes of gunfire from inside the round sandbagged bunker where he was firing his gun. I could also make out the dark shapes of several other men lying on the ground nearby.

As I watched him, I realised that he was moving around and around in a circle, firing at the sandbags surrounding his post. It seemed as though he was oblivious to everything around him and no one was able to get near to him for fear of being hit by a stray bullet.

Just then, I saw the flashes moving away from us, and leapt to my feet. I vaulted over the sandbags and disarmed him swiftly and without fuss before he or anyone else realised what was happening. As I took the gun from him, he just stood there, slack-jawed, his eyes glazed, not really aware of anything. Then he collapsed onto the ground. I picked him up and dragged him to the entrance of the bunker and stood there holding him for a moment.

'Medics! Where's the medics?' someone shouted, as the guys with the torches switched them back on and I saw that I was completely surrounded by men lying on the ground pointing their .303 rifles at me! It was a miracle that no one had been killed or seriously injured. Luckily, most of the bullets had gone into the sandbags.

When the medics arrived, they put Curran onto a stretcher and carted him off. I was still holding the gun. It was covered with blood and so was I, which I later discovered was from a wound on his left hand. He had trapped the end of his little finger in the slide mechanism of the Sten gun about four to five inches from the end of the barrel. This moves back and forth at high speed when the gun is fired, ejecting the used cartridges. He had been in such a state, he hadn't even noticed that the action had removed the first half-inch of his little finger! He had just kept on going round in a circle firing into the sandbags.

As soon as they took Curran away, I had to report to the guard-house to give an account of the incident.

'What's all this, Urwin? I haven't been away two minutes and I come back to find you've been jumping about like bleedin' Audie Murphy. What the hell do you think you're playing at?' the sergeant demanded.

'I haven't been playing at anything, sarge. He'd stopped firing and I just climbed over the sandbags and got the jump on him, that's all.'

'That's not the way I heard it. It was a crazy thing to do. Just who do you think you are, bloody Errol Flynn or something? Don't try that sort of thing again; you're not trained for anything like that.'

It was hard not to smile. 'Yeah, that's right, sarge, I'm not really trained for it, am I?'

A few days after the incident, I saw Sergeant Lupton crossing the parade ground, with that funny walk of his.

'Hi, sarge, any news on Curran?' I shouted to him.

'Well, well, if it isn't Geordie the hero. Taking a gun off a madman, eh? Bit of a crazy thing to do, wasn't it son?'

'It wasn't like that, sarge, it was empty. Anyway, how is he?'

'They took him to hospital at Nicosia,' he told me. 'It looks as though they'll probably discharge him in a couple of weeks and send him back to Blighty.'

He was right. We later discovered that Curran had in fact been discharged and sent back to England for further treatment. Although I felt very sorry for the young Greek woman, seeing her body like that didn't really bother me as much as it had others who talked about it for quite a while after. One or two of the guys made the odd remark about what they thought I did to disarm Curran but, after a few days, they lost interest. Nevertheless, I realised just how careful I needed to be so as not to draw attention to myself. During my next training session, I mentioned what had happened to Dynamo, Spot and Chalky.

'Oh, you mean the guy with the Sten gun?' Chalky said. 'Been doing a bit of practice on the sly, have you?'

'How the hell do you know about that?' I said, startled.

Dynamo leaned towards me and said quietly: 'We know when your toothpaste is running out, Geordie. We even know how many times you go to the bog.'

'What!'

'Only joking,' he laughed.

'Oh God, I wish you hadn't said that,' I groaned. 'I'll be watching everyone back at camp again now.' I had only just managed to stop thinking about who could be the 'inside man' at my platoon and now he had set me off again.

'I try to avoid getting into situations like that with Curran. But the harder I try the more it just seems to happen,' I explained. 'Besides, it's difficult not to tell my mates the truth when they're all talking about where they've been and what they've been doing during the week. Then they'll ask me what I've been up to and catch me off guard and I almost slip up and blurt out the truth.'

'Well, don't worry about it,' Dynamo said. 'They can't have any idea what is going on. As far as they're concerned you've just been digging another hole somewhere.'

'Anyway, if it bothers you so much, why don't you just tell them?' Spot said casually. 'But be careful.'

I was stunned. 'What do you mean, tell them? That doesn't make sense, Spot.'

'Well, Geordie, look at it this way,' he went on. 'Who's going to believe you, eh? It's so implausible. Just imagine you tell them that instead of delivering supplies around the island or digging roads, you were actually on a mission with a top secret unit, killing terrorists. They'll either think that you're kidding them or that you've gone barking mad like that bloke Curran. Just try it and see what their reactions are.'

Now I could see the sense in what they were saying; no one would ever believe me back at my platoon, even if I told them the truth. So, after that, whenever I got back to camp and Bill or Dave asked where I had been, I would joke with them.

'Oh, you know, just popped over to Cairo to sort a few of these Arabs out!'

It was strange. Actually saying it made me feel so much better somehow!

15. All together now

During the months following the operation in Cairo I was picked up and taken for training on a fairly regular basis, roughly every two or three weeks, but there had been no other missions since. Even so, our training was still as intense as ever and I was becoming increasingly restless.

I felt just as Spot had told me I would; I had not been the same since the job in Beirut. Killing that guy in broad daylight right under the noses of the guards and all of those people had really done something to me. It is hard to explain but I had felt great. It might sound crazy, but for me the next job could not come quickly enough; that was if there was ever going to be a next job.

That uncertainty was the one thing I did not like about being a part of all of this, the fact that I never knew if or when I would be picked up. I was living on a knife-edge, constantly keyed up, in a state of anticipation and disappointment. Every time they picked me up I thought this must be it, but for a long while, nothing happened.

This continued for some weeks. Then one Monday afternoon in the middle of a training session, the door of the hut suddenly burst open. Sweat was pouring off me and dripping into my eyes and I could just about make out the figure of Ken standing in the doorway with a big smile on his face.

'Well, lads, this is it! We leave for Jarâba tomorrow night,' he announced, rubbing his hands together.

I turned and looked at Dynamo. 'Where on earth is that?'

'I'm not quite sure, Geordie,' he replied. 'But I think it's somewhere near the Syrian border.'

'That's right, Dynamo,' Ken said, then turned to me. 'You've always wanted to meet the rest of the lads, Geordie. Well, you're going to meet the whole gang tomorrow night.'

'Great!' I said, grinning; this was more like it.

'It must be something pretty big if it's going to take all of us to do it,' Spot said.

'Well, it's big enough,' Ken replied. 'You'll be crossing through Lebanon and into the Israeli/Syrian border area. If things go wrong all hell will break loose.'

'What's the target this time, Ken?' Dynamo asked.

'Our intelligence is that a secret meeting has been arranged between some important civilians and military top brass, and if these particular people get together as planned, it will have enormous repercussions throughout the whole of the Middle East,' Ken explained. 'So it's our job to make sure that the meeting doesn't take place. We think they are up to something a bit naughty. That's why they don't want anyone to know what's going on, and why their meeting is taking place in the middle of nowhere. The fact that it's so secret will work to our advantage and make it much easier for us to get back. They won't want to draw attention to themselves by alerting the rest of the country to what is happening once we've interrupted their little get-together. My lads and I are taking care of the transport, so grab some tea and I'll go through the plans. There won't be time when you meet the others on the beach.'

Ken walked ahead of us into the office area, helped himself to a drink and sat down at the table where he spread out a number of photographs and a large map. The four of us followed suit and when we were all seated he began to outline the details.

'OK. We've got three things going for us: firstly, obviously the element of surprise; they certainly won't be expecting us. Secondly, although they're bound to be fairly well guarded, our information is that the place is surrounded by only a single perimeter fence; and lastly, the River Jordan is just about bursting its banks due to the heavy rain and snowfall up in the mountains around Mount Hermon.' Ken paused and sipped his tea before continuing.

'The bad news is that they won't all be there when we arrive;

two of them aren't due to get there until Wednesday evening. That means you've got a full day to make yourselves scarce. Right, here's the plan. I'll be here with the hack at 2300 hours tomorrow night to take you to within five miles of the mainland. A small fishing boat will be waiting for you there, which will take you to a deserted area eight miles south of Tyre.'

'Oh, no,' I groaned. 'Not Lynch and that flamin' boat again; I nearly broke my neck last time.'

'Never mind, Geordie, it'll be worth it for some of Lynch's greasy bacon and eggs,' Spot laughed. Ken finished his tea then continued.

'There's a railway and main road not far from the shore at that point; the other lads will be waiting for you there. I'm sure I don't need to remind you to make sure you are carrying nothing that will identify you in any way!' he said pointedly. 'You know the drill, no labels on your clothes, nothing that could indicate who you are or where you're from. Your watches and compass can be easily obtained anywhere so don't worry about them. I'll be back at the beach to collect you at 0100 hours Thursday.'

As usual I was curious to know more about the operation and how things were organised. 'Where does Lynch get the boat from?' I asked. 'Where does he keep it when it's not being used?'

'Forget it, Geordie, you don't need to know that, only that he will be waiting for you where I've said he'll be,' Ken smiled and winked, tapping an area on the map.

Dynamo, who had been shelling a hard-boiled egg as he listened intently to what Ken was saying, placed it on the corner of the table as he leaned forward to take a closer look at the map. The egg rolled off and across the dusty floor. Dynamo merely bent down, picked it up and stuffed the whole thing into his mouth. His cheeks bulged as he sat there chewing it, grinding bits of dust between his teeth then spitting these out of the side of his mouth. We all silently watched him in mock horror; he looked just like a hamster.

Spot nudged me. 'Ye knaa wot, he'd eat owt, him man, Geordie,' he said, in a near perfect imitation of my Geordie accent.

'Oh, very good,' I said, chuckling, then mimicked him in turn. 'You're spot on there, Spot, old boy!'

Dynamo looked at us indignantly. 'What's the matter with you lot? Waste not, want not: that's my motto,' he said with his mouth full. 'Anyway there's more to worry about than me and this bloody egg, what about those damn Israelis on the borders? It looks like we're going to be travelling pretty close to them, according to the route we'll be taking. You know how trigger-happy that lot can be!'

'There's no concern there, we've taken care of that and you won't be anywhere near them,' Ken replied, then continued. 'From your meeting point on the beach it's about 30 miles inland,' he said, taking the map back from Dynamo and spreading it out on the tabletop again. 'Bren will be driving a truck which will take all of you about 28 miles inland, to within roughly two miles of your target area just north of this place here, Jarâba, and not too far from the Jordan. You'll have to cross the river at that point then go on to your final destination on foot. Once you're across, you'll split up into your teams and meet up again at a pre-arranged rendezvous point up in the hills. There's the place and those are the co-ordinates,' he said, pointing out another spot on the map, as we each took notes.

'You shouldn't have any problems getting there, but getting back after the targets are taken out and the balloon goes up is when the trouble could start,' Ken said calmly and shrugged. 'We can't avoid that. The main thing you've got going for you on the way back is the damn river; you'll be able to cross it but they won't. That will be the key to you all getting back safely, as there isn't a bridge for quite a distance in either direction. As long as you all reach the river before they do, they shouldn't be able to follow you across. As I said before, there's been a lot of heavy rain in the area recently so the river will be really rough and totally impassable by ordinary methods. Anyway, some of the others will have booby-trapped the road, too, so that should slow up any of the buggers who make it that far,' he paused, grinning. 'You'll get an update on things at the beach.

'OK. Now, for the targets. There are actually five, and the least you know about them, the better,' he said, indifferently. 'As far as I understand, three of them are civilians and two are military. Rostin's team will be responsible for taking the targets out; the rest of you are there to assist them and ensure that he and his lads all get back out of the garrison in one piece. Believe me, they're really going to have a problem. The garrison is well guarded and there isn't much cover, just a small wooded area on the hilltop nearby.

'As you can see by the photographs of the place, it's going to be a hell of a problem for them just to get in, never mind take the targets out. We've really studied the place and it's just not possible for them to eliminate the targets without drawing attention to themselves, but that's not our problem: that's for Rostin's mob to sort out.' He slapped his hands onto his knees. 'And I'm really looking forward to seeing what they come up with.'

'Should be interesting,' Chalky murmured as Ken stood up. He went outside and returned a few minutes later carrying a couple of sacks, which he dropped onto the floor.

'Here's your gear,' he said, opening the sacks and pulling out four pairs of denim-type trousers together with four jerkin-style khaki tunics and a couple of Arab-style head-dresses. 'This is what you'll be wearing.'

'You'll need to take the usual stuff with you, set of ropes, cross-bow, pulley wheels, lines and dog-clips, and so on, and don't forget the veg grease, lads; you don't know what it'll be like near to the river. There's a new set of CTCs each in that wooden box, over there,' he said, pointing towards it, 'and the heavier fire power will be waiting at the beach for you.'

'Right then, my job starts now. I'll see you lot tomorrow at 2300 hours. Oh and by the way, make sure you have plenty to eat before we leave. It's likely to be all you'll get for a couple of days, apart from water and a few "dog-biscuits". And try to get plenty of rest tomorrow afternoon as well, you're going to need it, lads! See you tomorrow night.' And with that, he left as abruptly as he had arrived.

We continued with our training for the remainder of the day and turned in early. Tuesday passed uneventfully: we trained in the morning, then checked and prepared our gear in the after-noon, before eating and resting as Ken had suggested. By 2200, we were ready, dressed to look as much like the locals as possible, with our skin and hair darkened as on previous operations. We wore our sashes and boot knifes and stashed our MK1s with the rest of the gear in our holdalls together with a new CTC each.

Ken arrived with the hack promptly at 2300 hours and, as before, the helicopter created a huge cloud of suffocating dust when it landed. The four of us dashed forward and scrambled on board and he immediately took off. The noise was just as bad as I remembered it.

We swiftly flew out to sea and travelled uneventfully for roughly an hour before Ken indicated that we should look out for the boat. I couldn't see the actual shoreline but knew it was not too far away as I could clearly make out the tiny lights of villages in the distance. Dynamo was sitting in the front. He spotted the boat and nudged Ken who immediately turned the helicopter, dropped down low and headed towards it, then hovered overhead as we abseiled down onto its deck.

This time we all made it into the boat without any mistakes or mishaps. As before, once we were in the boat, Ken immediately took off, ropes still hanging, and the hack disappeared into the night.

Once the helicopter had gone and the noise from its engine and rotor blades faded, everything was quiet. The sea was flat calm and it was a warm still night, with a sky that was full of stars. There were no sounds other than the engine of the little boat as it sped through the millpond sea.

Lynch organised mugs of tea for us and as we sat drinking these, chatting, I looked around. It was pitch black. If it had not been for those few tiny lights on the mainland, I would not have known what direction we were travelling in. Just as we finished our tea Lynch pointed ahead.

'Righto lads, grab your gear: we've got less than half a mile to go.' How the hell he knew that was beyond me. I peered into the blackness, but still could not see the shore; it was just so dark. Minutes later he spoke again.

'This is it, lads,' he said and once more pointed towards the shore.

Just ahead of us, I could see a tiny red light flashing on and off. Lynch returned the signal then cut the engine and we drifted in the rest of the way until the bottom of the boat suddenly grated on the beach. Immediately two figures appeared out of nowhere and held on to it as Chalky and I jumped out of one side, Dynamo and Spot out of the other, landing up to our knees in water. We threw our bags ahead of us onto the beach and helped shove the boat back off the shore. It drifted slowly backwards, disappearing into the darkness. Then we heard its engine start and quickly fade again as Lynch sped off.

Picking up our holdalls, we began to make our way up the beach when we saw lights moving and flashing in the sky, like searchlights; vehicles were coming along the road.

'This way lads, quick!' one of the guys said, and led the way. We followed him for about 100 yards to the base of a railway embankment where I saw the huddled outlines of the others. There was a small, and very smelly, stream nearby but nothing else was visible in the dark.

'OK lads, get under here,' one of them said and they lifted over their heads a type of ground sheet, indicating for us to crouch underneath it too, as we heard a couple of trucks roll by along the road on the other side of the railway lines.

'That's been going on all night while we've been waiting here; it's the main road,' the guy nearest to me said. One of them produced a torch and switched it on, as another laid out a map on the ground. Seeing their faces for the first time came as quite a shock. They all looked so realistic, just like a bunch of dark and swarthy Arabs.

I sniggered, nudging Dynamo, 'Are you sure we've come to the right place?' The first guy spoke again.

'OK, chaps, we've got 10 minutes before the truck arrives.' It was weird to hear such a cultured and very English accent coming out of such a desperate-looking bunch.

'There's a sewer running underneath the railway and unfortunately we're going to have to pass through that rather than go across the top. We don't know when another vehicle might come along that road and we don't want to be seen crossing the railway lines,' he went on, pointing to the map in front of him. 'Now, we're here, there's the railway and there's the road; this is a bit of a dust track which is where our truck will be waiting. Oh by the way, lads, meet Geordie, 16.'

I wondered what he meant by that and nudged Chalky, raising my eyebrows.

'He means you're the last one in, Geordie,' he explained. 'You know, number 16.'

Still crouched under the canvas they all began to introduce themselves to me; it was a bizarre experience and I was dying to laugh. There they all were dressed up like locals but speaking perfect Queen's English, politely telling me the names they were known by in the group, as though we were at some vicarage tea party or something.

'Pleased to meet you, Geordie, lad.'

'Glad to have you on board, old chap.'

I felt a light kick on my backside and heard a voice behind us.

'Hey, Dynamo's bunch, grab this lot will you.'

There was a rattle of metal and, as we came out from under the canvas cover, a Sten was pushed into my hands, plus five magazines and some loose bullets. Dynamo and Spot were given .303 rifles, Chalky another Sten. It also looked as though they had been given several grenades. Quite a variety of weapons was being used, with each man having something slightly different from the others.

The guy who handed them to us spoke again. 'Don't forget, we want these back. Make sure you leave them in the truck when you return.'

Shoving the ammo into my bag, I slung the strap of the Sten over my shoulder and followed the others as they began to move off towards the large sewer pipe underneath the railway line. The pipe was about 30 yards long and roughly six feet in diameter; the stench inside was horrendous, and I felt my stomach heave. We stumbled and slid our way through, arms outstretched touching either side of the slime-covered walls as we followed the tiny red signal light of the guy at the front.

'Jesus, what a stink!' I said, revolted by the feel of what my hands were now covered in.

'Hey! Don't use that name around here,' someone said sniggering. 'You could start another bloody war.'

'What the hell do these people eat? It smells more like sheep dung.'

'Oh, you've tried the local speciality have you?'

There was a ripple of barely suppressed snorts and giggles from down the tunnel.

'OK, belt up, you lot,' someone said as we emerged from the pipe and gratefully filled our lungs with clean air before scrambling up the embankment to the road on the top. About 200 yards away I could just make out the tiny dots of vehicle sidelights and followed the others towards the waiting truck, tripping over loose stones and rubble on the rocky, uneven ground. Despite the fact that we now had the benefit of moonlight, it was still difficult to see.

At the back of the old army truck, which Bren had waiting for us, I threw my bag inside and was about to climb in when I felt a pair of strong hands grab me by the collar and hoist me up. I straightened up and I found myself face to face with a well built, strong-looking guy of about my own height, who leaned towards me to get a better look.

'Ah, you must be Geordie,' he said, shaking my hand. 'I've heard all about you.'

'I hope I got a good report,' I replied.

'That Cairo stuff, very clever, eh!' he said with a wink. 'My name's Rostin, by the way; I'll talk to you later.'

We settled onto the hard wooden benches fixed down either side of the truck and Bren drove off immediately. Half of the canvas meant to be covering the back of the truck was missing and from what I could see and hear, it appeared to be in a fairly dilapidated state. Each time we hit a rut or bump in the road the whole thing rattled so much that I thought it was going to fall to bits. I couldn't clearly see anyone's face in the poor light, but I could make out the shapes of the guys sitting opposite to me and was surprised to see that they all looked to be of about the same height and build.

Bren drove with the lights off, only switching them on every so often to make sure of his bearings. How he managed to see is beyond me. I was sitting next to the cab where a small square had been cut out of the canvas. Peering through this I tried to see through the windscreen, but couldn't make out anything other than a rough dusty track lined with huge rocks and boulders each time Bren switched on the lights.

'How the hell does he know where he is?' I asked.

'Don't worry, he practically lives here and knows the place

like the back of his hand; he's almost one of the locals. Nothing goes on around this area without us knowing about it; you could say he's our inside man,' the guy sitting next to me explained.

It was pretty rough going, as we jolted and bumped our way along the potholed track, and after about 15 minutes, it was obvious that we were climbing through a fairly mountainous area. The engine was straining and I wondered whether the old truck would make it. We travelled on slowly for over an hour and then began to descend steeply. Shortly afterwards Bren abruptly stopped the truck and immediately switched off the engine. Everyone jumped out at once.

'Righto lads, this is where I leave you,' Bren said. 'Try to keep in a straight line from here to the river. Don't go too far to the right; it's a bit marshy over there. You should find what's left of an old bridge only a couple of hundred yards away in that direction over there,' he said pointing. 'Dynamo, I'll be back for your lot early Thursday morning. Wait by those old ruins over there. I'll flash the lights twice and you'll know it's me.'

'What about the rest of them?' I asked Chalky.

'Everything's taken care of, Geordie, come on!' he said and made his way over to the others who were now huddled together near a group of trees on the hillside, checking our position.

'OK,' Rostin said. 'Let's get on with it.' And grabbing our gear, we started down the mountainside into the Huleh basin below. What little I could see of the area in the moonlight appeared to be flat open land. It was mainly dark and silent, the only sound being the roar of the nearby river as it ran through the valley below us. Judging by the noise of the rushing water, it appeared that Ken was right: it sounded pretty rough.

It was a cold, clear night; the moonlight seemed to have brightened a bit, which made it a little easier to see by as we headed towards the sound of the river. Gradually we began to see brief-flashes of water, silvery in the moonlight, and after about 20 minutes walking the firm ground began to soften beneath our feet. We had reached an area of marshland near to the river. It was beginning to get very cold now and I was very glad that Ken had warned us not to forget the veg grease. As we neared the tree-lined riverbank, the land rose a little and the marsh area gave way to drier, firmer ground.

'There are trees and bushes on this side but there's nothing for us to use on the other side at this point. So we need to find what's left of that old bridge Bren mentioned; it can't be too far away,' Rostin said. 'Once across, we follow an old track on the other side.'

Two of the guys immediately headed up river and another two went in the opposite direction to try to find the remains of the bridge, while the rest of us sat down to wait and tried to estimate just how wide the river was. It appeared to be about 30 yards across. After about 15 minutes, the two guys who had gone down river came back.

'We've found it, it's about 300 yards this way,' one of them said.

'You're right about it being old, Rostin; there's virtually nothing left of it, just a couple of posts sticking out of the ground,' the other added.

'OK, well let's hope there's something on the other side we can use then. Go and get the other two and we'll see you down there,' Rostin told him and we immediately set off south along the river-bank. After a few minutes we reached the remains of what had been some kind of bridge. The guys were right: there was very little of it left.

'Can you see anything on the other side?' Rostin asked, raising his voice slightly to be heard over the noise of the wide, swollen river as it rushed loudly past. Ken was right; it would be totally impassable for anyone using conventional methods of crossing.

The previously clear sky was beginning to cloud over and the moonlight was now intermittent. Even using our binoculars it was difficult to make anything out so far away in the dark. We waited for a few moments until the moon came out again.

'Look, there seems to be some kind of girder sticking about five or six feet out of the ground with another post just behind it,' a guy who had introduced himself to me as Reg pointed out. 'Can the rest of you see it?'

'You're right,' Spot said. The stubby remains of an H-girder stood out of the ground a few feet away from the edge of the embank-ment with another, smaller, wooden post sticking up a few feet behind it. Rostin scanned the opposite bank through his binoculars.

231

'Well, there doesn't appear to be anything else around,' he said. 'We'll just have to use that, Reg. Watch out for those bushes in the background. We'll get Spot to do this end of it.'

Reg and another guy named Den moved off about 30 yards further down the river until they were diagonally opposite the steel girder. Once there, they took out their light lines, crossbow and a snub-end bolt. Reg, the guy with the crossbow, fastened a light line to the bolt, the other end of which was coiled around a side spool attached to Den's belt. Den then positioned himself in the direction the bolt would take as Reg scanned the opposite bank through his binoculars in order to line up between the two obstacles on the other side, the steel girder and the wooden post. The object of the exercise was to fire the bolt between the two posts and a few yards beyond them.

All he needed now was a little bit of light from the moon and he waited until it came out from behind a cloud, then fired the crossbow. The line went screaming across the river and between the two posts as planned. Den stood where he was while Reg came back to let us know that they had succeeded. Although we had all been watching through our binoculars, it was still difficult to see the line lying there.

'OK, Spot, you're the man for the job, get yourself here,' Rostin said.

Spot also had a fixed side spool attached to his belt and immediately began to pull line off it, measuring out what he estimated to be the width of the river (his speciality) and allowing for a couple of yards past where we believed the line to be lying. We could not afford for his line to go any further than that in case his pick-up arrow became entangled in the several small bushes directly behind the posts.

When he had measured off the distance of line he required, he tied up the remainder of it on the fixed spool so no more would reel off. Then, picking up his crossbow, he dropped to one knee, and carefully placed the pick-up arrow in it before firing across the river. He aimed just to the left of the steel girder and slightly beyond, where he believed Reg's line to now be lying on the ground.

Spot's line also went screaming past the post on the other side then suddenly tightened and came to an abrupt stop before dropping to the ground. We could not see if it had in fact crossed the other line but Spot-On was not called that for nothing!

Slowly he began to pull the line towards him. If everything went to plan, the pick-up would collect Reg's line lying on the ground as Spot pulled it backwards. As he continued pulling, Reg came rushing back to us.

'It's on, it's on, it's picked up!' he exclaimed.

Spot grinned and winked at me. The line attached to the spool on Den's belt had begun to tighten as Spot pulled on his line, so Reg had immediately known they had been successful. Now Den began to release more of his line, as Spot pulled Reg's arrow over towards us. As it reached us, Den came back along the riverbank; his light line was now looped around the girder on the opposite bank and coming back to us. Spot removed the snub-nosed arrow that Reg had fired across the river, and tied our heavy abseil rope to Den's light line.

Now Den began to reel in his light line, bringing with it the attached heavy line, which looped around the girder on the opposite bank and came back to him. All we had to do was to tighten the heavy line using our pulley wheels and fasten ourselves on to the rope with our harnesses.

The whole exercise took merely minutes to execute and enabled all of us to cross the swollen, fast-flowing river in absolute safety, without getting wet. By using this method, it was impossible for any of us to fall into the river. Once the last man was across, a couple of the guys released the tension on the main line, allowing it to sink beneath the river. Then they scrambled down the embankment, pegged down the main line and hid the coiled remainder of rope in some bushes, thereby ensuring our method of escape.

The whole process was carried out quietly and efficiently. Hardly a word was spoken; no one gave any direct orders; it was unnecessary. We all knew exactly what to do and how to do it, and we all had the same capabilities.

On the other side of the river, a narrow track led away from the remains of the bridge. We followed it for about 500 yards to where it made a T-junction with a much broader, and by the look of it, fairly well used, dusty road. This road we knew led up into the hills and eventually to our objective, no more than half a mile away, with the town of Jarâba itself further south of this position.

In order to avoid detection, we now broke up into our groups and fanned out, all heading in the same direction, to our pre-arranged rendezvous point in the hills.

16. Jarâba

The earlier cloud cover had now passed by and the night became bright and moonlit once again. The air grew colder the higher we went but the steep climb up the hill kept us fairly warm. As we neared the rendezvous point, the road began to run around the base of a hill, over the top of which we saw a faint glow of lights obviously coming from the other side. It was time to get away from the road and into the sparse trees on its lower slopes.

As we began to climb, the trees increased in concentration until, as we neared the summit, they eventually formed a small thicket, interspersed with dense undergrowth and bushes. Our rendezvous point was just over the hill and slightly down the other side and as we made our way towards it through the trees, we could clearly see the garrison in the valley below us, about 400 yards down the hillside to the left of some old ruins.

Just below the brow of the hill, we came across Rostin and his lads crouched in the undergrowth and joined them, just as Reg and the others came through the trees to our right. For some time, we all sat quietly looking through our binoculars closely observing the scene below, taking everything in.

The garrison was built on a level area in a valley sheltered on three sides by the surrounding hills. The main gate was directly opposite our position and only yards from the side of the road that we had followed up through the valley. It wound its way around the base of the hill where we sat, past the garrison and continued on to the nearby ruins.

The garrison perimeter appeared to consist of a single mesh fence with barbed wire strung along its top. As Ken had pointed out, it looked to be a very flimsy and hastily thrown together affair, which was a surprise as we thought there might have been something far more substantial. Several vehicles and lorries were parked in a compound area just inside the fence and behind them was a two-storey building, which looked to be built out of breeze-blocks. To the left of this building was a cluster of smaller huts and outbuildings. To the right and outside of the perimeter fencing were the dilapidated remains of an old village. The compound area was well lit by several rows of light bulbs strung across it, suspended from wire.

The main gate was manned by two guards; a further two men were stationed outside of the main entrance to the two-storey building, while a guard with a dog casually patrolled the compound. They all appeared to be fairly relaxed, smoking and chatting to one another, clearly not expecting any trouble.

To the left of the main gate, inside the perimeter fence stood a small wooden-sided building. It was roughly 30 yards along the fence near to its corner, and about 15 feet away from it inside the compound. The structure had a two-foot gap right around it between the top of its walls and its corrugated tin roof, with a smaller gap between the bottom of the walls and the ground. This was obviously their toilet block, judging by the number of visits made to it by various soldiers who all emerged adjusting their clothing.

By now we had settled more comfortably into our position in the woods, opposite the main gate, from where we could continue to monitor movement within the compound. There were lights on in several of the rooms in the two-storey building, which made it easy to see what was happening inside each of these through the windows. Most had very little in them. However, there was a lot of activity going on in the last room on the second floor.

This was a big room at the end of a corridor. It had large, wooden double doors onto the corridor, which stood open, and opposite these, the rear wall of the room was draped with two flags. Although it was difficult to make out exactly what these were, we believed one of them to be Syrian. Most of the room was taken up with a huge polished wood table, surrounded by high-backed chairs.

'I think that looks like the room where the meeting's scheduled to take place. It would have to be the one at the farthest end of the building,' Rostin grumbled quietly.

'There isn't much going on down there at the moment, Rostin. I don't think we're going to learn too much more just now,' Dynamo said. 'I think we should get as comfortable as possible and try to get a couple of hours' sleep.'

'Yes, I think you're right,' Rostin agreed. 'Spread out a bit, lads, and get yourselves something to eat.'

A couple of the lads stayed on guard, while the rest of us settled down as best we could. We awoke to a truly breathtaking view. The early morning sun was shining on Mount Hermon in the distance to our north, tingeing the snow-capped peaks and slopes with a soft, pink-edged, gold. It was a beautiful and unforgettable sight.

'Well, it's your show, mate. How are you and Greg going to tackle it?' Dynamo asked Rostin, as he and a dark, broad-shouldered guy I took to be Greg joined us as we sat eating our meagre breakfast of dry biscuits and water.

'Well, it's obvious that the security here stinks; the place is lit up like a Christmas tree,' Rostin said in disgust. 'There's no one checking the hills overlooking their compound. It can't possibly be a military base, it's got to be some kind of old storage depot. Have you seen the gear that's lying about! The two military guys won't be here until later this evening and the only activity going on appears to be that lot going to the bog. There's another toilet block further back, which looks as though it's probably for officers' use only.'

Chalky had been watching the building through his binoculars. 'Take a look at this lot, the lucky swine,' he said. 'I bet they're not having what we're having!' Several civilians had entered one of the smaller rooms and were either sitting around in comfortable-looking armchairs or at a table laid out with food. They were obviously having their breakfast too.

'Never mind the "Last Supper"; this is going to be their last breakfast,' Spot joked.

'OK,' Rostin said. 'From what I can see it looks as though we need to get into that big room at the end on the second floor without anyone suspecting anything. The lads have had a look around and can't see another way in or out of that building, except for that one main door where the guards are, so no one should be able to sneak out the back if any trouble starts.'

Greg agreed with him. 'We can't wait until they're leaving the compound because they could be in there for a couple of days. Besides, they may not all leave together. So we'll have to take them out while they're having their meeting and they're all in one place.'

'Right, lads. This is what we've come up with,' Rostin continued. 'Greg and I have been studying their movements and as I said they all seem to be using this bog over to the left on a fairly regular basis. So, we've decided that I'm going to be the one to go in. I need to get into that bog and then if I can make them believe I'm one of their guys, I should be able to get into that room on my own. But I'll need everyone's help, including theirs.'

'What do you mean? How are you going to do that?' Dynamo asked.

'Well, this is the idea,' Rostin began. 'As I said, they're using that toilet block really frequently and most of the guys using it are coming from those huts in the background. Some of them go straight back to the huts again, but I've noticed a few of them are going into the large building and the guards don't seem to be taking very much notice of them. Now, before I make a move I need to know when the VIPs are all in that end room, because I need them all together, I don't want to have to look around for any of them. Greg and I are going to make our way down near to the corner of the fence over there at the rear of the toilet block. We'll put a hole in it under cover of dark and then I'll go through.

'Once we know all the brass are in that office, I'll get into the toilets from the back by using one of those vents in the top. From there I won't be able to see if anyone approaches the bog, but Greg will be in a nearby position where he'll be able to let me know if someone's coming. Actually, it would be better if someone does come when I'm in there, because the guards will then be expecting someone to leave. But I don't think it'll matter too much; they only seem to look in this direction if someone leaving the bog makes a noise with the damn doors. If somebody does come in, then I'll take him out. When I leave I'll let my Sten drag on the ground and fasten my trousers up as I walk across the compound towards the guards, so that you'll all know it's me.

'Now this is where I'll need back up and you all come in,' he went on. 'When I get to within a few feet of the guards on the door, I'll need you all to open fire on the building. That way I should be able to get inside while they'll all be rushing around in confusion.'

'Don't waste any ammo,' Greg added, 'but it would be useful if you put as many vehicles out of commission as possible.'

'That's right,' Rostin continued. 'It'll take me about a minute to run up the stairs and get to that room. With luck by then they'll have knocked the lights off and in the dark and confusion they'll just think that I am one of them. As I said, there doesn't appear to be another exit so I should be able to get to the targets. I can assure you there'll be no one coming out of that room alive!' he said, emphatically. 'Besides, by the time they do realise that I'm not one of them, they won't be in a fit state to do anything about it. So, with a bit of luck, I should be able to walk straight through the building and back out again,' Rostin finished, confidently.

'Well, that's the best plan I've heard yet,' Dynamo said, sitting back on his heels.

'It's the only one you've heard!' Rostin exclaimed.

'That's what I mean,' Dynamo laughed. 'Well, it's your pigeon, old man.'

'How many do you think there are of them?' Spot asked. 'I've counted about 25 but I think there could be more.'

'Well, I counted 30,' Greg said. 'But they've been in and out of the buildings so many times during the night I think I might have counted some of them twice in the dark.'

'So, unless the late arrivals bring more, we think there's between 25 and 30 of them,' agreed Rostin.

'Piece of cake then, isn't it?' Dynamo said.

'There's one other thing we could do, but it would mean taking out the two military guys before they get into the compound then use their uniforms and go in as them. But I don't really think it's a viable option; we don't know how many of them there'll be, they could have a large escort with them and any sound from outside the compound would alert this lot down here. I think there's just too many risks involved.'

'I agree,' said Chalky, nodding. 'It's an option but there's too much that could go wrong.'

Greg nodded too. 'The thing with the first plan is, if they think they're under attack down there, they'll switch the lights off, as Rostin said, which means that he has a greater element of surprise because he's already going to be inside by then.'

Both of Rostin's plans were discussed in detail as we finished off our biscuits. We were all in agreement that the second option was not a good one for the reasons Rostin had already pointed out.

'We need to immobilise as much of their transport as possible, to lessen the risk of being followed,' Dynamo said. 'And take out as many of them as we can in the process.'

'We need to keep a look-out for approaching vehicles,' Chalky pointed out. 'It looks as though this road is fairly well used and we need to be sure whether it's them or not.'

'You're right,' Rostin agreed. 'If they drive right up to the main entrance of that building, which they probably will, that truck parked at the side of it is going to block our view of anyone getting out of a car, unless they move it before the targets arrive. If not, we won't get a good look at anyone entering the building from here.'

'We won't be able to make out who's in the car coming up the road by then either, even with binoculars; it'll be too dark. Why don't I go down and hide by the roadside. I should be able to see them from there if I can get close enough,' I volunteered.

'OK, Geordie, make sure you find yourself somewhere reasonably comfortable where you can clearly see that it's our targets as they pass you,' Rostin told me.

Chalky was sitting nearby. 'And watch out for the snakes,' he teased.

'Aw, man, if it's not crocs, it's flamin' snakes,' I grumbled, giving him a shove.

Careful to stay well under the cover of the trees, we spread out through the woods to fully check out the whole area. A couple of the guys moved over to more closely observe the far end of the camp near to the ruined village, while several others moved through the trees setting booby-traps and tagging these so we could all clearly see each location.

I spent most of the day with Chalky at the furthest side of the wood away from the camp, overlooking the road, the river and the surrounding valley. It was baking hot, even though we were in the shade of the trees most of the day.

At around 1400 hours I looked through my binoculars and spotted a motorbike about half a mile away, heading up the road that led towards the garrison, its rider dressed in military clothes. Chalky had also picked him up. The guards on the gate seemed to be expecting him, as they opened the gates immediately and did not stop or check him. The bike rider shot past them into the compound without slowing down and drove straight towards the guards at the main doors to the central building. He stopped and dismounted then passed over a leather despatch bag to one of the guards, before climbing back onto his motorbike and speeding off through the main gates again and back down the road the way he had come.

It was an hour before we saw another vehicle approaching in the distance, during which time I had taken out my CTC and laid its sticky surface on the ground in order to pick up a covering of dust, twigs and leaves for camouflage. I checked the road through my binoculars again and saw there were actually two trucks, not one as I originally thought, and both were laden with fruit and boxes. Leaving Chalky to keep watch, I cautiously made my way through the trees towards Dynamo and Rostin.

'There are a couple of trucks coming along the road,' I informed them. 'I thought it was them but it's only a couple of trucks delivering food.'

'No, it shouldn't be them, it's too early. They aren't due until about six,' Rostin said. 'What time do you intend to go down to the road?'

'I'll make my way down there at about 1730. I've spotted a good position near to where we turned off the road last night, Dynamo. The hill's pretty steep and rough just there so they'll probably have to slow right down; I should be able to get a good look at who's in the vehicles when they go past,' I told them. 'I want to get down there in plenty of time. If I leave it until we spot them from up here they'll be reaching the place I've picked out at the same time as me!'

I went back to where Chalky still lay in the undergrowth on the other side of the hill, watching the road. At around 1630, the two delivery trucks left the compound and drove down the hill and back along the road. I waited a further hour then, while Chalky went to tell the others that I was now moving into position, I pulled my CTC around me for cover and made my way down the hill to the spot I picked out earlier.

There was a hollow in the ground at the edge of the road, where I could lie fairly level with the surrounding area. It was on a slight incline at the brow of a small hump in the road about two yards away from the road edge. I knelt down at the edge of the hollow then fell forwards downhill and crossed my forearms, which pulled my CTC completely around me. Then laying my forehead onto my folded arms, I shuffled around a little to stir up the dust that would help to make sure I blended in with the surrounding area. Then I pulled the hood over my head so that I was completely covered.

As I was facing downhill, my feet were slightly higher than my head as I positioned my binoculars ready and lay looking through them down the road in the direction the targets would be coming from.

After a while I glanced at my watch. It was 1900 hours and I had actually lain there for an hour and a half. Our targets were late. I knew I would be virtually invisible to anyone looking down the road as long as I kept very still, but I was beginning to grow uncomfortable; I wanted to move and wished that I had not been so eager to volunteer. Keeping still was proving to be difficult due to the number of insects crawling over me, probably ants.

The light was starting to fade and even looking through my binoculars I could barely see along the road now. Suddenly I heard the sound of fast-approaching vehicles.

Damn, I thought, annoyed. If it is them, they are travelling too fast for me to be able to see anything when they pass.

I could just make out three vehicles speeding along the road: an army lorry then a car followed by another lorry. I felt sure that these must be our targets, but I had to be certain. The first lorry raced straight past me, five or six soldiers standing in the back. Then, to my surprise the other two vehicles came to an abrupt halt about eight yards away from me. There were about seven or eight troops in the back of the lorry and two of them quickly jumped off. I thought they must have spotted me. But, moving slowly, I cautiously looked around to see why they had stopped. None of them appeared to be doing anything in particular, just stretching, yawning and chatting to one another. The two on the ground had now decided to relieve themselves only yards from me.

The car in front of the lorry was dirty grey without any markings. It was difficult to see exactly how many occupants there were inside, as there was some kind of partition behind the driver. However, I could make out one man sitting in the back, dressed in military uniform, staring straight ahead of him and calmly stroking his chin. After about two or three minutes the car driver suddenly beeped his horn, banged his hand on the outside of the car door and waved on the driver of the lorry behind. Immediately both vehicles moved off, with the two soldiers on the ground rushing to jump back into the lorry only inches away from me.

As they passed, the man in the rear of the car turned his head sideways and spoke to someone sitting next to him; I caught a brief glimpse of the two men in the back. The descriptions of them Rostin had given me were right. It was them. Our targets had arrived.

I lay still for a while longer until the sound of the disappearing vehicles had completely gone, before I gradually raised my head and had a good look around. The light was quickly fading but I could see that the coast was clear. My joints were a little stiff and sore from keeping still for so long, and I was covered in dirt, dust and insects. But I could not wait to get to the top of the hill and, itching and scratching as I went, I quickly scrambled back to where Chalky was waiting for me.

'Well?' he queried.

'Well what?'

'Was that them?'

'Yeah, it's definitely them!'

'Thank God for that; I couldn't stand another day stuck on this damn hill. For a moment there I thought they'd rumbled you.

When I saw them stop and those guys jumped off the back of that truck I thought I was going to have to come down there and give you a hand. That would've changed our plans, now wouldn't it? What was that all about anyway?' he said.

'I haven't got a clue; the two guys who jumped off just took a leak.'

'Come on, let's get back to the others.' We quickly made our way through the trees to where the rest of the lads were waiting.

'It's them OK; Geordie made a positive ID,' Chalky announced.

'Good!' Rostin said. 'It's just as well you went down there, Geordie. We saw the vehicles arriving but the car stopped where we thought they would, right outside the door of the main building, behind that damn lorry, and we couldn't see who was in it.'

'I didn't think they were going to get that far,' I said.

'What do you mean?' he asked.

'Well, the VIP car stopped just yards in front of me for some reason. I thought they must have spotted me,' I told him.

'Oh, so that's what happened?' he said. 'We couldn't understand what was going on either. The first lorry stopped just after it rounded that bend for some reason and they waved to the guards at the gates then reversed back. The next time we saw them the VIP car was right behind them,' he informed me. 'Don't ask me what that was all about. I've been in the Middle East for some years now and I've given up trying to understand these daft sods.'

'I wondered what the hell was going on but I couldn't see from where I was,' I said.

'Never mind, at least we know they're here now. Let's find a way to get rid of them.'

The lights were on in both the building and the compound, and it was easy to see the whole area. Two men dressed in military uniforms were walking around accompanied by a civilian, but we could not be sure if they were our targets or not. They disappeared for a short while then made their way back to the main building. Through the two windows on the first floor, just above the parked truck, we could see several people sitting drinking and talking, but our targets did not join them. Instead, they had made their way along the corridor to the large room at the end, where we believed the meeting was due to take place. They stayed there for some time then left the room together, returning shortly after with seven or eight other people who all began to seat themselves around the table.

'That's definitely them,' Rostin confirmed, looking through his binoculars just as someone in the room pulled a blind down over the window. 'Right, that's it, let's go. Dynamo, don't forget to warn the rest of the lads: if I get out of the building alive, I'll be the idiot rushing towards the gate firing my gun above your heads, with a red light on my chest. And by the way that's not a target, it's just to let you know that it's me,' he laughed. 'So, just make sure you don't get rid of the guards on the gate, I'll need them to open it for me,' he added.

'He might be a little bit crazy, but he's bloody clever,' Dynamo laughed.

'Come on, then, let's get on with it,' Rostin said to Greg.

We watched them stealthily make their way down the hillside, across the road to the corner of the compound and the darkened area at the rear of the toilet block. Then they disappeared from view. The rest of the group were getting ready to cover Rostin and Greg and Dynamo moved off to tell them what was happening. I looked at my watch; it was 2100 hours and very dark now. As soon as everyone was aware that Rostin had made a move, we all began to get into position and line ourselves up across the hillside in front of the compound. Each section had a target area of the building, mine being to cover the main entrance and to take out the nearby vehicles.

I moved slightly further down the hillside and got as close to the main gate as possible without being seen. Dynamo was just behind me to my right with Chalky, Spot and another guy slightly higher up. The others positioned themselves at various points to the right and left overlooking the compound. Greg would provide cover from his spot down to the left of the main gate near the toilet block.

Within minutes, we saw Rostin squeezing his way through the gap at the top of the toilets, out of sight of the guards on the gate. Just then, a soldier began to make his way across the compound towards the toilet block and we watched anxiously as he went inside.

Suddenly we heard the loud bang of a door being slammed shut and a figure emerged. The man appeared beneath the compound lights and began to walk towards the soldiers standing guard at the main door, dragging his gun along the ground and fastening up his clothing as he went. It was Rostin. He had done it!

'Let's wait until he gets within a few feet of those guards before we open fire.' Dynamo said quietly. 'Because once we start shooting, so will everyone else and I want to make sure he gets into the building.'

Rostin was only about four feet away from the guards on the main door when Dynamo opened fire at the windows and all hell broke loose as we all followed suit. The two guards at the door immediately ran into the building with Rostin right behind them and all the lights in the building went out. Confused soldiers began to pour out of the buildings towards the rear of the compound, running in all directions, yelling and screaming at one another. The guys lobbed grenades with deadly accuracy, and vehicles exploded all around the bewildered, panicking troops.

I hit the large truck parked at the side of the building, aiming at its tyres and where I thought the fuel tank was. It instantly burst into flames, just as a loud explosion came from inside the building and a body came flying out of one of the upstairs windows. It landed on top of the burning canvas covering the truck, which must have been carrying extra fuel because it suddenly erupted in a deafening explosion which sent fragments shooting high into the air and all over the compound.

The light from the burning vehicle brightly lit most of the area and we could see the poor bastards running around like ants. They had not expected a thing and were being slaughtered. They simply had no idea what was going on and where all of the gunfire was coming from or in which direction they should run for cover. It was like shooting fish in a barrel. Everywhere was noise, confusion, screams and yells.

'Concentrate on the entrance of the building,' Spot yelled. 'We'll need to give Rostin as much cover as possible when he comes out.'

Suddenly through the smoke and flames, I saw a guy running towards us, a small red light on his chest.

'There he is! That's him,' someone shouted behind me.

Rostin was out of the building and running towards the gate waving his gun in the air! We could clearly hear him above the noise shouting in Arabic at the two guards hiding near the gates. It was unbelievable; one of them actually ran towards the gates and opened them for him. Rostin immediately ran straight through, closely followed by the two soldiers who had been guarding the gates, with four or five other guys several yards behind them.

On the hillside, we were constantly moving and changing our positions to ensure none of us got hit if one of them got a bead on us, and I was now only yards away from Rostin and the following troops. I took aim to provide him with cover and take out as many of them as I could but Dynamo suddenly grabbed my arm.

'No, Geordie, wait,' he shouted.

At that moment, the ground in front of Rostin erupted and two figures stood up blasting the running men behind him just as he passed them. Two of his team had been lying in wait in their CTCs, which ensured they were completely hidden from everyone, including me. Lit up by the flames in the compound, from where we stood they looked like two giant hamsters standing up on their hind legs. They turned and immediately began to follow Rostin and ran with some difficulty down the road in the cumbersome coats, trying to undo the leg fastenings as they went.

Dynamo and I followed them with Greg closely behind us and, as we rounded the base of the hill, the others caught up with us.

'Take your time,' someone said. 'They must think there are hundreds of us.'

'Well, they certainly don't seem to have much transport left,' Rostin laughed.

We'd destroyed every vehicle in the compound. We briefly grouped together at the side of the road as Reg and Den removed their CTCs.

'You could have let me know they were down there,' I said to Dynamo. 'I nearly bagged one of them.'

'They went down there when you were watching by the road-side. Bloody good camouflage though, isn't it?' he laughed as we put our gear into our bags. 'Is everyone here? Everyone accounted for? Right, let's get the hell out of here and back to that damn river.'

As we made our way along the road we heard several explosions behind us; the lads' booby-traps on the hillside were obviously working. Back at the river, we headed slightly farther upstream of where we believed the old bridge and our ropes were, then worked our way down so we did not miss them in the dark. Without any great difficulty we found the spot, and were surprised to see that the river had risen by almost another two feet in the short time we had been away. We were lucky that it hadn't washed our ropes away, but it wouldn't have mattered anyway. We carried plenty of others and would have had no problems in repeating the process.

We swiftly crossed the river and the last man over tied the heavy line to both the wooden post and the H girder as we set up the pulley wheel system on the other side and tightened this to enable him to cross safely.

Meanwhile he had tied a light line to the dog-clip on the heavy line and brought the light line across with him. We then released the pulley wheels and slackened the line off, which enabled us to retrieve the dog-clip with the heavy line attached. Again, the whole process was accomplished in a matter of minutes and there was no trace left behind that we had ever been there. Once on the other side, we briefly discussed the operation with Rostin as we packed up our gear.

'Well, what happened?' Spot asked.

Rostin grinned broadly. 'I couldn't believe it. When you lot opened fire, I followed the guards into the building and got to the top of the stairs before the lights went off, so I managed to get a quick look around. I was lucky. There was such a commotion and racket going on that no one in the other rooms took any notice of me. They were all too busy trying to get you lot, so I just ran along to the end of the corridor and took out the guy guarding the room. They'd locked the door so I blasted it and lobbed in a grenade,' he said in a matter-of-fact way. 'Sorry I took so long but I wanted to make sure that I'd got them all before I left and it took a few minutes to check them using my torch. The five targets were definitely in there and I'm positive the other three were European. I wonder what the hell that was all about.'

'Well, we'll never know now,' Chalky said.

'So what, it's their fault they were there. At least we got the job done,' Greg said.

'There was so much noise and confusion I could have taken out everyone in the building; they just didn't have a clue what was going on,' Rostin continued. 'On the way back, I think I took most of them out in the rooms along the corridor. They were all firing out of the windows so it wasn't a problem. Besides, with all that racket going on they wouldn't know whether the bullets were coming from the outside or not,' he added. 'I definitely got all of them in that last room with a grenade just before leaving. I thought I might as well keep the numbers down and help you chaps out a bit,' he said, laughing.

'So that's why that guy came flying out of the window and landed on the top of that burning truck,' I said to Dynamo. We all crowded around Rostin to congratulate him, slapping him on the back and shaking his hand.

'Well, lads, this is where we part company,' Dynamo said. 'We can't stay here chatting all night.'

'No, you're right,' Rostin agreed. 'Well, Geordie, we didn't get our little chat but I'm pleased we met at last.'

The guys all shook hands, then, picking up our holdalls, we split up into our teams each heading off into a different direction. I had no idea where the others were going and by now I knew it was a pointless exercise to ask. All I was interested in was getting back to the truck and onto the helicopter. Dynamo, Chalky, Spot and I merely had to retrace our steps back across the valley to the rendezvous point on the top of the hill. There Bren would meet us later with the truck; we didn't expect to encounter any problems on the way and had plenty of time to get back.

As we moved away from the riverbank, we heard a commotion some distance away on the opposite side. They were apparently searching the area for us but we knew that there was no way they would be able to follow us across the river at this point, even if they had any idea where we were, which they obviously did not.

Although the trek back into the mountains was a steep climb, the four of us took very little time to reach the rendezvous point near to the ruins that Bren had pointed out. With plenty of time to spare before he was due, we sat down for a well-earned rest and after a short while I needed to take a leak.

'I won't be a minute,' I told the others as I got to my feet.

'Just make sure you're down wind,' Chalky called after me.

'And watch out for those snakes,' Spot sniggered.

'Oh, very funny,' I called back over my shoulder. 'You and your flaming snakes.'

'And scorpions,' Dynamo added.

The nearby dirt track ran between the steeply sloping hillsides and on the other side of it, at the base of the hill, I spotted a clump of convenient bushes and made my way across to them. Further down the track I saw a flash of light. Bren must be early, I thought, and carried on with what I was doing.

As I started back across the track, I heard the sound of an engine then saw another flash of light as a truck slowly made its way around the base of the hill. I stopped where I was in the middle of the track and waited while the truck drove right up to me then stopped a few feet away. I couldn't make out the driver with the headlights shining in my face but I heard the sound of the door opening and someone making their way towards me. To my surprise, a voice called out to me in Arabic.

Very funny, Bren, I thought. Again, the voice called out. I had no idea what he was saying. I called back. 'OK, OK, cut the joking, Bren. You know I can't understand a word you're saying.'

The man was fairly close to me by now and I suddenly realised that it very obviously was not Bren. The passenger side door opened and the guy turned to jabber something to another guy behind him. There were two of them.

Just as I was about to take the first guy out, I noticed that the second man was holding something in his hand. It looked like an iron bar but I couldn't quite make it out because of the headlights behind him. By this time, I was standing directly between the men in front of the truck and where I had left the others. I knew they wouldn't be far away but would not want to show themselves at this stage. They would not be able to use any firepower either because I was in their line of fire. Besides, we didn't want to draw attention to ourselves; a gunshot could be heard a long way off.

I quickly decided to let the second man get nearer to his mate so that I could deal with them both at the same time; I knew I could handle the situation easily. At that moment, I saw a glint of metal in the headlights and realised that the second guy was actually holding a knife. The first man spoke again, then the second guy lunged straight at me. In that instant, the machine took over.

I blocked the knife with my left hand and swivelled on my left heel in order to swing my right leg behind me. But my right heel caught on a large stone and I couldn't get it completely out of the way. The knife was longer than I thought and I felt a sharp agonising pain as it thudded into my thigh, penetrating down to the bone. Despite the acute pain, I hit underneath the man's nose hard with the base of my right hand, pushing the nose bone towards his brain. He instantly crumpled to the ground, pulling the knife out of my leg as he fell. In the seconds it had taken for this to happen, the lads had quietly despatched his mate.

Chalky and Dynamo grabbed my shirt then dragged me off the track towards a pile of rocks and lay me against them.

'Kill the bloody lights on that truck, Spot,' Dynamo said, as Chalky ripped open the top of my trouser leg, which by now was saturated in blood. The pain was excruciating, waves of nausea and dizziness washed over me and my leg felt like a solid lump of lead.

'This would happen when everything's gone perfectly so far,' Chalky commented wryly as he closely examined the wound.

'Trust me to mess things up,' I moaned back at him.

'Don't knock yourself, Geordie, this could have happened to any one of us. None of us are that clever; we've all got scars of some sort. Besides, it's the other guy who's dead, not you!' he reassured me. 'The trick is to get back alive.'

'Come on, Dynamo, give me a hand,' Spot said, dragging one of the bodies towards the truck. 'If we shove this lot over the side it'll look as though they've had a accident.'

They loaded up the two bodies and pushed the truck off the track where it quickly disappeared and crashed down the steep hillside. They had just reached Chalky and me as we heard the sound of another truck, its headlights flashing off and on as it rounded the bend in the road. It stopped quickly and Bren jumped out.

'Where the hell have you been?' Dynamo asked him.

'What do you mean? I'm early!' Bren replied cheerfully.

'Not early enough. Shame you didn't get here 10 minutes earlier,' Spot told him. 'Never mind, you're here now; give us a hand to get Geordie onto the back of the truck.'

'What happened?' Bren asked, concerned.

'We had a bit of bother with a couple of locals and Geordie's been stabbed in the leg. We'll tell you about it on the way back,' Chalky said.

Bren produced a small first aid kit from the truck, which he gave to Chalky. 'Let's get out of here quickly, then,' he said.

Dynamo and Bren climbed into the cab of the truck while Chalky and Spot jumped into the back with me. Chalky gave me a couple of painkillers and then got to work on my leg. The journey back seemed to take forever, and I felt every bump and jolt, but by the time we reached our drop-off point near to the railway embankment the painkillers were working and my leg was not feeling too bad. Bren stopped the truck and came around to the back to help Chalky and Spot get me down as Dynamo took the guns out of our canvas bags and left them in a sack on the back of the truck.

'Take care, Geordie,' Bren said. 'Got to go, catch you later.' And with that, he jumped back in the cab and drove off.

Dynamo rushed ahead with the bags as Chalky and Spot hoisted me up, one arm around each of their shoulders, and dragged me along. My leg could not take any weight, which made getting back through the stinking sewer pipe incredibly difficult. It was pitch black and we had to go through it sideways, as it was only wide enough for one person to walk through properly. The stench seemed to be even worse this time, and for a moment, I thought I was going to retch. Dynamo came back after dumping our bags on the beach and shone a torch in front of us, which made it easier.

Once through, we sat on the sand for about 10 minutes before we heard someone coming towards us along the beach. Dynamo and Spot quietly got to their feet, ready for any problems. But it was Ken looking for us.

'What's happened here?' he asked.

'We'll tell you on the way. Let's get out of here,' Chalky replied.

'OK, this way. I've got the hack further along the beach; it's a bit too close to the main road just here. I've been here for about 15 minutes and there's been quite a few vehicles passing by.'

They helped me along the beach for about 300 yards or so to where Ken had landed, and lifted me inside onto the floor. Chalky put a set of headphones on me as the helicopter quickly took off, and both he and Spot clung on to me all the way back. We had had no sleep for over 24 hours and I was suddenly very tired. With the help of the painkillers and the constant drone of the engine, I quickly fell asleep.

The next thing I knew we were back at the hangar. Chalky had lifted the headphones off me and the racket of the helicopter woke me up. He and Spot helped me out and, as usual, Ken wasted no time in taking off. It was early Thursday morning and I seemed to spend the hours to lunchtime drifting in and out of sleep.

Chalky dressed my wound in a type of elastic bandage, which he wrapped right around my leg. The ends of the bandage on each side of the cut were sticky and laced up together like a shoelace. It was quite strange. I had never seen anything like it before, but it was very effective. He placed a lint pad covered with antiseptic onto the cut itself and laced up the dressing, drawing the edges of the wound together.

'It's a clean cut; it won't be infected and should heal up fairly quickly as long as you change the bandages every couple of days. Whatever you do, don't let anyone see this or you'll probably have to report sick,' he warned, as he gave me a couple of spare bandages and some more painkillers. 'That should do you. But make sure that no one sees this,' he said, pointing to the strange bandage.

'You'll have to work on that leg,' Spot said. 'We've got until four o'clock tomorrow afternoon to get you back on your feet.'

The rest of that day and the next I hobbled about, trying to put more and more weight onto my leg, and, by the time I was ready to leave I just had a slight limp. Once back at camp, I had the rest of the weekend to work on it. If anyone questioned what had happened, I decided to say that I had caught it on a broken bedspring. This was a fairly regular occurrence around the camp, so no one would question it.

17. Coming home

At 0900 hours on Christmas Eve 1959, I was sitting on the jetty at Limassol. The place was swarming with thousands of troops, all like me with their kit, all chatting excitedly about going home, all looking forward to it eagerly. But, gazing towards the distant, snow-capped Troodos Mountains, I sat quietly lost in thought.

'Oh, boy, I'm certainly going to miss those guys. I wonder what they're doing right now?' I said to myself. 'Could it be the end for them too? Perhaps they're sitting here in amongst this lot.'

I eagerly scanned the faces of the waiting troops but saw no one I recognised. I must have sat like that for 15 minutes when I felt a hand on my shoulder.

'Don't tell me you're going t'miss t'place, Geordie?' a voice said, close to my ear.

I turned quickly. For one brief moment I thought (hoped) it might be Dynamo, Chalky or Spot, but it was just Bill, sitting next to me.

'What's t'matter? You were miles away. You're not really going t'miss this stinking place, are you?'

'No, of course not, Bill,' I replied quietly. If only he knew, if only I could tell him what I was really going to miss and what I was going through right at that moment. It was as bad as the wrench I felt leaving my family two years before: similar yet very different, and for very different reasons. But I felt just as empty.

For the last 18 months, those guys had become the brothers I had never had: no one in my life so far had treated me the way they had. With them I had been a man among men. Yet we had never once discussed a single personal thing; they had merely accepted me for what I was, for what they knew I could be, for what I became. They had always treated me with respect, as their equal. With them I always felt that I truly belonged. The worst thing about leaving was the absolute knowledge that once I left there could be no turning back: I would never see them again.

I had hated every single minute of being in the army, the regular army that is, and was really longing to see my family again. But I had changed completely and part of me desperately wanted to stay behind with the guys. I had never wanted medals or glory, just the chance to prove to myself that I was not thick like my Dad thought. Ever since I was a kid, I'd always felt different, the odd one out. But I knew even then that I was better than what he said about me, that I was not, as he thought, stupid.

But now, when for once in my life I had done something that would prove just what I was capable of, I was completely unable to tell a soul about it. How could I? It would be to betray their trust and besides, who would believe me anyway? I was just a young Geordie lad doing his national service in the Pioneer Corps.

Now, sitting looking at the mountains with the moment of leaving only minutes away, I felt so alone and empty. There was a hollow, sickly feeling in the pit of my stomach. Is this the end then, or just another beginning? Just how far could I have gone with them, I wondered? One thing I was absolutely certain of: I would never, ever meet their like again.

It was a few weeks since I had last seen them, but it felt like only yesterday when Ken had told me the bad news. His words were imprinted on my brain. I will never be able to forget that day. It was the day that a part of me died, the day that for the first time in my life I wanted to shout and swear using every disgusting word in the book.

I had been collected and taken up to the old tin hut as usual but had been surprised to see Ken there as, on the way up in the jeep, Chalky had not said anything about there being a job on. Ken had said he wanted to see alone but I had never dreamt that it would be to tell me what he did.

He stood in front of me and immediately I sensed that something was seriously wrong. His whole manner was so different; his face had a look of sadness and he even stammered slightly as he began to speak.

'Er, Geordie, um, I don't want you to misunderstand what I'm about to say, but obviously I can't explain in too much detail because of security. When I heard that you wanted to sign on for another three years it really was the best news we could have received, and when I say "we" I mean all of us in this tin hut, as you call it.' He smiled briefly.

'Believe me, Geordie, it really was the best news. You surprised every one of us here, far beyond what we expected. So you see, Geordie, lad, you really were one of us more than you could ever imagine, which is why it's killing me to tell you this. But I'm afraid your time is up, old boy. You're going to have to go home with the rest of them, which really should be good news, shouldn't it? But it bloody well isn't.'

It felt as if the bottom had just fallen out of my world. I was speechless, totally dumbstruck by the shock of his words, and just stood there staring at him in utter disbelief. Surely he had to be joking, I thought. But I could see by his face that he was not. He looked utterly wretched.

'It's like this,' he went on, his voice seeming to come from a long way off. 'As you know, in February this lot buried the hatchet, the government allowed Makarios back in March and has agreed to let this lot have their way. Early next year it's going to become a republic. National service is all washed up and your lot are off home soon. We've known about it for some time now but we were hoping that we could find a way around it. Believe me we've tried but it seems that there are some things that are impossible, even for us.

'You see, Geordie, if you signed on now you would be signing on for the regiment that you're in, but that whole regiment is now going back to Blighty and it will be very difficult for us to recall you. There are going to be some big changes for us too, but I can't say what they are. It has suited our purposes for you to be where you were and in the outfit you were in. Although 518 Company will be staying behind, the things which have helped to make all of this possible won't be here then, so even getting you transferred to them would be pointless, if you understand what I am getting at,' he said, meaningfully. 'The changes about to take place on this island are going to affect all of us. We have to have you where we need you, Geordie, and that just isn't possible with your regiment being sent back. I'm afraid that the only thing that you're going to get out of this, Geordie, is some crummy active service medal,' he said, his voice heavy with sadness.

'No, Ken, no!' I burst out, suddenly finding my voice. 'Don't say that, it's not true. You're totally wrong, I've got something that I've wanted all of my life. You've made me what I've always wanted to be, you've given me what I've always wanted – my confidence. All I ever wanted was pride and self-confidence and it doesn't matter to me if no one ever knows, I'll know it. That's the only medal I want and believe me, Ken, I'll wear that badge with pride for the rest of my life.'

For the rest of that afternoon we did nothing. The five of us just sat drinking tea, laughing and talking about the jobs we had done, the places we had been together and how we had made fools of them all. The lads did their very best to cheer me up, but nothing really could. A huge part of me had died.

I knew that they, like Ken, were genuinely saddened by the situation. I left them as I had joined them, knowing nothing more about any of them than that they were, beyond a shadow of a doubt, the finest, most remarkable men I would ever meet.

They each shook my hand in turn, not saying much. I just could not speak, I was choked, totally gutted by the fact that I would never see them or be with them again.

I had thought long and hard about signing on and believed that it was merely up to me to make a decision and that once I had, they would be able to sort everything out as they always had done before. It had never occurred to me that anything like this might happen.

Ken placed his hand on my shoulder, his gaze steady and direct, and his voice heavy with regret. 'You were a soldier of the future, Geordie,' he said. I did not quite understand what he meant. 'Things will be different, believe me; one day you'll see. Look after yourself, lad.' Then, turning quickly, he walked away without looking back.

'Take care, Geordie.' Spot spoke quietly and gripped my hand, then he too turned and followed Ken.

Dynamo shook my hand vigorously and leant over to whisper

in my ear. 'I'll tell you a secret, Geordie. I come from the place where they make the best cheese,' he said quietly, then stepped back and looked directly at me. 'Never mind, nothing lasts for ever you know, does it? But we certainly showed them how it was done, eh?' he said with a wink. Then he too turned away and was gone. I stood rooted to the spot.

'Come on, Geordie, time to go. Let's not hang about,' Chalky said quietly and for the last time I climbed into the jeep alongside him.

'You were the best, Geordie, the fastest learner I've ever seen. Always remember that,' he said as he started the engine.

'You don't have to try to cheer me up by saying things like that,' I told him, my throat constricting as eventually I managed to speak.

He shook his head. 'No, honestly, Geordie, believe me. I'm serious.' We did not speak again until he stopped to drop me off. 'Take care, Geordie,' was all he said, then winked and spun the jeep around and drove off in a thick cloud of dust. I just stood there watching him disappear, shocked and numb.

I was supposed to have been working at another camp that day and waited at the side of the road for the working party truck to come by and pick me up. I wanted to be on my own, not with a bunch of noisy joking blokes. For a while I sat quietly, not joining in or making conversation with the other lads.

'Cheer up, Geordie; it might never happen.' The lad next to me poked me in the ribs. Suddenly I remembered what Dynamo had whispered.

'Where do they make the best cheese in England?' I demanded.
'Eh! What do you want to know that for?' he asked in surprise.
'Never mind! Where is it?'
'Well, there's stacks of places, depends on what you consider to be the best, I suppose. There's Cheddar, Cheshire.'
'Lancashire,' someone else chipped in.
'Leicester.'
'Wensleydale.' Suddenly, they were all at it.
'Well, I like Caerphilly.'
'What about Derby?'
I burst out laughing as I realised that in the end Dynamo had

told me nothing about himself at all. I thought he had broken the rules, but I should have known better.

I looked up at the ship we were about to board, *The Devonshire*. It was a fairly small ex-passenger liner, which had been drummed into service as a troop carrier during the war. We were told that torpedoes had hit it on a couple of occasions and obviously it had not sunk, but whether this gem of information was to make us feel more secure or not was difficult to say.

Well, the enemy didn't get us but it looks as though some stupid civil servant probably will, by trying to save a few quid and cramming as many of us onto this old tub as possible, I thought. Looking at it, it seemed impossible to me that it could carry so many men.

'Not to worry, lads,' the officer in charge told us. 'We know it looks a bit on the small side but it was designed to carry 2,000 civilians and it's been altered to carry all of us.'

'Oh, well, that's made us feel a lot better, sir,' I said.

We were kept hanging around for a few more hours, for whatever reason nobody knew, before we eventually started to board the old rusty bucket. Fed up with having to wait around for so long, by this time most of us could not have cared less what it looked like, as long as it got us home.

Going up the gangplank ahead of Bill, I kept stopping and looking back. I had some stupid notion that a miracle might happen: that there would be a sudden change of plan and they would say that we were not leaving; that there were just too many of us and we had to disembark immediately. I hoped that somehow The Sixteen had managed to fix it. For once, I actually wanted to hear some big-mouthed sergeant calling out my name, telling me that I had to stay behind.

'Come on, Geordie, get a move on.' Bill nudged me. 'You'd think you didn't want t'go 'ome; are you sure you're not going t'miss t'place?'

We had been told that as soon as we boarded we were to go straight to our allocated sleeping quarters, but it was a struggle to get through the doors with our rucksacks and rifles. The sleeping quarters consisted of row upon row of hammocks and I quickly picked one near a porthole. There was nowhere to stow our gear so we just threw our things on the floor; dozens of us were crammed into a room probably designed to accommodate half a dozen civilians.

The majority of us went up on deck and hung around there until, after another couple of hours, we felt the ship move. A huge cheer went up and we watched as Cyprus, our home for the last 18 months, slowly and gradually began to fade from view.

I stood alone leaning on the rail and kept on watching long after most of the others had become bored and gone off elsewhere. Were Dynamo, Chalky, Spot and Ken up on that mountain somewhere practising, possibly sitting with their binoculars trained on the ship watching me, I wondered? Perhaps they were already off on another operation, or maybe, just maybe, they were here on board amongst all of these thousands of troops. And if they were, what would I do if I saw them?

The thought had occurred to me that they might already be training someone else, my replacement. But I really did not want to think about that and pushed it as far to the back of my mind as possible.

I was glad that it had all taken place, not from any political point of view, as I really neither knew nor cared about that and never discovered whether what we did actually made a difference, but for the change it had brought about in my life. It had given me the opportunity to become me.

Eventually, when I could see the island no more, I went to join the others, as there was not really anything else to do. Within minutes of going below deck, sweat was pouring off me. Now I just wanted to get back home as quickly as possible.

None of us had used a hammock before and we had a lot of laughs trying to get into them. By the time we did manage it, we were so worn out that we just lay there with our arms hanging over the sides chatting to one another, cracking jokes. This went on for hours until we finally docked at Malta, the place it had all really started for me.

Some of the lads went ashore in the brightly coloured gondolas that came alongside the ship. All they could talk about before they left was a place called 'The Gut', a notorious area full of bars and prostitutes. But that was not for me and after they went I lay in my hammock thinking. Nothing had changed for these guys: they were all two years older but none the wiser. Yet everything had changed for me and about me.

We stayed overnight in Malta and then were on the move again, our next stop being Gibraltar. About an hour out of Malta all hell broke loose: the sea became so rough that most of us were thrown out of the hammocks and crashed onto the deck. The waves were huge and *The Devonshire* was tossed about like a cork. Then the seasickness started. Hardly anyone escaped it and even those who did felt pretty rough.

It was with immense relief we finally docked at Gibraltar. Again some of the lads went ashore but most were just too ill to move. I was OK, just a little queasy. None of us thought it could get any worse than what we had just been through.

'If you think that was bad wait until we hit the Bay of Biscay,' one of the ship's crew cheerfully informed us. He was dead right.

We left Gibraltar and steamed into the Atlantic. Things were uneventful for a few days, then the ship began to be thrown about like a matchstick. It was much worse than before and I really felt sorry for the lads who had just recovered. Again, I was not actually seasick but it was a pretty awful few days. Apparently, even the captain was ill.

Eventually, the weather improved, and things settled down again after a couple of days, but by now everyone was worn out, bored and fed up with a journey that seemed to be taking forever. Suddenly someone came dashing in.

'It's land! It's Blighty!' he yelled. Everyone flew up on deck and there it was. At last, we were home. It was 4 January 1960 and the journey had taken us 12 days.

By now just about everyone on board was on deck, excitedly talking to each other. The sky was grey and leaden, it was bitterly cold and I was shivering, but I didn't care because I was almost home. The icy wind was clear and fresh and I felt that it was blowing away the last remnants of heat, flies, sand, dirt and sweat. It was wonderful.

As we sailed closer we began to see hundreds of people waiting there on the jetty, waving and cheering as the ship drew nearer. All of a sudden, everyone began dashing about, rushing below deck to grab their gear; we all just wanted to get off this flaming bucket as quickly as possible.

The ship slowed almost to a stop and then began its docking manoeuvres. We had to parade on deck as the gangplank was put in place. People were shouting and screaming as they saw their husbands, boyfriends and sons, and lads were shouting back as they spotted their families in the crowd. There was even a military band playing for us. The noise was incredible.

Everyone seemed to have someone to hug, someone waiting to greet him. I stood alone on the cobbled jetty glad to be back on terra firma, but I knew that there would be no one waiting for me. I glanced down at my feet and there to my surprise I saw words engraved on the piece of marble I was standing on: 'The Mayflower left here in 1620'. I stood there looking down at it, wondering for a moment what that ship must have looked like and whether any of those people felt as I did right now.

All around me lads were hugging and kissing their girlfriends, wives, mothers. I suddenly I felt very cold and desperately lonely. Although my mother had written to say she could not afford the fare down, it was still a bit of an anti-climax as I stood alone surrounded by a sea of happy faces. I could not help but think how lucky they all were and realised just how much I longed to be home to see my family for the first time in two years. It was a very long while since I had thought of my father but now suddenly he came to mind. What a shock that little waster's going to get when I get back, I thought. His days as a tough guy are well and truly over.

I took one last look out over the sea and thought of Dynamo, Chalky and Spot, then made my way with everyone else towards the huge convoy of waiting trucks. It had been two long, incredible years. But now I was going home and back to reality.

Appendix: Background
to the Middle Eastern conflict

19 October 1954
Egypt and Britain conclude a pact on the Suez Canal, ending 72 years of British military occupation. Britain agrees to withdraw its 80,000-man force from the Canal Zone within 20 months, while Egypt guarantees freedom of canal navigation.

13 January 1956
Syria and Lebanon sign a mutual defence pact providing for joint retaliation if either is attacked by Israel. This is in response to the 11 December 1955 Israeli attack on Syrian positions along the Sea of Galilee. On 19 January the UN Security Council votes unanimously to censure Israel for the attack as a ' flagrant violation' of the Palestine armistice.

10 May 1956
It is announced by the UN Secretary General that unconditional cease-fire agreements have been signed by Israel, Egypt, Jordan, Syria and Lebanon.

13 June 1956
British 74-year military occupation of the Suez Canal zone ends as the last British soldier leaves Port Said, in accordance with the 1954 British-Egyptian treaty.

26 July 1956
Under a nationalisation decree, President Nasser seizes the Suez Canal after denouncing the Western withdrawal of financial

support for the Aswan Dam project. Nasser intends to use canal revenues to build the dam.

1–2 August 1956
In reaction to the Suez Canal crisis, Britain, France and the US hold high-level talks in London. At the same time, a war scare is touched off by British and French deployment of forces in the Mediterranean. Tension eases by 16 August when representatives of 22 nations open Suez discussions in London; only Egypt and Greece refuse participation.

29 October 1956
Israel invades Egypt's Sinai Peninsula. After Egypt rejects cease-fire demands made by Britain and France, the two nations bomb Egypt, beginning on 31 October, and land forces on 5–6 November. The US condemns the Anglo-French attack, support-ing a cease-fire demand by the UN. Egypt and Israel accept the cease-fire, and Britain and France follow. Fighting ends on 7 November. The truce is supervised by a UN international police force. The British and French capture the upper quarter of the Suez Canal, and Israel gains control of the Sinai and the Gaza strip. The Canal itself is blocked by scuttled and sunken ships and destroyed bridges. Egypt emerges from the war with the US and USSR as virtual allies, at least on this issue.

29 December 1956
UN salvage crews begin clearing the Suez Canal of sunken vessels and other obstacles. The canal reopens to vessels on 7 March 1957.

CYPRUS
In Cyprus, following the deportation of Archbishop Makarios in 1956, thousands of British troops are barely managing to contain EOKA terrorists. Under the leadership of General George Grivas, these terrorists are commiting many atrocities including the shooting of innocent civilian families in their bid to achieve full union with Greece. A number of terrorists are executed by British troops.

5 January 1957

President Eisenhower asks Congress for the right to use military force to resist communist aggression in the Middle East. With the offer of US aid to Middle East nations to resist communism, this policy becomes known as the Eisenhower Doctrine and becomes law on 9 March.

6 March 1957

Israeli forces complete their withdrawal from Egyptian territory as UN Emergency Forces take control of the Gaza Strip and Sharm el Sheikh.

13 March 1957

JORDAN/GREAT BRITAIN

Termination of the 1948 Anglo-Jordanian treaty of alliance severs economic and military ties between the countries. All British forces are to withdraw within six months. Jordan is to pay $11.9 million over six years for British military installations and supplies left behind and the British end their annual $35 million subsidy to Jordan.

28 March 1957

CYPRUS

Archbishop Makarios is released by the British from exile in the Seychelles Islands, after he agrees to issue a call for an end to violence in Cyprus. He is forbidden to return to the island.

14 April 1957

JORDAN

King Hussein quells a revolt led by pro-Egyptian elements in his army. To affirm support for Hussein, the US moves its Sixth Fleet to the eastern Mediterranean. King Hussein announces that the crisis is over on 5 May.

3 June 1957

The US joins the Baghdad Pact (METO) at a Karachi conference and reaffirms its determination to aid the member nations – Turkey,

Iraq, Iran, Pakistan and Britain – in countering communist aggression.

26 December 1957

CAIRO

Delegates from 40 African and Asian states and colonies open the Afro-Asian Peoples Solidarity Conference, which adopts resolutions backing Soviet appeals for peaceful co-existence, condemning Western imperialist and colonialist policies and attacking the Eisenhower Doctrine. A Soviet spokesman offers economic and technical aid to all Asian and African peoples.

December 1957/January 1958

18,000 British troops are dispatched to the Middle East.

1958

Throughout the Middle East the year of 1958 marks a period of dangerous instability with subsequent events posing a huge threat to the Israelis and peace throughout the area. Repercussions of the Anglo-French invasion of Suez in November 1956 are still being felt. Britain's action in sending troops into Port Said is widely condemned and President Nasser of Egypt is in the unique position of having the US and USSR in agreement in their public condemnation of the British activity.

21 January 1958

The USSR warns the Baghdad Pact nations against any Western attempt to introduce nuclear weapons and missile bases into their various national territories.

1 February 1958

Egypt and Syria merge as the United Arab Republic (UAR) with Nasser as president per results of a 21 February election. Yemen joins the union on 8 March. On 14 February Jordan and Iraq counter this move by merging as the Arab Union.

1 May 1958

EGYPT/USSR

On an 18-day state visit to the USSR Egyptian President Nasser has the place of honour at Lenin's tomb for the traditional May Day Parade in Moscow. The USSR and Egypt sign a joint statement committing Nasser to support Soviet foreign policy and the Soviets to promote liberation of all Asian and African peoples.

14 July 1958

Following the overthrow of the monarchy in Iraq, the Jordan/Iraqi union breaks down and on 19 July Iraq joins the UAR formed by Egypt and Syria. The threat to the stability of the Middle East, and to Israel and Jordan in particular, at this time is a very real one. The UAR is allegedly supported by the USSR in the provision of weapons and advisers to the Arab countries.

15 July 1958

LEBANON

Greatly concerned about this turn of events and the threatened growth of communism in the area, President Eisenhower orders US marines into Lebanon at the request of the Lebanese President Chamoun, who fears that the Lebanon will be unable to survive the threat of Muslim rebels, allegedly supported by the UAR and USSR. The arrival of 3,500 US marines in Beirut to support the pro-Western Lebanese government and to protect American interests, is condemned by the Soviet Union. Withdrawal of US troops begins on 12 August after calm is restored.

The situation for a time seriously threatens the fragile stability of the world following the Second World War and also threatens to escalate into full-scale war.

17 July 1958

JORDAN

Following the Iraqi revolt, King Hussein also fears an imminent attempt by the UAR to create internal dissension and the overthrow of his monarchy. Prime Minister Macmillan sends 2,000

British troops to Jordan at King Hussein's request. British forces do not withdraw until 20 October.

23 October 1958

EGYPT/USSR

Following the withdrawal of US financial support for the Aswan Dam project, the USSR offers to lend Egypt $100 million towards the construction of the Aswan High Dam on the Nile River. Included in the offer are Soviet technicians, machinery, and materials. The proposal generates strong pro-Soviet sentiment in the Middle East.

The interpretation of events shown above is adapted from Chronicle of 20th Century History *(Magna Books, 1989 © Bison Books Ltd)*.

What Nasser's intentions were in this period of uneasy peace from 1956 to 1967 is unclear, but it may be assumed that at some stage he intended to have another go at Israel; as a military man he felt deeply the Egyptian defeats of 1948 and 1956 and this alone, independently of any feelings he might have had about the destruction of Israel as a state, would have impelled him to war.

Soviet motives in meeting his demands for arms are a little clearer. Moscow intended that Egypt should be strong enough to hold its own against any US-backed Israeli attempt to suppress the 'progressive' regimes in Cairo and Damascus. The Soviet government had persuaded itself that the West would refuse to allow the new Syrian and Egyptian regimes to exist in peace and would at the right moment take action through Israel. The 1956 war was regarded as confirmation of this view, more attention being paid to the belligerent actions of France and Britain than the cease-fire that had been imposed, in effect if not blatantly, by the US. On the other hand, the prime aim of the Soviet government was to avoid any risk of an armed conflict with the US. This not only led to Arab disappointment at the lack of expected Soviet support at critical junctures, but also determined the shape of the Egyptian, Syrian (and to a lesser extent Iraqi) armed forces.

These forces were moulded by the types of weapons which Russia sent, and Russia was determined not to give these three

Arab countries the kinds of weapons with which they might obliterate Israel, for that would provoke a war in which the US might intervene. Instead the weapons were to be sufficient to deter Israel from aggression and to give the three progressive Arab states the means of backing their diplomacy with the appearance of military power. This is not how Russian activity was portrayed in the Western or Israeli press at the time, or indeed later.

The above text is adapted from History of Middle East Wars *(Bison Books, 1984 © Bison Books Ltd).*